ADVANCED KRAV MAGA

קרב מגע למתקדמים

A complete Reference

Tested in battle:
No-nonsense Self Defense techniques from today's most effective Fighting System

By

Marc De Bremaeker

Fons Sapientiae Publishing

Advanced Krav Maga - A Complete Reference. Published in 2018 by *Fons Sapientiae Publishing*, Cambridge, United Kingdom

Please note that the publisher and author of this instructional book are NOT RESPONSIBLE in any manner whatsoever for any injury that may result from practicing the techniques and/or following the instructions given within. Physical and Martial Arts Training can be dangerous, -both to you and others-, if not practiced safely. If you are in doubt as how to proceed or whether your practice is safe, consult with an accredited coach, physical trainer, Krav Maga teacher or a trained Martial Art master before beginning. Since the physical activities described maybe too strenuous in nature for some readers, it is essential that a physician be consulted prior to any type of training.

Copyright © by Marc De Bremaeker
All rights reserved. No part of this publication may be reproduced or utilized in any form or by any means, electronic or mechanical, without prior written permission from the author and/or the publisher.
martialartkicks@gmail.com

ISBN of the printed version: 978-0-9957952-5-9

Recommended reading, by the same author:

"Krav Maga kicks - Real-world Self-defense Techniques from Today's most effective Fighting System" (2017)
"Joint Kicks - Destruction of the Opponent's Limbs" (2018)
"Isoplex - Musculation Program for an Aesthetic and truly Athletic Body (2017)
"Sacrifice Kicks - Advanced Martial Arts Kicks for Realistic Airborne Attacks (2016)
"Stealth Kicks - The Forgotten Art of Ghost Kicking" (2015)
"Ground Kicks-Advanced Martial Arts Kicks for Goundfighting" (2015)
"Stop Kicks-Jamming, Obstructing, Stopping, Impaling, Cutting and Preemptive Kicks" (2014)
"Low kicks-Advanced Martial Arts Kicks for Attacking the Lower Gates" (2013)
"Plyo-Flex-Plyometrics and Flexibility Training for Explosive Martial Arts Kicks" (2013)
"The Essential Book of Martial Arts Kicks" (2010) by Tuttle Publishing
"Les Coups de Pied au Sol" (2018) in French
"Les Coups de Pied d'Arret" (2017) in French
"Les Coups de Pied Bas" (2016) in French
"Le Grand Livre des Coups de Pied" (2016) by Budo Edition (In French)
"i Calci nelle Arti Marziali" (2015) by Edizioni Mediterranee (in Italian)

DEDICATION

*This volume is dedicated to a lifelong friend now facing adversity.
To true friendship, youthful dreams and the inexorable march of time and senescence.
Hang in there, Rui...*

Rui Ramon Monteiro, Meu amigo.

Dear Reader,

In this day and age, the life of a serious author has become quite difficult. The proliferation of books and the explosion of internet content has made it nearly impossible to promote work based on extensive research and requiring complex lay-out.
Please enjoy this book. Once you are finished, I would ask kindly that you take a few short minutes to give your honest opinion. An unbiased Amazon review, of even a few words only, would be highly appreciated and encouraging.

Thank You,

Marc

**Good words are worth much and cost little.
~George Herbert**

Acknowledgements

Without the active support of my wife and life companion, **Aviva Giveoni**, this book would not have come to life. Being an athlete in her own right, she understands the meaning of hard work and dedication.

Sensei Shlomo Faige

Aviva

Among many teachers and heads and shoulders above, my late Sensei, -**Sidney (Shlomo) Faige**-, should be mentioned with longing thankfulness. Sensei Faige founded the Shi-Heun style of Karate and Krav Maga.

Special Thanks to my life-long friend and training partner, **Roy Faige**, for his help and support. Roy is now heading the Shi Heun school is also my co-author of *The Essential Book of Martial Arts Kicks*. His influence and advice is felt in nearly every page of this work and the previous books in the series, where he appears in many photos.

Roy and Marc

Thank you to **Ziv Faige, Gil Faige, Shay Levy, Dotan De Bremaeker, Nimrod De Bremaeker, Eric Collet and Itay Leibovitch** who helped by painstakingly posing for some of the photographs.

Most photographs have been taken by the author, by Roy Faige and by Aviva Giveoni. But special thanks have to be extended to my friend **Yariv Gai** and to talented **Grace Wong** for some shooting sessions. Thank you also to professional photographer **Guli Cohen**: some of the photographs in this book have been extracted from the photo sessions he gracefully did for previous volumes.

The drawings in this book are mine. Everything that I have learned about line art, I have done so from professional Illustrator **Shahar Navot**, who illustrated *The Essential Book of Martial Arts Kicks*. Thanks Shahar!

הבא להורגך השכם להורגו

"If someone comes to kill you, get up early to kill him first."
-Babylonian Talmud, Sanhedrin 72:1

Contents

Dedication 3
Acknowledgements 7
Disclaimer 10
General Foreword 12
Introduction to Krav Maga 14
Part One: The Kicks of Krav Maga 18

Part Two: The Vulnerable Points to Target 24

Part Three: Victimology - The Theory of Aggression 39
    3.1 Awareness 40
    3.2 The Verbal Phase of an Aggression 41
    3.3 The Physical Phase of the Aggression 43
    3.4 Danger Detection 46

Part Four: Krav Maga Strikes 47
    4.1 The Headbutt 48
    4.2 The Shoulder Strike 50
    4.3 The Elbow Strikes 50
    4.4 The Knife-hand and Forearm Strikes 55
    4.5 The Punches 61
    4.6 The Palm Strikes 62
    4.7 The Eyes Attacks 66
    4.8 The Hammer-fist 74
    4.9 The Throat Attacks 78

Part Five: More Offensive Techniques (Range Covering, Combinations, Guard Neutralization) 84
    5.1 Range Covering Techniques 85
    5.2 Guard Neutralization Techniques 89
    5.3 Natural Combinations 93
    5.4 Special Techniques 98

Part Six: Defenses against Stick Attacks..................117
6.1 The Stick..................118
6.2 Preemption..................119
6.3 Defense against a Downward Stick Strike..................129
6.4 Defense against an Horizontal Inwards Stick Strike..................139
6.5 Defense against a Backhand Stick Strike..................141
6.6 Defenses against Baseball Bat Attacks..................144

Part Seven: Defenses against Knife Attacks..................150
7.1 The Knife..................151
7.2 Training for Knife Defenses..................152
7.3 Training Progression..................153
7.4 Minimizing damage..................156
7.5 Preemptive attacks against a knife-wielding attacker..................158
7.6 Disarming Principles..................162
7.7 Close proximity Knife Threats..................164
7.8 Downward 'Icepick' Knife Attacks..................177
7.9 Straight Pokes and Stabs..................183
7.10 Slashes..................195

Part Eight: Defenses against Gun Threats..................207
8.1 Body evasion and Disarming..................209
8.2 Threats from the Front..................214
8.3 Threats from the Back..................221
8.4 Threats from the Side..................226
8.5 Long Gun Threats..................228

Part Nine: Improvised Weapons..................235

Afterword..................248

CAUTION – Additional DISCLAIMER

This special disclaimer comes in addition to, but not instead of, the general disclaimer presented on the first page of the book regarding the practice of Krav Maga and other physical activity.

Most techniques presented in this book are crippling and potentially lethal. They are designed to be used in real self-defense situations where life and physical integrity are threatened.

The Author and the Publisher decline all legal responsibility for the possible consequences of using these techniques in training and in real life situations. The reader and practitioner is solely responsible for keeping an ethical behavior and for remaining in the legal framework for self-defense of the jurisdiction in which he is at the moment of use of said techniques.

Utmost caution and restraint are required both in training and in a real aggression. Krav Maga techniques have been designed for survival in extreme situations and common sense is required by the trainee.

All this having been said, the Author thinks that life is sacred, starting with yours and that of your loved ones. All normative citizens, because of their observance of social graces, are often reacting too slowly to obvious aggressions by criminals. Common Sense should always trump political correctness, although with caution. But honest folks should remember that, in extreme circumstances, it is *"Better to be judged by Twelve than carried by Six"*.

General Foreword

In 2017, we published a first book about Krav Maga in our 'Kicks' series. This "**Krav Maga Kicks**" was intended to explain the Krav Maga approach to kicking for self-defense, which is different than traditional and sport Martial Arts. We presented the kicks used in Krav Maga and the way they should be executed. But the book did also present in detail the general Krav Maga principles, the sensitive points targeted by all strikes and kicks, the general offensive techniques used to preempt an attack and the basic self defense techniques against an unarmed assailant. All in all, it was our intention to give the 'Kicks' series a little peek of the world of modern no-nonsense survival fighting.

This treatise was very well received, but many reactions did indicate a need for a more complete presentation of Krav Maga. The need for more advanced techniques, the need for a description of the upper limbs strikes and the dealing with armed opponents were clearly missing for many readers. This was due to the limitations of being part of the 'Kicks' series, and certainly not done on purpose.

This is why we have completed this first work with the present book (*Advanced Krav Maga*), and its contents answer the requests of most of the commenting readers to date.

'*Advanced Krav Maga*' is not about overly sophisticated techniques! This would be contrary to the KISS principle ("Keep it simple, stupid"). It is about simple techniques against more complex and dangerous (armed) attacks and that therefore need more drilling to become natural. The book will also cover the Krav Maga strikes that were omitted in the previous book about kicks, and we shall go into more details about the range-covering techniques for a safe preemptive attack. We shall also conclude the book with a short Chapter about the use of everyday items as self-defense weapons.

This book has been written as a complement to 'Krav Maga Kicks', but it also needs to be able to stand alone as a Krav Maga treatise. It is also independent from the successful 'Kicks' series. Therefore, we had to duplicate some of the data found in 'Krav Maga Kicks' into this book. We apologize to our faithful readers, but these duplicated parts, necessary for new readers, will be kept to a minimum and will help the coherence of 'Advanced Krav Maga'.

Introduction to Krav Maga

Foreword מבוא

Krav Maga (קרב מגע) is a Hebrew word meaning basically "Close Combat". 'Krav' means combat or battle, and 'Maga' means contact in the sense of very close. Until its world fame as an effective Martial Art, the word was interchangeable with its previous generally accepted denomination: *Kapap* (קפ"פ). Kapap is the Hebrew acronym for: Krav Panim el Panim (קרב פנים אל פנים), which translates as 'Face-to-face Combat'. Basically, it means the same thing: Close Combat.

Krav Maga and/or **Kapap** is a self-defense system developed for the **Israel Defense Forces** (צה"ל) that consists of techniques based on simplicity and gruesome efficacy, and drilled in very realistic training. It is renowned for its focus on real-world situations and its brutal counter-attacks. As a rule of thumb, it emphasizes fast threat neutralization, simultaneous blocking and countering and an always offensive mindset. *Krav Maga* used to be used mainly by the Israel Defense Forces' special units, but it started to trickle down to regular army units, then to law enforcement and intelligence organizations, and finally, in a toned-down version, to the general public in Israel, and more recently internationally.

History היסטוריה

Imre Lichtenfeld (aka *Imi Sde-Or*) was born in 1910 in Budapest, Hungary and grew up in Bratislava (Slovakia). Lichtenfeld grew up to become a gifted wrestler and boxer. When, in the mid-1930s, anti-Semitic riots began to threaten the Jews of Bratislava, he became a street fighter and organized and trained Jewish young men to defend their neighborhoods against the growing numbers of Nazi and anti-Semitic hooligans. Finally, Lichtenfeld had no choice but to escape from Europe with his family in 1940.
Arrived in Palestine, he joined Israel's "Haganah" (הגנה), a pre-state Jewish paramilitary organization protecting Jewish refugees from Arab marauders and also fighting for the establishment of a homeland for the persecuted Jewish people...

... It is then and there that Lichtenfeld met the *Kapap* training system already in place to teach Jewish refugees physical education, stick fighting and the rudiments of an evolving self defense system. Names associated with *Kapap* in the 'Haganah' and its special forces (called *Palmach*) were, among others: Gershon Kopler, Yitzhak Sadeh and Maishel Horovitz. In 1944, Lichtenfeld began training fighters in his areas of expertise: physical fitness, swimming, wrestling, boxing and both armed and unarmed street fighting. In 1948, when the State of Israel and the IDF (Israel Defense Forces) was founded, he became Chief Instructor for Physical Fitness and Close Combat (*Krav Maga*). He served in the IDF for about 20 years, during which time he developed and refined his unique method of hand-to-hand combat, based upon scientific principles and battle experience. The Middle East is a 'tough neighbourhood', to paraphrase Chief of Staff Ehud Barak. It is therefore by necessity that the Martial Art of *Krav Maga* evolved into the most realistic for the 20th and 21st centuries.

Imi Lichtenfeld

The Art evolved through trial and error, and through cross-fertilization with the experience of numerous Jewish Martial Artists who came and immigrated to Israel in its formative years. These Artists and their students did all meet through the special units of the IDF and influenced one another for the betterment of Krav Maga. Among a few, one can name **_Sidney Faiga_** and **_Dennis Hannover_** who, in 1960, immigrated together from South Africa to settle in Moledet, Israel. *Sidney (Shlomo) Faiga* later founded the *Shi Heun School of Karate and Krav Maga*, and *Dennis Hannover* went on to found the *Hisardut* (Survival = הישרדות) Organization.

Dennis Hanover and Sidney Faiga

Sidney 'Shlomo' Faiga

The fights and growth of the young State of Israel were the fertile soil in which all these influences brought about the genesis of a new and fully practical Martial Art umbrella: **Krav Maga.**

BASIC PRINCIPLES עקרונות בסיסיים

Although **Krav Maga** encourages civilian students to avoid confrontation, it promotes finishing a fight as quickly as possible if it becomes unavoidable. Attacks are always aimed at the most vulnerable parts of the body, and training promotes the deliberate causing severe injury. Drills provide maximum safety to students by the use of protective equipment and by emphasizing caution and power control. *Krav Maga* is about 'real world violence, which unfortunately is still too common. And the key principle behind it is **KISS** (Keep it simple, stupid!).

The other general basic principles of *Krav Mag*a are:

• **Attacking preemptively** or Counterattacking as early as possible. Take the initiative as soon as possible.
• **Keeping an offensive attitude**. Project confidence and proficiency. Avoid retreating and keep the pressure *forward*.
• **Targeting attacks to the body's most vulnerable points** (eyes, neck, throat, nose, ears, solar plexus, groin, lower ribs, knee, foot, fingers,...).
• **Maximizing efficiency** for fast neutralization.
• **Using an offensive Defense**: simultaneous attacking and blocking
• **Maintaining constant awareness of the battlefield** (assailant's accomplices, surroundings, escape routes, weapons or useful everyday objects)
• **Retzev** (רצף). This probably the most important tenet of Krav Maga. *Retzev* in Hebrew simply means: sequence or continuity. But the connotation of the word in modern Hebrew is very much about un-interruption, smooth continuity, no stopping in a sequence of different steps until finished. American Krav Maga has it translated as 'Continuous Motion', which is a fair image. The idea of 'Retzev' is pretty simple: after your first offensive move [preemptive attack/attack/offensive defense/counterattack] you keep striking with no interruption until the fight is over: no resting, no interruptions, no retreating for assessment. And ideally, you should vary the type of attacks (punches/strikes/kicks), the height of attacks (low/high/medium), and the angle of attacks (inside/outside/back) in order to better overwhelm the opponent. Just do not make the mistake of assuming that this is about speed first; it is not! It is about continuity and full-powered intelligent strikes. Speed is good if it does not impact the focused power of the chain of strikes. Applications in the text will make the concept clear.

The Late Sidney Shlomo Faiga in action

**It is not because it is difficult that we do not dare; it is because we do not dare that it is difficult.
~Senecus**

Part One

The Kicks of Krav Maga

הבעיטות של קרב מגע

The kicks of Krav Maga have been presented in detail in our previous volume 'Krav Maga Kicks'. The reader is invited to consult that book for more details. In this book, we shall simply list the kicks briefly for completeness.

The Kicks of Krav Maga will be simple to execute in order to utilize the body natural reflexes to their maximum. They will never be 'High Kicks', so as to remain safe and stable, and as to keep the groin protected. They will target vulnerable points only. That's it! The whole story in brief...

Again **KISS**! Keep It Simple, Stupid.

1. The Penetrating Front Kick

2. The Upward Front Kick

3. The Phantom Groin Kick

4. The Low Front Kick

5. The Pushing Front Stop Kick

6. The Front Stomp Kick

7. The Penetrating Side Kick

8.   The Pushing Side Stop Kick

9.   The Low Side Kick

10.   The Stomping Side Kick

11.   The Small Roundhouse Kick

12. The Bent-body Long Roundhouse Kick

13. The 'Low Kick' or Straight-leg Roundhouse

14. The Penetrating Back Kick

15. The Short Back Kick

ADVANCED KRAV MAGA

16. The Upward Back Kicks

17. The Small Heel Back Hook Kick

18. The Crescent Kick

19. The Outside Crescent Kick

20. The Outward Ghost Groin Kick

Part Two

The Vulnerable Points to Target

נקודות התורפה

This Part is <u>exactly</u> as found in 'Krav Maga Kicks'. It is reproduced Verbatim in this book because the targeting of sensitive points is one of the basic principles of Krav Maga. This work must stand alone and needs to present the Vulnerable Points to the reader who has not read 'Krav Maga Kicks'.

One of the main attributes of *Krav Maga* is the <u>exclusive targeting of vulnerable points</u>. This is a no-nonsense fighting system that is supposed to work in stressful situations. Unless you are a lifelong dedicated Martial Artist, hitting esoteric pressure points or striking the opponent randomly does not work. One must also bear in mind that in high adrenalin-state, feelings of pain are dulled and therefore an assailant's body can easily take much more punishment that you can imagine from your armchair.

By concentrating on a limited number of targets, *Krav Maga* makes the acquisition of good habits and effective techniques much simpler: you can drill the maneuvers many more times and you will basically often execute the same strikes in different '*Retzev*' all the time. These automatisms will serve you right when your body will be on autopilot in a stressful 'real world' situation.

Krav Maga is also not for the faint-hearted; it is a system developed for survival in warfare and in life-threatening situations. Survival trumps all social norms, and training is required for a normative citizen to acquire self-preserving reflexes that are not in line with his social education and background.

We will describe here the main **Vulnerable Points** to target in training (*carefully*) and in case of need (*at full power*). The targets mentioned in this book are not restricted to those you should kick; all main targets will be mentioned. They can be kicked, punched, palm-striked, elbowed, kneed, and even bitten if your survival depends on it…

If you find yourself in a fair fight, you didn't plan your mission properly.
~Colonel David Hackworth

1. First Line Targets

The First Line Targets that must be hit with priority whenever possible are:

1. The Groin
2. The Groin
3. The Groin.

This pun is intended to underline the importance of the *testicles* and of the general *groin area* as a vulnerable point to strike in a survival situation.

I once had a Tai Jitsu instructor, very good but rather foul-mouthed, that used to say: "In real combat, you do not have an opponent, you have a floating pair of balls in front of you". This is a quote and I apologize for the language; but it expresses very clearly the state of mind required and the importance of making targeting the groin a second nature.

You can and should hit the groin from the front, from the back, with your feet, with your knees, with your palms, with your elbows, with your head; you can even try to grab them...

The testicles are an exception to the adrenalin-pumped pain theory: nearly everyone will experience excruciating pain when hit. The physical damage is also very serious. But this does not mean that you have to stop your 'Retzev' after a successful groin strike. Remember that *Krav Maga* series do not stop until the opponent is fully neutralized; you may need to repeat the groin strike, follow with other strikes to sensitive targets, or destroy the assailant's joints to make sure the danger to you or your loved ones is over.

Krav Maga first line targets

KRAV MAGA'S VULNERABLE POINTS TO TARGET

2. SECOND LINE TARGETS

The Second Line Targets must be targeted when the groin is well protected, out of reach, or has already been hit, or has been feinted towards to elicit a reaction. *Second Line Targets* are crippling targets, but they still have always to be part of a 'Retzev' and followed up until complete victory.

Unlike in traditional Martial Arts, they are not pinpointed vulnerable points to be struck with precision and with specific natural weapons: They are general areas rich in such points! *Krav Maga* takes into account the stress of real life threats for normative people not used to violence. It would be difficult for them in such situations to react with pinpoint precision!

The Secondary Targets List reads as follows:

2.1 The Nose ('Middle of the Face' Target).

The *nose* is a great target: easy to find in the middle of the face, and very sensitive. When you hit someone's nose hard, you overload his senses: shock his sense of touch with the impact, blurr his vision with the watering of his eyes, disturb his ability to breathe through the nose, and make him smell and taste blood,... The preferred kicking weapons are the *knee* or the *top of the foot* when you have caused him to bend forward, and the *bottom of the foot* if he is already on the floor. The preferred punching weapons are the *fist* and the *palm of the hand*, although *elbows* and *head* butts are not to be sneezed at. The author tends to prefer the Palm to the Fist for 2 reasons:
- it is safer to the fingers, especially in stressed situations where the fist is not necessarily well-rolled.
- it has the fingers visiting the area around the opponent's eyes, which is very disturbing to the attacked.

The nose is also a great target, because, being in the middle of the face, it lends itself to misses that are still good targets: the eyes and orbital bone, the cheekbones, the lips,... Of course, after scoring on the nose, you have to keep hitting until your assailant is fully subdued.

Head Butt to the nose

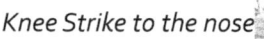

Knee Strike to the nose

2.2 The Throat (Adam's Apple and the general Larynx area).

The **throat** is not always easy to reach, but when possible, it is a crippling target, even to the extent of being lethal. This, of course, underlines the need for utmost caution in training and in actual 'real world' use. If your life is not in danger, you should avoid targeting the throat; this is not for stopping an inebriated acquaintance fooling around! A crushed larynx will cause breathing difficulty that can lead to asphyxiation and death. On the other hand, if your life is in danger from several real thugs or an armed mugger, you should use your *knuckles*, the *sword edge of your hand*, the *webbed part between your thumb and forefingers* or the *sword edge of your foot* to strike the throat. If you miss slightly, you are still in a sensitive target-rich environment: the chin, the carotids, the lips and the clavicles.

Knuckle Strike to the throat

Striking the throat with the weapon seized from the attacker

2.3 The Eyes (and the Orbital Cavity Ridge).

The **eyes** are an obvious but often underused target. Poking the eyes is, of course, a very painful and crippling move that can cause blindness. Poking with the *straightened fingers* or *protruding knuckles* is a very serious and dangerous technique to be used only in life-threatening circumstances. But the eyes can also be attacked in serious but milder ways: you can punch or palm-strike the *general eye area* to damage the orbital cavity, or you can **rake or whip-strike** the eyes to cause an atavistic reaction that will include lifting the hands (and therefore uncover the primary target). The <u>Whipping Strike towards the eyes</u> is an extremely fast and effective technique to be used any time possible; it has milder consequences than a poke, but it as effective in the very short term needed. When you are going with a Punch or a Palm Strike for the general eye area, you are in a good neighborhood: should you miss, you still could hit the nose, the temple or the higher cheekbone.

Fingers Poke to the eyes

2.4 The Back of the Neck (Cervical vertebrae).

The **Back of the neck** is a potentially crippling target that can even cause death. Be extremely careful in training and in real-life use. In the unfortunate life-preserving circumstances, it must be struck with a penetrating blow *that goes through*. The weapons used are the *knife of the hand*, the *elbow*, the *forearm*, and in the right set-up the *foot*. We cannot underline enough the seriousness of striking the cervical area: be wise and calculated.

Elbow strike to the back of the neck

2.5 The Knees.

The **knee** is an important target: it is easy to reach, especially if your opponent has a high guard to protect his face or if you have provoked his lifting his hands, for example with a feint towards his eyes. The knee should be hit from any side possible: front, back and sides: it is a very sensitive joint. Most serious kicks will damage the knee, cause pain and hamper the assailant's mobility; their crippling potential should also be understood. The knee can be attacked with straight, circular and stomping Kicks; one has just to remember to kick *through* the target. No surface-slapping!

It is also important to target the knee with *precision*: the traditional 'Low Kick' (*Circular*) is usually delivered to the thigh; it hurts but it is a bad self-defense habit. Go for the knee with precision, because you want to destroy the ability of your attacker to move and to stand.

Stomping the knee

Krav Maga's Secondary Targets

KRAV MAGA'S VULNERABLE POINTS TO TARGET

3. Third Line Targets

Attacking the **tertiary target**s is damaging and painful, but not easily crippling. Striking them will nevertheless cause a shock to be used for following up in the *Retzev*, preferably towards the groin or at least towards more serious secondary targets. Hitting these sensitive points causes physiological reactions that will (1) hurt the opponent, (2) add to the overall shock of the previous strikes and (3) give you enough time (in milliseconds) to keep attacking without allowing for a counter. *Tertiary targets are always part of a Retzev*, as a transition or as a distracting move (leading to something else).

Here comes the Tertiary Targets List:

3.1 The Side of the Face.
This 'target' goes from the *temple* through the *ear* all the way to the *mandibular joint* (jaw hinge). The *temple* could be a secondary target if it was not difficult to pinpoint exactly in a stressful situation: a collapsed temporal area is crippling and can even be fatal. The *ears* are full of sensitive nerve endings and can tear easily, but the best way to attack them is with a *Palm Strike* (preferably Twin Strike to both ears) that will tear the eardrum (*tympan*) and cause a serious loss of balance control. Remember not to 'slap' but to strike forcefully through the target, like always. If you miss the ears and strike the hinge of the jaw, no big deal: it is very painful and can cause a serious dislocation that will win you the fight. The weapons of choice for the Side of the Face area are: the *Palm*, the *Knife-hand*, the *forearm* and the *elbow*; of course the *knee*, the *top of the foot*, the *tip of your shoe* and the *fist* are valid as well.

Palm Strike to the side of the face

The concussing Ears Twin Palm Strike: simple but very damaging

3.2 The Side of the Neck (Carotids and Vertebrae).

The **side of the neck** is a good target because of the veins and carotid arteries, as well as many nerve endings. You must strike powerfully 'into' the target and not just 'slap' the surface. By doing so, you will also shake the cervical vertebrae. This sensitive target can be attacked with the *Knife-hand*, the *forearm*, the *elbow*, the *palm*, the *fist* and the *foot*. Should you miss slightly because of your opponent moving, you would still probably strike the side of the head, the back of the neck, the throat or the clavicle...

Knife-hand Strike to the side of the neck

another type of Knife-hand Strike to the side of the neck

Another side-of-the-neck strike

3.3 The Collarbone (Clavicle).

The **clavicles** are an underused target: these are bones that are relatively easy to break, which is very painful, causes serious internal damage and basically takes the corresponding shoulder out of the game immediately. The ideal point to strike, diagonally from above, is at about one third of its length from the throat side, but anywhere will be very effective and reverberate from the shoulder all the way to the neck. The collarbone can be attacked with the *fist*, the *hammer-fist*, the *forearm*, the *elbow*, the *Knife-hand*, and, in the right set-up, with any part of the *foot*.

3.4 The Solar Plexus (Celiac plexus).

This network of nerves at the pit of the stomach is very sensitive to a reverberating strike; it is close to the stomach and the aorta. The general area to target is in the middle of the trunk just below the chest-bone (*sternum*). On top of being very painful, a strong blow causes the diaphragm to spasm, and hence difficulty in breathing. It can also affect the nerve plexus itself and damage the viscera. Knocking the wind out of an opponent will, of course, allow you to follow up easily. Pinpointing the exact *solar plexus* point is not always easy in stressful situations, but a powerful penetrating strike in the general area will generally be good enough. Kick with any part of the foot, but kick 'into' the target. The *straightened fingers*, the *knuckles*, the *fist*, the *elbow* and the *knee* will make good penetrating weapons too. The *head* and the *palm* can also be used if their striking trajectory comes from below or straight on (not from above).

3.5 The Floating Ribs (False and Floating Ribs).

The term '*floating ribs*' is loosely used in Martial Arts, as it usually also includes the so-called 'False Ribs'. The False Ribs (Ribs 8 to 10) are so called because they are not directly attached to the chest bone (sternum), but are so through a cartilage link to the 'Real' Ribs above them. The Floating Ribs (Ribs 11 and 12) are not attached at all to the sternum in any way. The common denominator is that they both are 'weak' ribs that do not protect very well the internal organs under them. Moreover, well-delivered Kicks can easily cause damage to the ribs themselves. You can also use the *knee*, the *fist*, the *elbow* and the *forearm*.

Lower back Kick

3.6 The Kidneys (Lower Back Area)

Kicking the **lower back area** is very efficient: it is painful and causes a disturbing concussion that will open the assailant to easier follow-ups. You should kick '*into*' the general area just above the belt: it encompasses the sensitive kidneys, but also the vertebrae. A powerful Strike will reverberate along the whole of the spine and into the lower internal organs like the liver. It also often kicks the wind out of the opponent because the shock causes the diaphragm to contract. Pinpointing the *kidneys* with the *knee*, the *fist* or the *hammer-fist* is possible, but targeting this area is more the realm of a kick, especially the Circular Kicks connecting with the *ankle* or the *shin*.

3.7 The Elbow Joints.

Striking the **elbow joint** with power can destroy the opponent's ability to keep fighting, but breaking the elbow will only come if you strike the elbow of an extended arm from outside while keeping the wrist in place. Most regular strikes to the elbow will numb and cause pain to allow for a follow-up. Remember to strike *through* the elbow, all the way. Use the *Knife-hand*, the *forearm* or the *crescent kick* presented in Part One. The other good way to destroy the opponent's elbow to prevent further attacks, is to <u>stomp</u> the elbow of an opponent on the ground, which is entirely justifiable in the case of a life-saving situation (especially against an armed assailant).

Elbow Break attempt: Knife-hand Strike while keeping the forearm in place

3.8 The Hands (Wrist and Fingers).

Damaging the opponent's **hands** will prevent his ability and will to keep on fighting. That goes without saying. Striking the wrist of an assailant with the *knife-hand* or the *forearm* can rattle him, but the best way to take the attacking hands out is to stomp on them when the opponent is on the ground. Do not hesitate: crushed fingers are very painful and will seriously diminish your opponent's abilities and belligerence.

3.9 The Feet (Ankles to toes).

What is true for the hands/wrists/fingers is doubly true for the **ankles/feet/toes**. The only differences are: that you can (1) crush those also when your attacker is still standing, and (2) that a damaged foot will hamper the opponent's ability to move and stand. Foot Stomping is an underused maneuver, which makes it usually more surprising. It is very easy to perform and fiendishly effective. You should do it nearly automatically whenever possible. The only drawback is that it requires you to be close to the opponent. But if you find yourself close for any reason, go for it...

3.10 The shin (Tibia and Fibula Bones).

The **shins** also undeservedly make for underused targets. The shins are very rich in nerve endings and the shinbone is pretty prone to damage. Kicking the shins is also pretty easy to do with fast kicks, if you execute them stealthily without moving the upper body, or if you kick just after feinting high with the hands. Kicking the shins is always a great opener, or a fantastic diversion before a decisive attack; it is extremely efficient if you have *hard-tipped shoe*s. Shin Splints and Stress Fractures will be the mildest results of a hard-soled shoe striking 'through' the tibia. Drill the Kick and use it whenever possible.

Kicking the sensitive shins. With shoes!

KRAV MAGA'S VULNERABLE POINTS TO TARGET

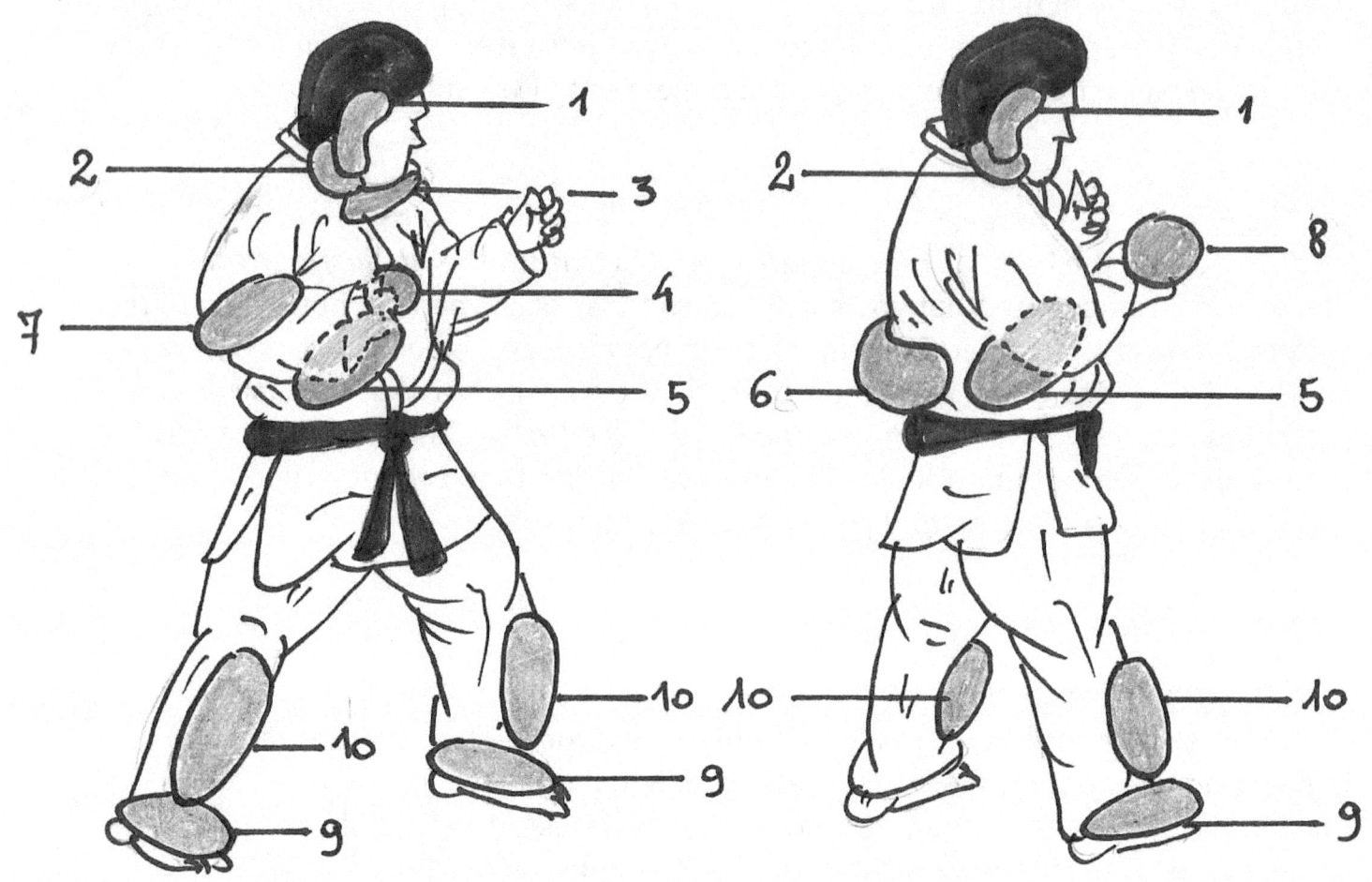

The Tertiary Targets of Krav Maga

36 **ADVANCED KRAV MAGA**

Palm Strike to the face area: nose crush and fingers near the eyes

Self defense is the clearest of all laws; and for this reason - the lawyers didn't make it.
~Douglas Jerrold

KRAV MAGA'S VULNERABLE POINTS TO TARGET

Part Three

VICTIMOLOGY

The theory of aggression

איך לא להפוך לקורבן

3.1 *Awareness*

The world is a dangerous place, but most of our readers live in countries where security is provided reliably by the State. Such people are educated to reject violence and to behave civilly towards their fellow citizens. This, in turn, makes it difficult for them to deal with serious aggression by asocial elements of society. And unfortunately, muggings, violent break-ins, sexual attacks, car-jackings, hate aggressions, bullying for ego-boosting and terrorism are not uncommon anymore. It happens, and it can happen to you, even though you are a normative socially responsible tax-paying citizen who expects to be protected by the authorities.

The first step to avoid becoming a victim is **vigilance**. Be always ready! And use common sense: do not carry more money than necessary, separate big bills from the pocket money needed for everyday transactions, do not take nightly long walks in deserted places, be aware of your surroundings when using the ATM, do not flaunt jewelry and expensive watches, do not open your car before you have checked the surroundings, lock your doors at home and in your car, do no attract unnecessary attention…

The second step is to try **not to look like a victim**. Research has shown that human predators definitely choose their victims intuitively, based on their demeanor and on their gait. You should walk around with self-assurance, alertness, a straight spine and a purpose. Look around and scan your environment. In problematic areas at least, avoid at all cost the earphones and the smartphone screen.

In times of crisis, there are only two things we can try to control: *emotions and behavior*. They must be handled as well as possible under the stress caused by the outside environment. Of course, how to handle an aggression will be very dependent on your personal history, on your fighting abilities and on the way that you are impaired by said stress. That is why, once you have mastered the techniques, you must drill them realistically, and that means: *under pressure and under stress*. The atavistic stress reaction of Freeze/Flight/Fight must be rewired to 'fight only', because the 'freeze' (to stay unnoticed by predators) and 'flight' (from said predator) are not relevant to the modern animal we have evolved into. Familiarity of dealing with attacks under some training stress will teach our unconscious brain to react immediately to an aggression. That is what the practice of *Krav Maga* is all about.

Your general fighting abilities are very important when you are challenged: the more comfortable you feel about being able to handle an aggression, the more relaxed you will be in the verbal handling of the challenge, and the higher your chances of defusing the situation. Therefrom derives, again, the importance of **serious training** in self-defense techniques.

If the aggression materializes, *your worse enemy is stress*: it will impair your reactions and your common sense. It is where training comes, again, to the rescue. Learning *Krav Maga* or other self-defense methods is not about collecting 'miracle' techniques. **It is about achieving muscular memory with intensive and repetitive drilling.** In a stressful situation, your body is basically on its own: if you have trained hard, it is a good thing. Your body will react instinctively and use automatically the most suitable techniques in its muscular memory. This is why hard work and *the focus on a few good techniques* is so important.

The other important attribute that is needed for survival in times of crisis is: **determination**. You have to be ready to do what is needed to survive, and it is not as simple as it may seem. As a normative citizen living in a protected society, your survival instincts have been dulled by social rules and a regulated environment. When you are being attacked, you find yourself in a different world where all rules have been abolished by your assailant. Be it for sexual, ideological, hate or financial reasons, your physical and psychological integrity is at risk. If you are a woman about to be raped, are you ready to stick your thumb into the predator's eye? You should! And you should think about it and familiarize yourself with the possibility, because it is probably not natural to you. Considering the consequences, you have no other real choice; but you should not have to think about it then.

3.2 The Verbal Phase of an Aggression

Conflict avoidance should always be your first priority. Self-defense is all about protecting your body, not your honor or your pride! If you have invaded someone's personal space, bumped into him or done anything wrong, apologize sincerely while staying vigilant and assertive. Do not reply to insulting comments or challenging stares (look sideways, not down!); just ignore and *walk away*. If someone starts to bully you verbally, to annoy you in order to elicit a reaction or to make himself look good, *walk away*. It is not cowardice but the intelligent and moral thing to do. Nobody knows how serious the consequences of a fight can be. Of course, walk away with vigilance and heightened attention. If the potential aggressor wants your wallet or your watch: give it to him. Within reason, no worldly possession is worth your life, your physical integrity, the safety of your loved ones or a long prison sentence for having won the fight. Just remember though that this 'giving up' does not include rape, the infliction of pain or the kidnapping you or a loved one away to another place.

The legal framework around the right to self-defense is very similar in most of the Western and Westernized World: if using force, you have to be able to prove that there was no alternative (like *walking away*), that there was true intent to cause you physical harm, and that you have used a responsible and *proportional* amount of force to place you out of danger. The reader should realize how heavy the burden of proof is for the winner of the fight, especially to a few judgemental people in armchairs in a climatized room and who are not in a state of justified stress! Several American States have on their books the right 'to stand your ground laws'. These laws are based on a sound and rightful principle: normative citizens should not live in fear and be cowered into fleeing or giving up their wallets when challenged by bullies and criminals. The author agrees fully with the ideas and principles behind these laws, but must remind the reader that it is better to be wise than to be right. An apt comparison would be the right of way at a roads crossing: even if you have the right of way, it would be wiser to yield to a crazy driver flying through without slowing! In case of an aggressive challenge, the modern Hebrew aphorism "Be wise, not right" (עדיף להיות חכם מאשר צודק) should also be heeded. Even if you are right and indignant: *walk away if you can*. A fight has always serious consequences: you could make a mistake and get seriously hurt (just for your ego or some money); you could win the fight but could have to live with having caused serious injuries to another human being and you could find a jury mistakenly disagreeing with the amount of force you have used. Stress can make you bypass your logical brain and go overboard. Even if the law allows you to stand your ground: be wise and walk away if you can. The emphasis is: If you can...

A disagreement should be negotiated <u>before</u> it turns into a challenge, and then into an aggression. Usually, a bully will become violent if he does not obtain what he wants by demanding and threatening. If you are verbally challenged, you should remember that the exchange will decide whether this turns into a fight or not. Most assailants will not challenge or attack anyone they do not expect to beat easily; it is a law of nature true even in the animal realm. **The victims are <u>chosen</u> by the predators. It is important not to look like a victim.**

In most cases, the potential aggressor feels threatened or affronted by you, or he is looking to assert his social dominance (just like with social animals). In those cases, it is sometimes possible to defuse the situation by responding verbally to the problems *in an assertive but non-threatening way*. Of course, if the potential aggressor is inebriated, under drug influence or in a psychotic rage, reason and de-escalation will not work; it is best to ignore the person and walk away immediately if possible. Always remember: **It is never too late to negotiate and it is never too late to flee!**

When challenged verbally, you have first to become psychologically ready. Remember that, in such an exchange, **your body language and the tone of your voice are even more important than the words you utter**. As a matter of general principle, you should avoid threatening, challenging, ordering or defying the protagonist. Be assertive, but all the while, get your body ready to act and to preempt if necessary. You should be basically ready to press the button that turns you from a normative citizen into an animal in survival mode, because, -make no mistake-, the stress of a violent altercation brings out animal behavior on both sides.

If your potential aggressor starts talking louder and becomes more threatening or more insulting, let him express himself while staying fully ready if you discern the start of a physical attack. Talking out could help him calm himself. Listen to him empathically with no insulting or bored mimic, without interrupting and without contradicting him. When he is over, you should try the reformulation of his grievances in order to start what is akin to a de-escalating negotiation. But stay vigilant, it is possible that nothing you say can stop the coming assault. Use a neutral voice that does not mimic his tone and aggressiveness and reformulate his diatribe; for example: "If I have understood you correctly, you think that I have made fun of you?". If he answers positively, you have started a 'negotiation' during which you can assertively but calmly convince him that you have not done so...

But it should be clear to the reader that most aggressions will happen anyway, the attacker having already decided that he will have no problems to physically beat you. If it becomes necessary, you should make clear that, although unnecessary in your eyes, you will do whatever is needed to defend yourself. Do so without lifting your fists or threatening him; just assertively and in a state of full readiness. In some cases, it can be what is necessary to convince him that you are not the victim he thought you were. If not...

3.3 The Physical Phase of the Aggression

You now understand that nothing will prevent a physical altercation. You have to be ready, and you must have been thinking about it in your training to get familiar with the possible situation.

Here are your options:

1. **Flee**. No shame in that, whatsoever. '*He who fights and runs away, may live to fight another day (Tacitus)*'. If you are in an inferior situation, outnumbered, clearly outmatched, or unarmed against an armed assailant, *run*! Throw your wallet and *run*. Throw your gym bag or attaché-case and *run*. No shame whatsoever. If you flee, run from darkness towards light, towards crowds, towards upper ground and towards first aid stations like police and hospitals.

2. **Pre-empt the attack,** as the preferable option of *Krav Maga*. Launch your attack as soon as you 'feel' that he is about to launch his. It is easier than it reads: just trust your gut and your sixth sense heightened by stress. You may look like the aggressor, but it is better than being struck first.

3. **Stop-strike the opponent's attack,** and start your own series of uninterrupted attacks until victory (*Retzev*). Second-best *Krav Maga* option.

4. **Block and Counter**. Start a *Retzev* as soon as you have scored with a counter.

The big problem is that most people are not truly ready to do a preemptive attack, or even to counter 'all-out' until the opponent is vanquished. Social conditioning and ethical/religious upbringing make us to be 'shy' or fearful of strong reactions. Just as we are 'afraid' to ask for a salary raise, we are 'afraid' of preempting an attack. We are 'afraid' of asserting our right to self-preservation and we are inhibited to cause harm to others even if justified. In these extreme situations, this is a fatal paralysis. You need to imagine such situations, you need to understand the possible consequences and you need to be psychologically ready to do what is required to protect yourself and your loved ones.

The natural stress reaction in such dangerous situations also hinders our abilities to react. It can cause fear paralysis and a distortion of straight thinking. This is why we need to train and drill: *we need to become familiar with comparative situations*. Stress causes a spike of some hormones, like adrenalin and cortisone. This has several consequences: a reserve of energy becomes available, the blood regresses from the periphery to the internal organs, the emotional part of our brain (*limbic*) takes over from the rational frontal cortex, and we lose some of our peripheral vision and hearing capacities (*auditory exclusion*). And we are afraid, which is totally natural.

Remember that we are all 'afraid' before a confrontation. Afraid means normally apprehensive; it does not mean cowardly or paralyzed. Do not think that it is shameful: it is normal. As a competitive fighter, I always had butterflies in the belly before climbing in the ring or on the mat. Action takes that away instantly.

Stress gives control to your emotional brain, which will cause you to react *instinctively* and *according to muscle memory*. The stress does not disappear, but it can be managed by acting in a well-rehearsed and rational way. Just like policemen or firemen do act professionally and according to their training when their services are needed, so can you base yourself on your training to cope with the stress in an actionable way.

Action can be first simply taking an 'appeasing' guard: be fully ready to attack or to stop-strike, but do it with the hands opened. Do not use an aggressive tone and try to defuse the situation. You have one foot forward and your legs are slightly bent. Your hands are up but open in a widely accepted calming posture; keep your chin slightly down and all your senses on alert. See first Drawing.

An alternative that disguises even more the fact that this is, in fact, a guard is to keep your hands up, as if naturally busy: holding your chin dubitatively, holding the lapels of your jacket, or your hands clasped as if wondering… See the second set of Drawings.

The appeasing guard

Alternative non-threatening guards: holding the chin or clasped hands held high

VICTIMOLOGY

3.4 Danger Detection

The most important way to avoid violence is to remove yourself from a place or from a situation before anything can happen. For that you need to be constantly aware of your surroundings, and you need to trust your gut. I personally have been 'jumped' on (aggressed by surprise) twice during my (long) life, by criminal elements (I grew up in then very unsafe Congo); in both cases, my sixth sense warned me in advance that 'something was not right'. Everybody will have those intuitive warnings if he is aware of his surroundings. When that happens, do remember that social graces do not apply: it is not rude to let a question stay unanswered, or to cross the street to the other side. If you feel uneasy and something bothers you, it is OK not to come to somebody's help; you can take your distance and call for help, or you can first assure yourself that the situation is kosher. *Intuition* is based on a long experience of gathering social clues and of analyzing body language. If your gut tells you that something is out of sync, it is usually right and you should listen to it and ignore social inhibitions. By moving away from dodgy places or from weird individuals, you can prevent a dangerous physical confrontation.

Someone asking for directions, sweet-talking you or presenting his hand to shake could be preparing a surprise attack, especially if there is nobody else around. Be aware and trust your gut... Remember that it is your 'gut' that reads body language, and it is this sixth sense that will alert you if there is a disconnect between the protagonist's words and his real intentions.

Just like animal predators, human predators will try to ambush and surprise you. They will trick you, distract you and place you in an inferior setting from which there is no escape. Usually they will make sure they have the advantage of numbers or weapons. That is why **general awareness** is so important, and listening to your gut can be literally a life-saver.

Self-defense is not just a set of techniques; it's a state of mind, and it begins with the belief that you are worth defending.
~Rorion Gracie

PART FOUR

Krav Maga Strikes

מכות בקרב מגע

We have covered at length the *Kicks* of Krav Maga in the previous volume, and briefly in this one. It is now time to read a brief overview of the other **Strikes** commonly used in *Krav Maga*.

4.1   The Headbutt

The Headbutt is a very easy technique to master and execute at close quarters. You simply must connect with the upper rim of the skull, about where the hair starts growing. And you must target *only soft and vulnerable parts*, preferably the **nose**.

There are two things to keep in mind:
-1.   If you are close enough to execute a headbutt, <u>you are also close enough to receive one</u>.
-2.   The natural reaction when detecting an incoming headbutt is to evade back, and therefore lift the chin. This can cause you to connect with the opponent's chin or teeth, which are 'hard' targets that can cause *you* open wounds.

A forward Headbutt to the nose with head pull

Generally speaking, exploding into a headbutt to the opponent's nose is usually very surprising and usually successful. It causes bleeding, tearing of the eyes, restricted breathing and shock. Follow up immediately; a Groin Knee Strike will usually flow very naturally. The power of the headbutt can be enhanced by grabbing the opponent's head and pulling it in during the strike: you can grab the hair or just the head as such, but the best option is to grab the ears (preferably after having slapped them).

The headbutt can also target the *side* of the head, as will be illustrated. The back and side of your skull crown can also be used for 'stopping strikes'.

The headbutt should be drilled on a focus pad held at the right height by a partner.

A finishing headbutt to the nose of a faltering opponent, with ear grab and pull

48   **ADVANCED KRAV MAGA**

Arm Pull with a Head Butt to the side of the opponent's head: go for the general ear area

Applied offensive Headbutt

 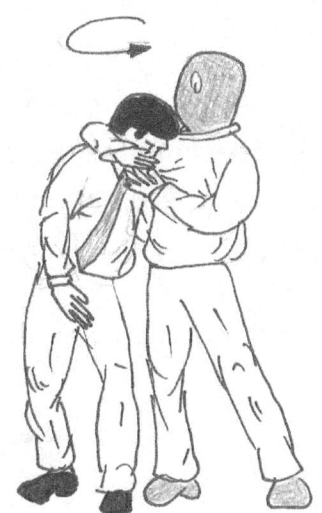  

Headbutt as a stopping strike for a Rear Choke Attempt

Applied **Side** Headbutt against a rear hair grab attack

KRAV MAGA STRIKES

Applied Rear Headbutt, in a rear Bear Hug

Roy Faiga and Marc De Bremaeker, early 1990ies

4.2   The Shoulder Strike

The **Shoulder Strike** is an effective but underused technique for close combat. It is quite surprising and allows for very hard follow-ups, like the headbutt for example. Its main advantage is to protect you from a headbutt as you are close: your head will be besides his, and you will strike with your shoulder, then follow up. The important points are to strike with power and to aim at the **nose**, again.

There is not much to add: use it when you can. Drill it for familiarization and try to use it in free fighting. You'll become used to it and it will pop out automatically in clinching.

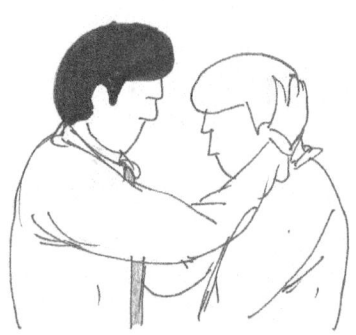  

The simple but efficient Shoulder Strike: aim for the nose

4.3   The Elbow Strikes

Elbow Strikes are very powerful because they use the big muscles of the trunk, and often are propelled by the hips. Moreover, the striking areas of the elbow are very resilient and will not be hurt by the strikes (unlike the fist); this is important because there will be no unconscious hesitation at striking, the way it can happen with an injured fist.

Krav Maga, at least at basic and intermediate levels, will limit itself to the use of the *simple* techniques only, as they are to be used under severe stress. For this reason, we shall present the important Elbow Strikes only and we shall omit the more sophisticated ones in spite of their efficiency (the Spin-back circular and the Vertical upward ones come to mind, for example).

All Elbow strikes should be drilled for familiarity and for t*he use of the whole body*, against focus pads held by partners. It is important to get used to strike a few inches **into** the target, with hip power, and not to merely slap the surface of the target. Drill them and do not take them for granted; it will give you a powerful weapon if you take the pains to work them out.

a.   The Circular Forward Elbow Strike

The principle of the strike is simple and illustrated in the Figures below. Just remember to strike *through* the target and to use the twisting *power of the hips*. The usual targets for the *Circular Forward Elbow* are the side of the head, the nose, and in certain respective positions, the throat. This elbow strike lend itself to easy and harsh follow-ups with the same arm.

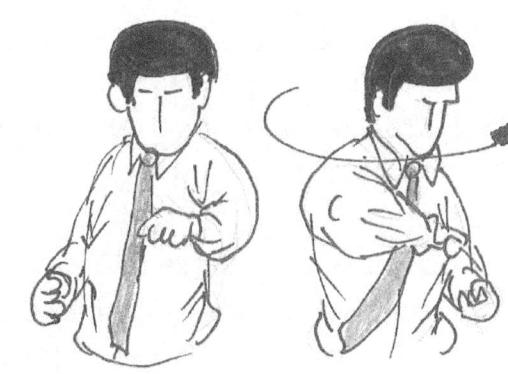

The basic technique for the Circular Forward Elbow

Applied Elbow Strike to the side of the head

Circular Forward Elbow to the Jaw Hinge; look at the hips

Offensive Applied Circular Elbow and natural Hammer-fist follow-up

b. The Lateral Elbow Strike

The *Lateral Strike* is simple and natural, as illustrated below. Just use the power of the retraction of the other arm, and put your body weight into the strike. Again, aim for the side or the center of the face, **or the throat if possible**. If you are in a low or very low stance compared to the opponent, you can target the solar plexus or the groin. It is a very fast strike, to be used whenever adequate.

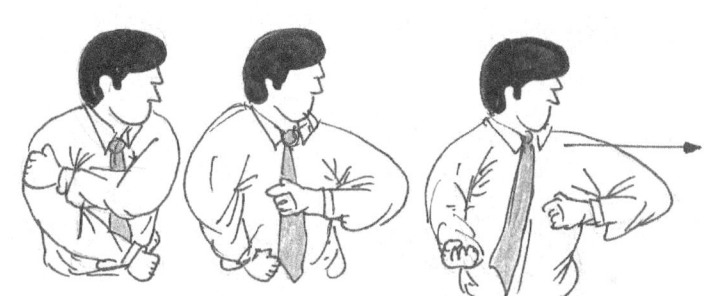

The straight Lateral Elbow Strike, fast and powerful

Applied Lateral Elbow to the throat

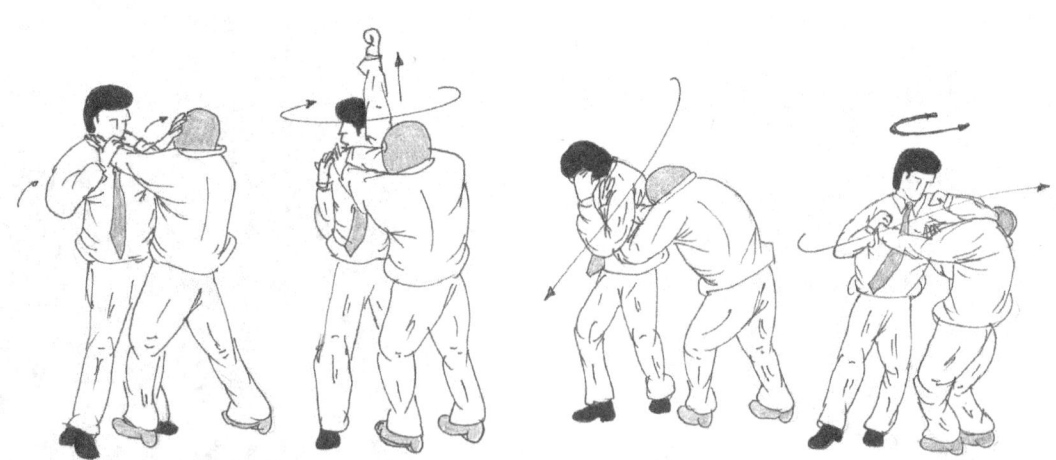

Applied Lateral Elbow in an attempted front choke release; look at the use of the body in the release and in the strike itself

Preemptive applied Lateral straight Elbow

c. The Straight Back Elbow Strike

The **Straight Back Elbow** is even more natural: just hit back behind you. It is very powerful because of the back muscles involved. It is of course a situational technique, to be used in very specific situations of attacks from the rear. It is worth drilling the strike though, to make it powerful when used. The targets are the solar plexus, the armpit, the floating ribs, or the groin if you can crouch low enough.

The Straight Back Elbow Strike

Applied Straight Back Elbow in a Rear Bear Hug attempt defense; strike with all the power you have

d.   *The Circular Back Elbow Strike*

The **Circular Back Elbow Strike** is even more powerful than the straight one because it adds the power of the hip twist. Strike *through* the target, usually the head, and follow up. The technique lends itself naturally to follow-ups that use the pivot and the strike-through, for example a Circular Forward Elbow Strike with the other elbow that uses the momentum of the original hip twist. The Strike exists also as a redoubtable Spin-back attack, but not to be recommended to *Krav Maga* beginners because of the blind spot while spinning back.

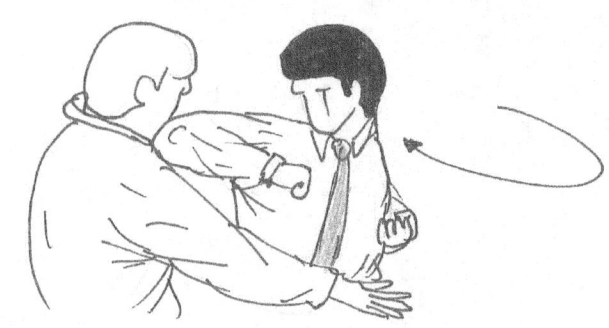

The basic Circular Back Elbow Strike

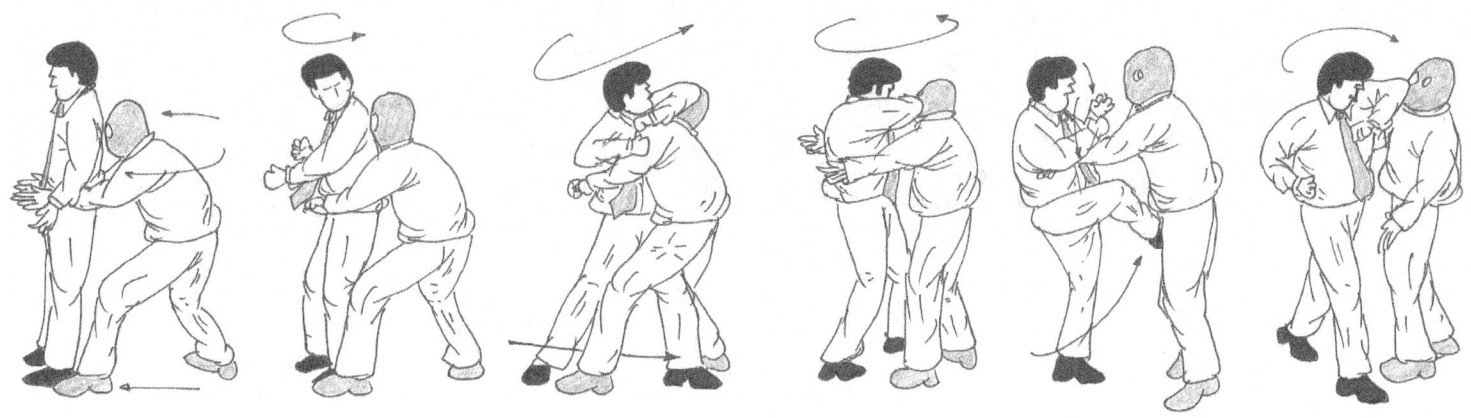

Applied Circular Back Elbow against an attempted Bear Hug Hold; the naturally following technique is a Circular Forward Elbow with the other arm, and then more

e.   *The Vertical Downward Elbow Strike*

This is a very easy to understand strike, used usually against the *back of the head* or the *back of the neck* of a crouching opponent. It is a very dangerous technique to be used with extreme caution. The strike is obviously a very good follow-up to a successful Groin Kick that causes the opponent to bend in pain. But it can also, in certain situations, target the clavicle or the upper back between the shoulder blades.

Applied Downward Elbow to the back of the head

The Vertical Downward Elbow Strike

Downward Elbow to the back of the neck

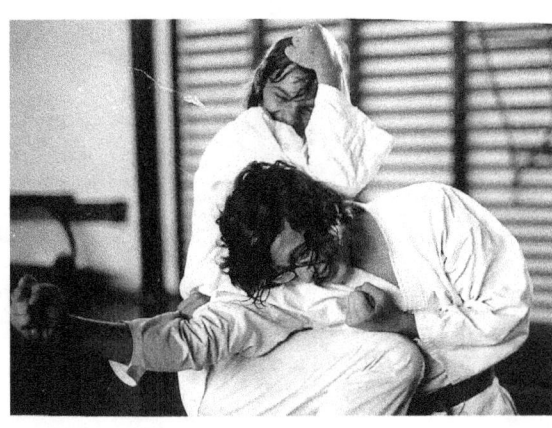

Downward Elbow to the neck held in place by a Knee Strike; Serge Coucke on Marc in the 1970ies

4.4 The Knife-hand and Forearm Strikes

We present the **Knife-hand and Forearm Strikes** together because they are identical in execution. You can connect with the blade of the hand ('Karate chop') or with the forearm, according to the distance or the requisites of the situation. These strikes aim exclusively at soft targets, like most of the time in *Krav Maga*. The most common target will be the **neck** from all sides: the side of the neck, the throat or the back of the neck of a bent-over assailant. But these strikes can also target the side of the face, particularly the jaw hinge, and the nose. The Downward Knife-hand Strike is also sometimes used to attack the clavicle.

There are **Four** basic and effective ways to strike with the open hand (or with the forearm): outwards, inwards, vertically down and straight forward. The Illustrations and Photos will provide the necessary examples.

It must be noted that all four executions can be made to connect with the forearm o*r with the hammer-fist* instead of the blade of the opened hand, according to the distance, the target and your personal preferences. The Forearm Strikes are usually more of the 'straight-forward' type, and the Hammer-fist should be preferred for all strikes that do not target the neck (where the 'thinner' open hand has more chances to connect with the carotid or the throat).

1

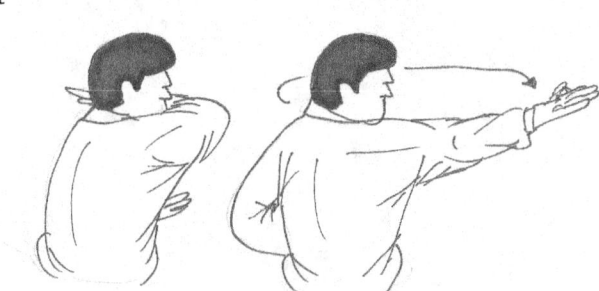

The **Outward** Knife Hand Strike

2

The **Inward** Knife Hand Strike

KRAV MAGA STRIKES

The Downward Knife Hand Strike

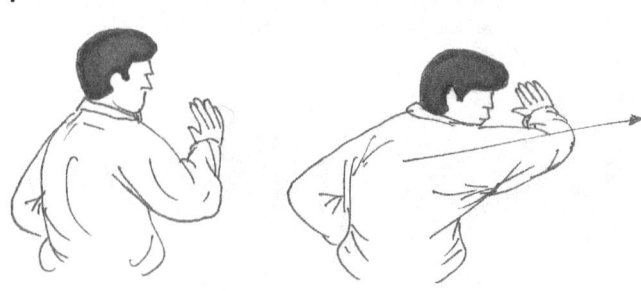

The Forward Knife Hand Strike

4.4.1 The Outward Knife-hand Strike is probably the most effective, practical and naturally-flowing. It is executed *with the whole body*, usually after a blocking or attacking move that has taken you sideways relatively to the opponent. It should target the throat or the side of the neck, preferably.

For example, in the next set of Photos, the Release technique from the Choke places you sideways, in perfect position for the *Outward Knife-hand* to the neck.

Pivot inwards for the Release, come back outwards with the Strike

The release technique from the wrist grab in the next example also places you in perfect position for the Outward 'Chop'"

Strike the grabbing hand while releasing and get in position for the outward strike

It can also be a same-hand Downward Knife-hand Strike that places you in good position, like in the next example.

Use a Downward Knife-hand Strike to help release your grabbed wrist: you are now sideways and ready to attack his neck with an Outward Chop

4.4.2 The Inward Knife-hand Strike is a less natural and more sophisticated technique that requires training to be useable in stress situations. It also has the disadvantage of 'opening' your guard while you are chambering. But it is very suitable in certain situations, or if you are a trained Martial Artist. Go exclusively for the **throat** or the **neck** though.

Inward Knife-hand Strike to the neck on evading a Kick; Marc on Rui Monteiro in the 1970ies

Chambering the Inward knife-hand in an appropriate situation; go for the throat

The Inward Knife-hand Strike to the neck in a Defense against a surprise low Knife attack

KRAV MAGA STRIKES

4.4.3 The Downward Knife-hand Strike is, on the other hand, very natural. Striking down on something comes easily and intuitively. The Strike is best used with a clenched fist in 'Hammer-fist' style, unless it targets the arm, the neck (of a bent-over opponent) or the clavicle of the opponent. The Hammer-fist is stronger, more massive and safer for the hands. The Knife-hand is best used for narrow-access targets (throat).

Strike downwards on the fleshy part of the forearm, near the elbow

 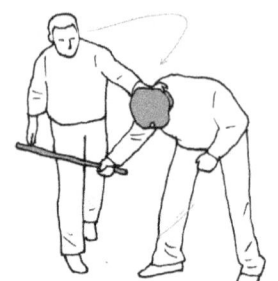

Downward Knife-hand to the exposed back neck of a bent-over opponent: more examples

Downward Strike, impact clearly with the Forearm

Downward Knife-hand Strike to the back of the neck; **Master Sidney Shlomo Faige** *in Krav Maga demonstration in the 1980ies*

4.4.4 The Forward Knife-hand Strike is slightly less powerful than the previous 'chambered' Strikes, but it is fast and it uses the body to support it in its forward momentum. It is also often slightly 'outward' because of the position of the hand at the start, which confers it some more power from the hips. As will be illustrated separately, it is often used advantageously *with the forearm* as the connecting weapon. It should also limit itself to attacking the **neck** area under the *Krav Maga* principle of targeting exclusively the most vulnerable points possible. If you can grab the opponent's arm to keep him in place, the power of the Strike will be multiplied (See further).

Target the neck

58   **ADVANCED KRAV MAGA**

Block, grab to keep in place, execute fast Forward knife-hand neck Strike

The Forward <u>Forearm</u> Strike is similar to the previous Knife-hand version, but executed from close to the attacker. It is used with the whole body pressing forward and targets, again, the neck or the throat. Its best execution will have your other hand catching the opponent's head to pull it in as you strike (See below).

The technique needs familiarization and training on the heavy bag to become a very powerful weapon in your arsenal.

The Forward Forearm Strike

It is a forward-going move; go for the throa

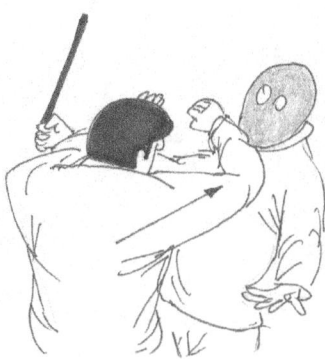

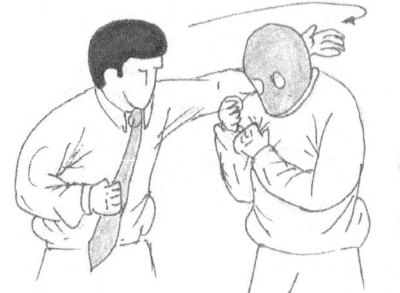
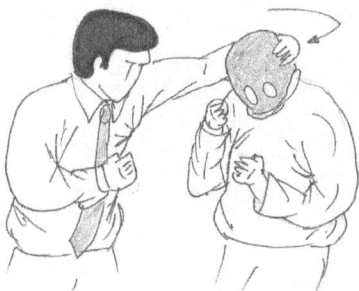
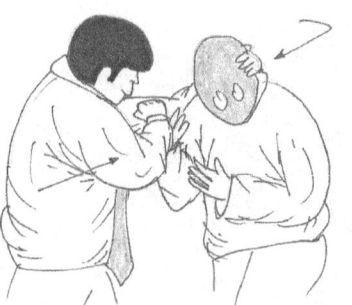

More effect if you can pull the opponent's head in; the nose can be a target

KRAV MAGA STRIKES

The Inner Forearm 'Clothesline' Strike is a different Forearm attack, but we present it here with the other Forearm Strikes. The use of the internal ridge of the hand or the internal forearm is part of traditional Martial Arts, but too sophisticated for the *Krav Maga* use under stress. But the *Clothesline* move is an important exception because it is easy, natural and extremely effective. It is used with a diagonal forward evasion and aims at letting the opponent run himself into the strike, like into an invisible rope stretched at throat level. You simply overtake your momentum-driven opponent and strike at throat level. The rushing-forward opponent adds his own momentum to the power of yours and of your strike. At contact, you should go *through* but also *diagonally up* with your arm (to lift his chin).

The Clothesline Maneuver

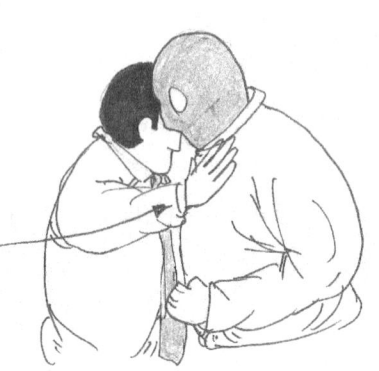

Go through and slightly up after contact

Applied Clothesline Forearm Strike against a straight kick

4.5 The Punches

The reader is obviously familiar with punches and there is no need for over-presenting them. But here is the place to explain the author's views on the use of Punches in self-defense. **I think that punches should be avoided as much as possible in the drilling of self-defense techniques**: they should be replaced by *Palm Strikes*! Unless you can strike with some certainty and accuracy the nose, the solar plexus or the floating ribs, punching can cause damage to your wrists, hands and fingers in the midst of the fight. Remember that these techniques are to be used in very stressful situations, where technique can become sloppy because of your hormones. Remember that your hands are not bandaged and gloved like those of a boxer. Remember that you are not necessarily a thoroughly experienced boxer, *karateka* or kickboxer. Remember that your opponent has hard bones here and there, and teeth...

Even in sporting context, the author has suffered and witnessed numerous hand injuries from punching the opponent, and this, in spite of the relative protection of the rules of engagement, of bandages and of gloves of different types. The author has also witnessed trained individuals getting open wounds and joint damage from real-world punching.

Losing a weapon (your hand) in the middle of a fight will not be conducive to a fast and easy victory. Of course, it could NOT have to happen: you could succeed in your punches with no injury. But is it not better to increase the odds in your favor by not taking the risks? Your choice.

But it is the author's advice that, unless you are a well-trained boxer and unless you can target with confidence soft targets, *you should avoid punching as much as possible*. Replace your straight punches by identical Palm Strikes (to be presented later).

We present below, for illustrative completeness only, the main trivial Punches.

The Jab

The Cross

The front-hand Hook

The rear-hand Uppercut

4.6 The Palm Strikes

As explained above, the author thinks that Punches should be replaced by straight **Palm Strikes** for reasons of safety, to keep your hands and fingers unharmed. Most Punches can simply be replaced by identical techniques executed with an opened hand. Impact is with the lower and fleshy part of the palm, close to the wrist. Strike the nose, the chin (slightly upwards), the side of the face, the floating ribs,…

The Palm Jab

The Palm Cross

Palm-striking **the nose** is especially recommended: it is an easy and very sensitive target in the middle of the face, and, while striking it, you also have your fingers landing in the general area of the eyes!

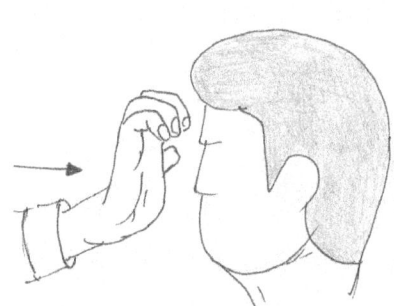
Strike the nose straight on and look where the fingers are

Strike straight a few inches into the middle of the face and let your fingers claw the eyes

ADVANCED KRAV MAGA

Another important use of the Palm Strike is the classic **Twin Slap to the ears,** very fast and easy to place when you are very close. It must be executed like a *strike-through* and not as a surface slap; think of having your hands meet in the middle. Well-executed, this technique will cause searing pain and a loss of balance. Follow up though.

The very efficient Twin Ear Slap; keep your Retzev going after that

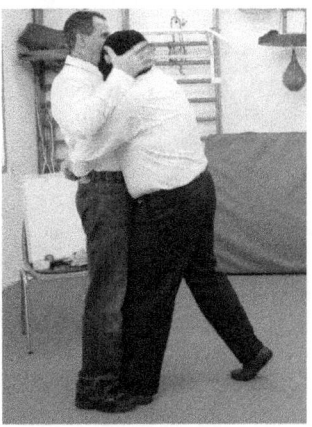

Applied Twin Ears Palm Strike against a bear hug attempt from the front

Applied Twin ears Strike against a choking attempt from the front

An important variation of the straight Palm Strike is the **upward attack of the chin**. The vector is diagonally upwards in order to catch the chin and strike it up. This also causes harm to the cervical vertebrae; a very powerful and brusque strike can be crippling or even lethal. **CAUTION IS WARRANTED!**

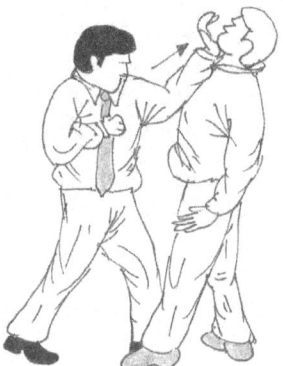

The Upward Palm Strike to the chin: a dangerous strike

Same attack in Photo; look at the neck

Applied chin strike against a Haywire Punch or an Overhead Strike; look at the naturally-flowing follow-up: an Outer Reap Takedown

KRAV MAGA STRIKES

Applied chin strike against a lapel grab

Hit the chin up and through, then push down; Marc on Serge Coucke in the 1970ies

Of Course, a direct Palm Strike to other soft targets can be as efficient, especially if the assailant is going or falling into the strike. See example below. Aim for the **ear** and strike a few inches *into* the target.

Slightly curved direct Strike to the opponent's ear or temporal area; use the hip twist for power

Evade and strike down a Low Side Kick, palm-strike the side of the attacker's face, and flow into a Rear Naked Choke

A very different type of Palm Strike, but surprisingly efficient, is the simple **Slap**! Yes, slap him! Of course, it is not a surface strike like the common slap. It is, in fact, the Palm version of a Hook Punch, or a Swing punch: it is a relatively circular attack that uses the whole body to strike *through* the opponent's head. This maneuver is fast, surprising and punishing. It requires some training to become efficient and familiar: drill on the heavy bag and on focus pads held by a partner.

➔

64   **ADVANCED KRAV MAGA**

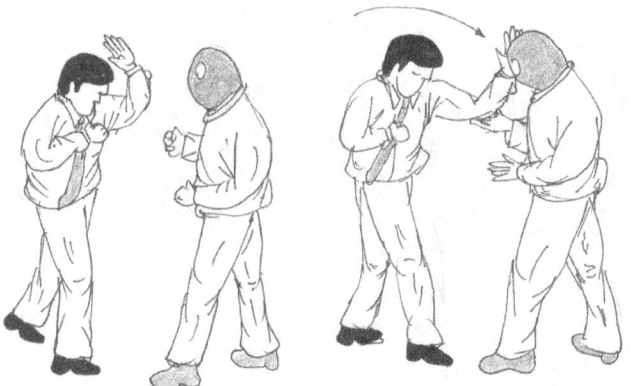

The Slap: surprisingly efficient

An applied Slap: look at the full use of the body to strike through

There are many other Palm Strikes, but *Krav Maga* does focus only on the most effective and most naturally-flowing in stress situations. The last technique presented here is certainly *Krav Maga-worthy*: it is the **Palm Groin Strike**! Strike the opponent's groin upwards with your open hand, but make sure you strike up and *through* the target: train to *not* make this a 'surface slap'. After the strike, you can then grab his genitals if clothing permits.

The Groin Palm Strike; use it any time you are in a suitable position

A sneaky offensive version of the Groin Palm Strike: feint a Slap and go down for the groin as he lifts his hands; best execute after one or more real Slap attempts

KRAV MAGA STRIKES

An applied defensive Groin Slap against a Front Kick: evade, block, slap the groin as he comes down and finish with a straight Palm to the face

4.7   The Eyes Attacks

The eyes are a basically *the second-best target after the groin*. It is quite obvious why. There are two things the reader should bear in mind though. First, not everybody is psychologically able to poke, rake or claw somebody else's eyes. There is a strong educational, squeamish and moral barrier to cross. You should think about it seriously and drill safe strikes in order to get familiar with the idea that you could have no choice but do it. The second point is that there are ethical and legal considerations to take into account: this kind of technique should only be used proportionally and when you are truly attacked with no possibility of retreat (and have no other choice to protect your physical integrity). Therefore, to sum it up: get used to the idea, but try to avoid it.

There are **3** basic ways to attack an assailant's eyes. In order of seriousness: the Whip, the Rake and the Poke.

4.7.1 The Eye Whip is a very important technique that must be mastered by all serious '*Kravists*'. It can be used in most situations because it is more a Feint or a Combination Opener than a crippling strike. That does not mean that it is not dangerous, but it is more likely to cause reparable damage than the next Eye Strikes. In any case, it is guaranteed to cause a violent and atavistic combined reaction: *closing the eyes, lifting the hands and pulling the head back*. Of course, this opens your opponent to a multitude of follow-ups, especially towards the groin.

The advantage of the **Eye Whip** is its speed, because of the way it is executed (with muscles totally relaxed). The Principle behind it is true 'whipping'. Think about a whipping towel strike, of the kind going on in teen-agers cloakrooms: you throw the towel you are holding by a corner forward and as the opposite corner reaches the target, you violently pull it back like a true whip. It cracks and liberates a lot of energy at the far corner. You will now do the same thing with your arm: your relaxed fingers are the striking corner, and your flexed elbow is the 'held' corner. With muscles completely relaxed, you extend the arm and throw your totally relaxed fingers towards the opponent's eyes (their trajectory is direct but naturally curved by the straightening of the arm). As soon as your fingers touch his eyes and face, you pull them back brusquely and fast to their starting position, trying to make them 'crack' like a whip. It is easier to understand by doing than by reading: get a towel first, try a few times and then try to mimic with your arm. Concentrate on speed and on pullback. This move requires some training and familiarization, but it is surprisingly easy. Drill for speed and use it whenever possible. The movement is similar to the fast Backfist of non-contact Karate (*Uraken Uchi*), just with an open hand and loose fingers. You can drill with that in mind 'against a hanging towel or a focus pad. You should also drill in front of a mirror for explosiveness and non-telegraphing.

The Eye Whip: make it fast and untelegraphed

The well-known Whipping Towel Principle

KRAV MAGA STRIKES

Front View of the Eye Whip: pull back fast

The Whip, from a video recording

The Eye Whip: fast and relaxed

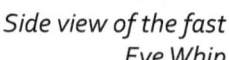
Side view of the fast Eye Whip

ADVANCED KRAV MAGA

Eye Whip Training with a towel

The Eye Whip can be used in the midst of your *Retzev*, in combinations and to help close the gap to your opponent. But it is especially suitable *for the start of a preemptive strike*, whether the is just starting an attack or if he is only gearing himself for it. If it is clear that violence is going to break out and if you do not have the possibility to walk away, go for it! You can start with a diversion, like looking and pointing behind the opponent; you can even call out to an imaginary person behind him. He'll have to look back, even for a millisecond. Whip his eyes immediately as he turns his head back towards you, and start your *Retzev*.

Cause the opponent to check behind him, and whip his eyes as he looks back to you

KRAV MAGA STRIKES

4.7.2 The Eye Rake is a more aggressive technique, and slightly slower. In this maneuver, you attack the opponent's eyes with the tips of your fingers horizontally from the inside outwards. It is as if you are trying to cause a horizontal scratch on his corneas. The move is slightly slower than the Eye Whip because your muscles cannot be completely loose. You extend the front arm to your in-side so that the fingers are a few inches to the side of his eyes and you go horizontally to the other side of his face, touching his eyes on the way. In the classic execution, your palm is facing the floor. It is pretty simple; just be economical in movement, and make sure you do not telegraph you intention to move.

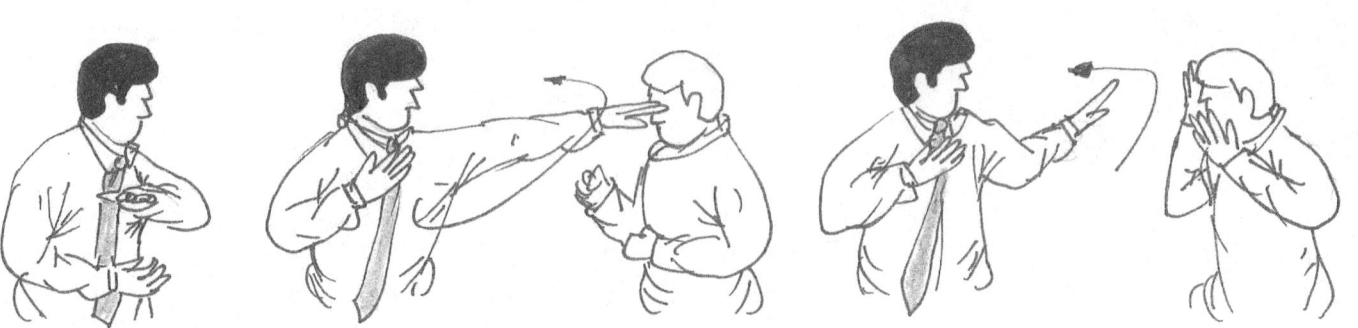

The orthodox Eye Rake: scratch his eyes in a short horizontal move

There is a drawback with this technique: if you go deep into his eyes or if he blocks even partially, you could get your fingers hurt. The technique is a fast *surface strike* on his eyes; if your fingertips meet something more solid, the fingers joints get jolted sideways, which is not their natural range. And remember that you are to use this technique in a stress situation in which you could lack precision. A preferred embodiment of this technique is presented below: while you extend the arm towards his eyes, *you also turn your hand to have your thumb pointing down*. The horizontal rake is identical, but if your fingers hit something hard, they'll just bend backwards a little.

This version is less natural than the orthodox move, and therefore, it needs drilling. Train in front of a mirror and drill on a marked heavy bag or o focus pad held by a partner at eye level. Then work speed on a hanging towel.

The preferred version of the Eye Rake

Front view of the improved Eye Rake

Side view of the optimal Eye Rake

Front view of the rake: lighting fast and easy

The orthodox Eye Rake with partner

KRAV MAGA STRIKES

Improved Eye Rake move - training with towel for explosive speed

The Eye Rake is, again, a great combination-opener or preemptive strike. You can use the same preparatory diversion presented for the Eye Whip. Or you can suddenly start shouting to startle him before launching. Or, as illustrated below, you can point at his midsection to distract him, and start the move *directly from this hand position*.

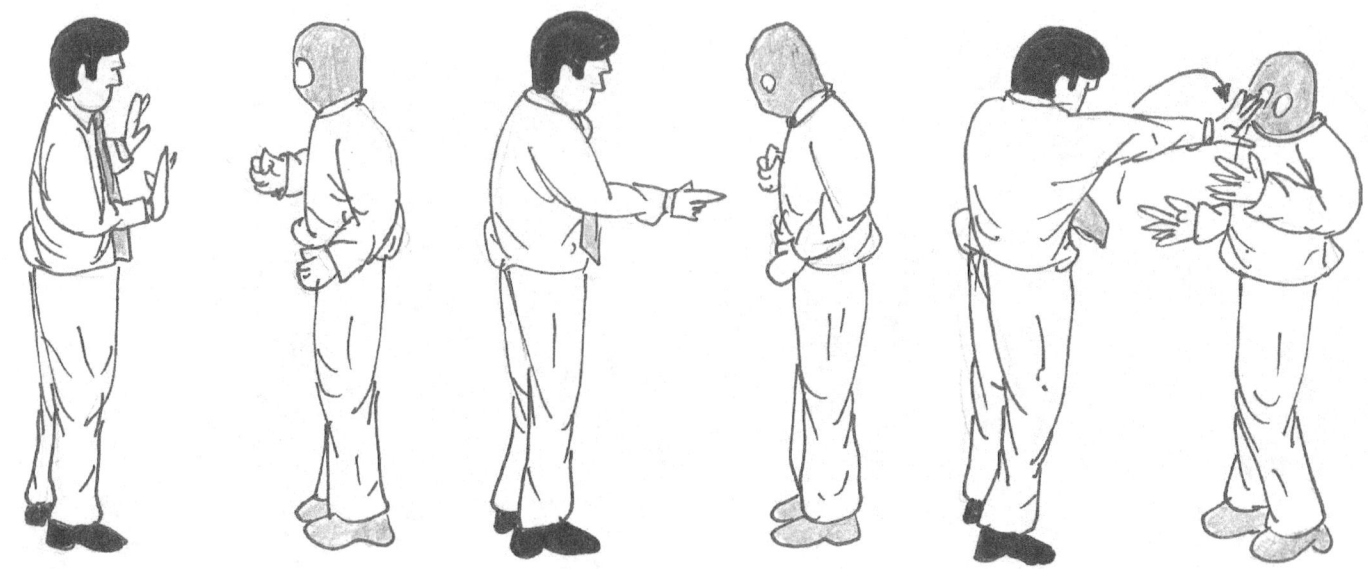

What is this? Bam!

72   ADVANCED KRAV MAGA

4.7.3 The Eye Poke

4.7.3 *The Eye Poke* is simply a straight strike to the eyes with the stiffened fingers. Just like a Jab, you extend your arm fast to hit his eyeballs with one or several fingers. You can strike *fast* because no power is really necessary, and even shallow penetration into the target will cause serious damage; and in any case, it will allow you to follow up. **This is a dangerous technique to be used only in situations justifying it. Be careful in training as well.**

There are several ways to use your fingers to poke: the 2-fingers fork, the 5 spread fingers, the 1 finger poke and the 4 fingers hand-spear. There is no need to go into details: use what suits your personality and habits; just poke and follow up. The only thing to add is that you need to familiarize yourself with the impact on your fingertips: drill hitting <u>soft</u> targets with your stiffened fingers. You need to get used to it and get the feeling (No need to drill in sand buckets and get calluses like in some traditional Martial Arts).

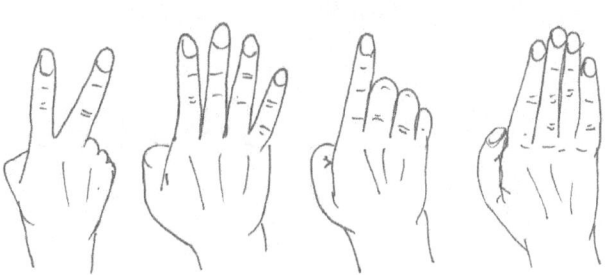

The various fingers set-ups for poking

The Eye Poke is delivered fast like a Jab; here a spread-fingers open hand

The 2 Fingers-fork version of the Eye Poke

The 1-finger Eye Poke

The 5 Spread Fingers Poke - Claw Style

Towel-Drilling the Poke for explosive speed

One could add to the various fingers set-ups the use of the thumb and the clawing of the eyes. These are more close-up techniques for grappling, used for holds and grabs releases. They are trivial and presented in context when necessary. They are not striking techniques to be used from some distance, with the exception of thumbing in certain circumstances.

Applied Eye Clawing in a Release; not a strike!

Thumbing the eye from some distance; go fast, no need for power

4.8 The Hammer-fist

Hammer-fist Strikes are, generally-speaking, very similar to Hand Blade Strikes. They are more powerful (mass of the fist) and safer for the fingers. Therefore, if the target is not narrow and does not require the edge of an open hand, close the fist and do exactly the same movement. Impact is with the fleshy part of the bottom of the hand.

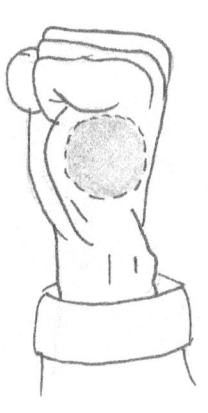

ADVANCED KRAV MAGA

The Hammer-fist Strikes relevant to Krav Maga are: the Downward Strike, the Outward Strike, the Straight Strike and the Hammer-fist Punch.

4.8.1 The Downward Hammer-fist Strike

is executed just like the Hand-sword Strike, but with the fist closed. It is usually targeting the back of the neck of a bent-over opponent or the clavicle. It can also be used to attack a limb or the throat (if it is exposed by pulling his head back).

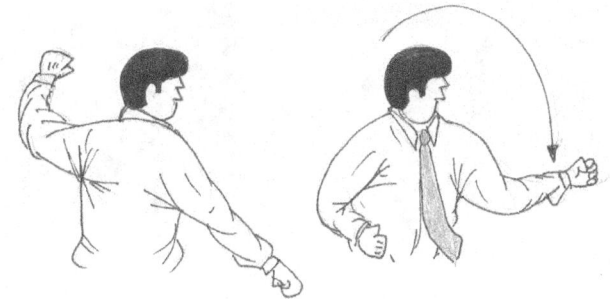

The Downward Hammer-fist Strike

Applied Downward Hammer-fist to the back of the neck

4.8.2 The Outward Hammer-fist Strike

is exactly like its Sword-hand counterpart. It is used to attack the opponent's nose if he is sideways, or the side of his head. It is usually not suitable to attack the throat or the side of the neck, because the fist is too big to get there cleanly. But the Strike is very powerful because it is powered by the hips, and it can also be used on the body: solar plexus, floating ribs, kidneys.

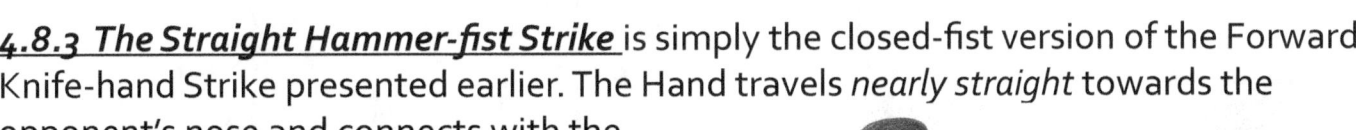

The powerful Outward Hammer-fist Strike: the closed-fist version of the Hand-sword Strike

4.8.3 The Straight Hammer-fist Strike

is simply the closed-fist version of the Forward Knife-hand Strike presented earlier. The Hand travels *nearly straight* towards the opponent's nose and connects with the 'hammer-fist' part. Simple and straightforward, but it always needs to be followed up. It is not the most practical attack in its orthodox form presented here, but it is worth drilling for a fast response. The better option will be the Hammer-fist Punch presented just after.

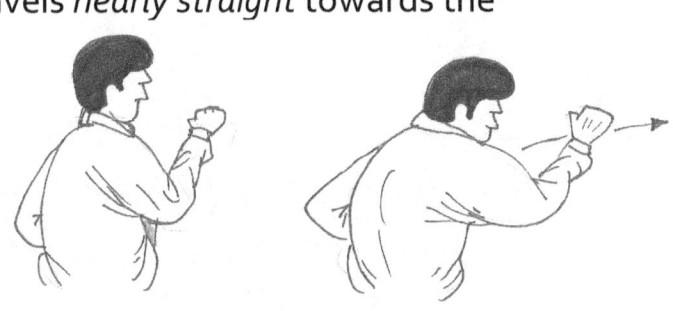

The Straight Hammer-fist Strike

KRAV MAGA STRIKES

Applied Hammer-fist

4.8.4 The Hammer-fist Punch is a very important technique. It is a <u>hybrid</u> between the Downward and the Straight Hammer-fist Strikes. It is more powerful than the Straight version and much less telegraphed than the Downward version. <u>But its importance resides on its exploding directly from a natural high covering guard</u>. When attacked with punches, you will instinctively will lift your arms to cover and protect your head. From this position, you will strike directly without lowering the hand first to a regular guard position from which a jab usually starts. Striking directly is both fast and surprising. Lowering your striking hand first takes time and exposes your intentions. Instead, you will extend your hand directly towards the opponent's nose in a flattened arc. Punch the nose but keep going and drive your fist to a classic guard position. *It is not a surface hit*: strike <u>into</u> the nose for an inch, but keep going through. This is a very surprising strike, and surprisingly effective too. It needs drilling for familiarization (on the heavy bag and on focus pads), but once mastered, it is pretty easy to use.

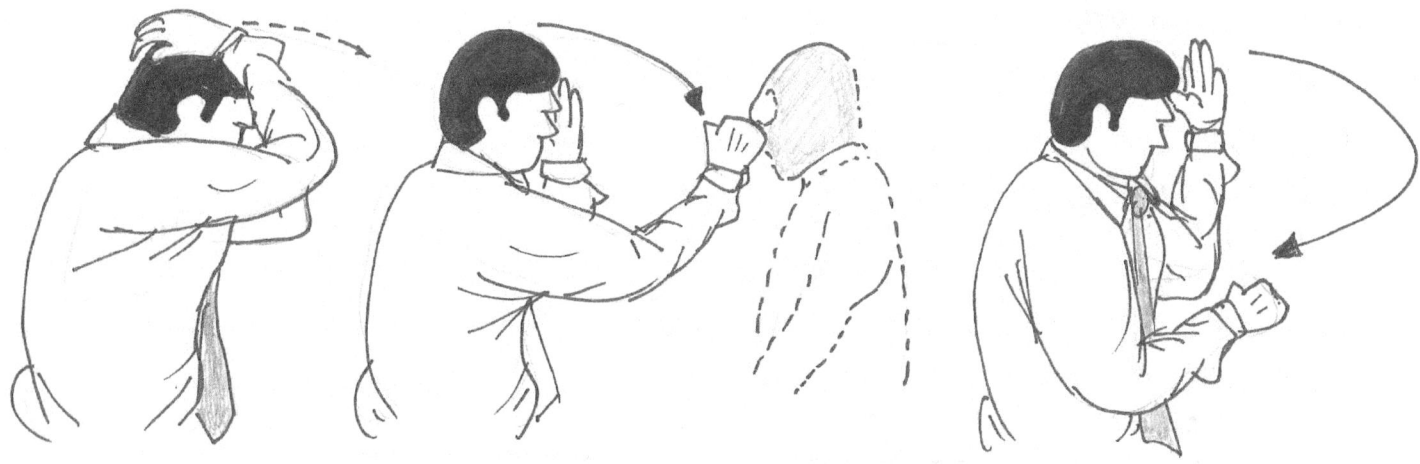

The fantastic Hammer-fist Punch, directly from the Covered Guard position

ADVANCED KRAV MAGA

The Hammer-fist punch- side view

Target the nose!

Front view of the Hammer-fist Punch; straight from the covered 'helmet' guard

Impact and keep going straight through before pulling back

KRAV MAGA STRIKES

This fantastic little technique lends itself to a multitude of naturally-flowing follow-ups, in the spirit of *Retzev*. One possible option is presented below. Design your own and drill it for familiarization.

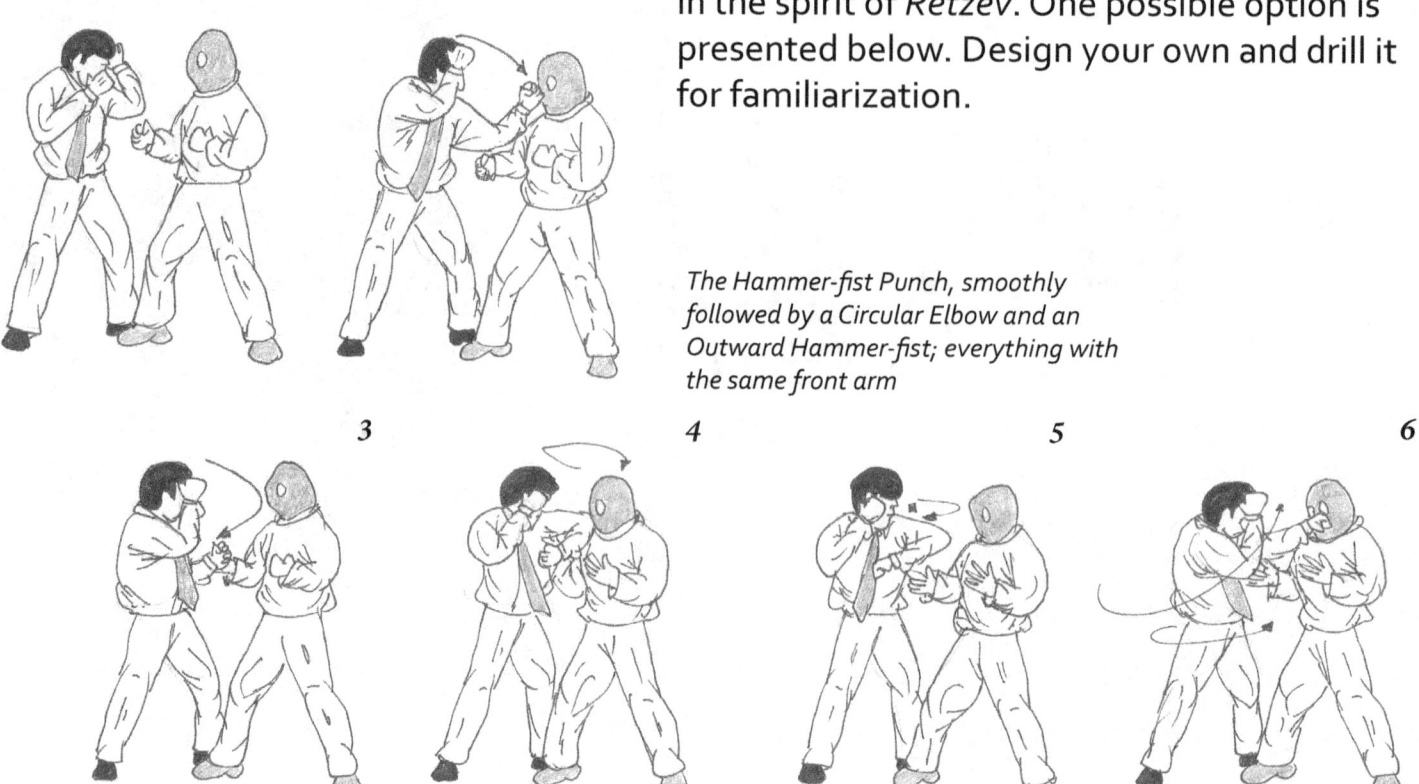

The Hammer-fist Punch, smoothly followed by a Circular Elbow and an Outward Hammer-fist; everything with the same front arm

4.9   The Throat Attacks

The **throat** is a secondary target, ranking in importance with the groin and the eyes. Striking the throat is potentially debilitating and even potentially lethal. A controlled attack will cause difficulty to breathe and enough pain to stop the fight. Drill carefully and use only in serious circumstances. The throat can be attacked from any angle possible and with any suitable hand configuration; it is sensitive enough *to require more precision than power*.

You can theoretically attack the throat with any of your natural weapons, but it is not always easy or practical. The preferred ways to attack the throat are presented in the Drawings at the top of next page:

- the '*mouth of the hand*' (the webbed part between the thumb and index fingers) which lends itself to following up with trachea pinching techniques.
- the '*leopard paw*' (the first knuckles of the three middle fingers) which is very hard but narrower than the fist.
- the *knife-hand* ('karate chop') for circular techniques.
- the *Ridge-hand* (opposite side of the Knife-hand) for circular attacks as well, with the thumb and index finger knuckles.

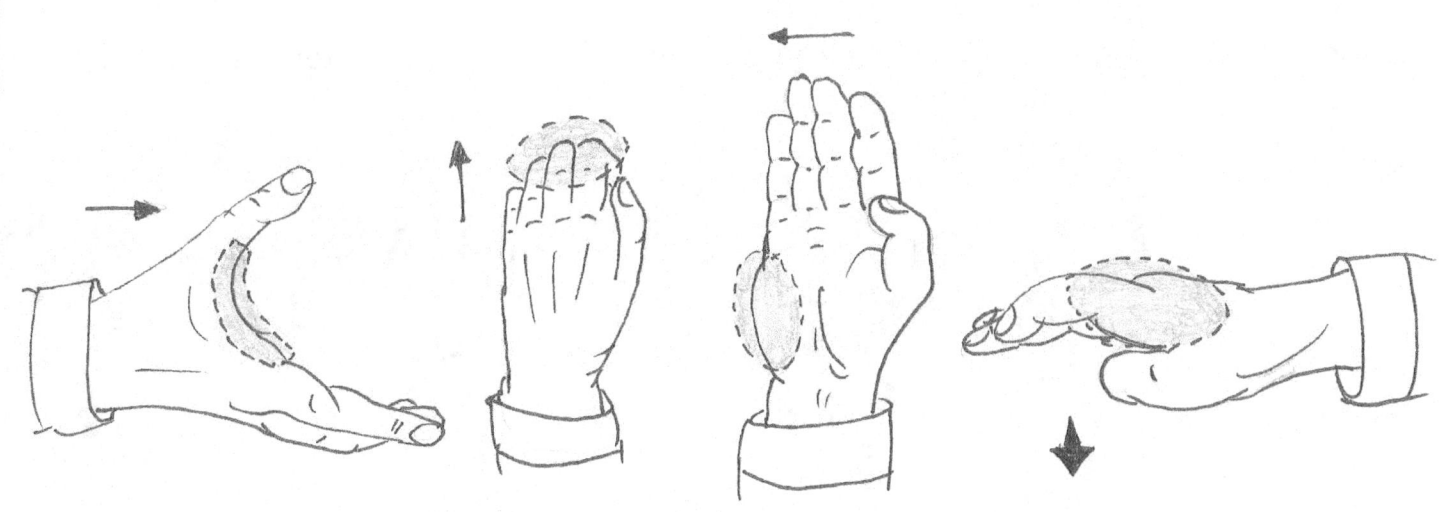

Natural weapons for attacking the throat

Other ways to attack the throat are valid in certain cases, but they require more concentration and more complicated approaches, which is not in line with the simplicity required by *Krav Maga* for use in stressful situations. For example, a regular Punch to the throat will be very efficient in dispatching the opponent; but most fighters keep their chin down to protect both throat and chin, which makes access difficult. If the circumstances are right, you can either come with an upward punch or pull the opponent's head back (by the hair or the eyes to 'open' the throat. The coming Figure shows such an 'opening' of the throat for the delivery of a Hammer-fist Strike in a similar technique. The use of the stiffened fingers to strike straight with the tips of the fingers requires impact training not in line with the KISS principle of *Krav Maga*. You can even use a Kick to attack the throat, as illustrated (In extreme cases, you can even stomp-kick the throat of the opponent thrown to the floor).

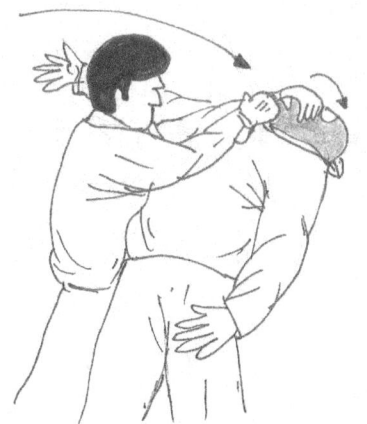

Downward Hammer-fist Strike to an exposed throat – use only in special circumstances

Side Kicks to the throat – requires lots of training and unnecessarily sophisticated for Krav Maga

KRAV MAGA STRIKES

It is therefore recommended to concentrate on the **4** hand configurations presented above and drill them for familiarization.

The 'Bear Mouth' Hand strike to the throat

Applied Circular Outward Knife-hand Strike to the throat in a Choke Release

Leopard Paw 'punch' to the throat

Circular Ridge-hand Strike to the throat

The 'Mouth of the Hand' straight Strike is highly recommended: it is natural, it is easy to perform, it can come diagonally up from down out-of-the-field-of-vision, and it lends itself to a mean trachea pinch follow-up. It can be delivered from the lead hand, as a jab, or from the rear hand as a cross. Get familiar and use it, but remember that it is a <u>Strike</u>, not a choke or a push. Hit <u>fast</u> and dry. Only after impact of *a few inches into the throat*, should you eventually start grabbing for a choking follow-up.

A full-powered 'Mouth of the hand' throat attack: pull him in by the grabbed wrist

Only after you have mastered the technique as a dry 'punch', should you start drilling **the subsequent grabbing of the throat** for the mean follow-ups it allows.

These special and *very dangerous techniques* have to be drilled very carefully and used only in the direst of situations where your life, or that of your loved ones are in clear danger.

➤

80   **ADVANCED KRAV MAGA**

After impact, you should grip the opponent's trachea between your thumb and your other fingers. You are *not* to try to choke the whole neck by squeezing everything (including the carotids). It is simpler to try to pinch the larynx only by going in with your fingers as if trying to encircle it to pull it out. It is enough to squeeze the trachea itself to cause immense pain and difficulty to breathe. Squeeze only as much as the situation dictates; this is very dangerous, especially coming after the throat strike.

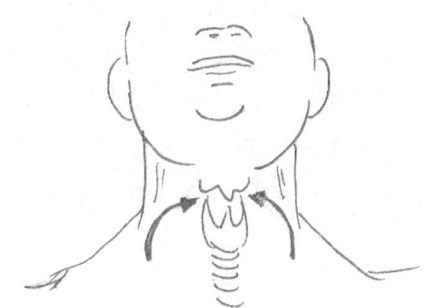

Try to pinch behind the Larynx Box

Once you have pinched the trachea, you have to prevent the opponent to pull out of the grab. You can do that by throwing him to the ground or by catching the back of his neck and pulling it forward into your grip.

You can take the opponent down by reaping his leg and twisting him into the throw by pushing his throat. See Illustrations below. You can also simply push his head straight down while holding his lower back to prevent him retreating (See second set of Figures). In both cases, you should use the technique *to slam his head to the ground*, not just to take him down [*If you have had to use a trachea pinch, it means that the circumstances were life-threatening*].

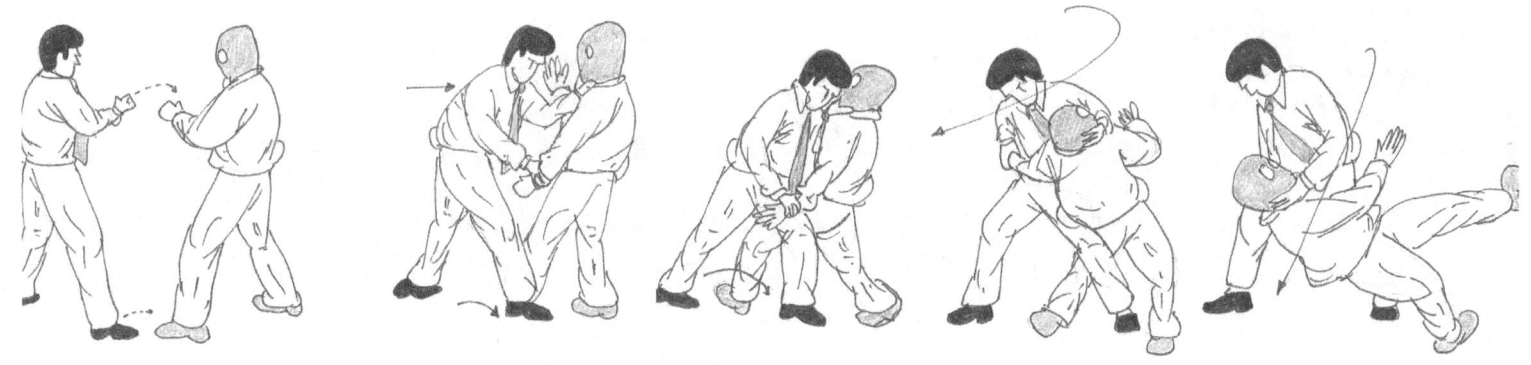

Throat Strike to Trachea Pinch to Outer Leg reaping Takedown

Throat Strike and Trachea Pinch on a Haywire Punch Defense; push his head directly down into the ground

KRAV MAGA STRIKES

If you do not want to take him down but rather to keep striking him, you should use the Trachea Pinch after the Throat Strike, *and immediately catch the back of his neck* to prevent his retreating. Pinch hard and squeeze the hands together for a painful maneuver, but keep striking. This is not a static technique like a choke, **but a dynamic transition**. The natural follow-up is one or several Knee Strikes to the groin, before you let go ... to keep Striking.

Double Hand Squeeze as a transition technique between a Throat Strike and a Groin Knee Attack

When it comes to self defense, it is better to have the power and not need it than to need it and not have it.
~Kevin B. Shearer

ADVANCED KRAV MAGA

PART FIVE

More Offensive Techniques: Range Covering, Combinations, Guard Neutralization

סגירת מרחק, קומבינציות וניטרול ידיים

*This part of the book corresponds to the Chapter about **Offensive Techniques** in our previous 'Krav Maga Kicks'. Our previous book was skewed towards kicking, although it did present general offensive techniques often starting with a hand movement. We will now elaborate with more rounded offensive techniques, with maneuvers for Range Covering, with Naturally-flowing striking combinations, with 'special' attacks and with guard neutralizations.*

These are all offensive techniques, even if they appear after a defense in the middle of a fight. They should be drilled in the Krav Maga spirit of <u>always being offensive</u>. In fact, they all should be looked at as Preemptive Techniques, to be used as soon as you 'feel' that the assailant is about to launch his own attack.

The trainee should not aim at mastering all the techniques presented. As already mentioned, he should aim at truly mastering only a few techniques to be drilled assiduously. But the trainee should drill all of them and try to use them in training and in free fighting. This is the only way to become familiar with the possible maneuvers, and then let the body decide which are most suited to your specific physique and psychology.

5.1 Range Covering Techniques

Mastering **Range Covering** is very important for all Fighting Arts. As a fight generally starts from the outrange from which neither protagonist can land a strike without a step move, you have to learn *how to get into striking range as safely as possible*.

Krav Maga is all about being <u>offensive</u> from the start and all the way to the end of the fight. This means that, if confronted in a no-escape situation, you should go on the offensive as early as possible. *By doing so, you take the initiative and hopefully keep it, you assert your status as a 'no-victim' and you try to place your potential assailant on the defensive.*

Our previous book (*Krav Maga Kicks*) did already present a few **Range Covering Techniques** in the Chapter about 'Offensive Techniques'. They were not specifically presented as range covering, but they are obviously so. They were generally deep-lunging forward maneuvers with some protective arms configuration. And further in this section, we shall present *Guard Closing Techniques*, which are also, in fact, Range Coverers: the closing of the opponent's guard neutralizes his upper limbs for the time needed to get into close range. So the concept of **Range Covering** is very wide and encompasses many possible techniques. The few that we are going to present below are more specific to getting into striking distance from relatively far away. *The explosion forward is supposed to surprise a potential assailant who feels safe where he is and expects you to cower in place or to retreat in front of his threatening attitude.*

The illustrated examples presented further in the text will make the concept abundantly clear.

In order to become **a good Range Coverer**, it is imperative to develop Explosive Power and to learn to avoid any Telegraphing of the impending jump forward.

Explosive Power can be achieved by:
- Intense drilling of the techniques,
- Calves building in the gym,
- Daily Rope Skipping (at least 20 min),
- Lower Body Plyometrics.

Non-telegraphing can be perfected by:
- Drilling the explosion forward in front of the mirror,
- Drilling the disconnect between upper and lower body during the forward jump (upper body stays in exact same position while the legs push forward),
- Training with a partner that 'spots' you.

Once you have mastered the techniques presented, you should complete them with your own *Retzev*: once you have closed the distance and struck your opponent, there is no stopping until the fight is totally over.

(1) The simplest type of Range Covering is by feinting high and kicking low.
Feinting high, even if you cannot even reach the opponent will nevertheless elicit an instinctive reaction and draw his attention high while letting him feel safe because he is out of range of the punch. The very simple example below shows how you feint with a hopelessly far Cross Punch, while in fact stepping close enough for a successful long Front Kick to the groin area. Follow up, of course.

Lunge forward with a high out-of-range Punch, but kick long to catch him in the groin

86   ADVANCED KRAV MAGA

The next example is based on the same principle, but from **a shorter distance**. In that instance, you feint a Cross to the body that has no pretention to score, but only to make the opponent retreat slightly to stay out of range. You follow with a front-leg Sweep Kick to the front inside ankle that will place the opponent off-balance while *you lunge forward* with a real Cross Palm Strike to the face. You can naturally flow into a Groin Knee Strike as you take hold of his head (eventually striking his ears). From there, the *Retzev* is yours.

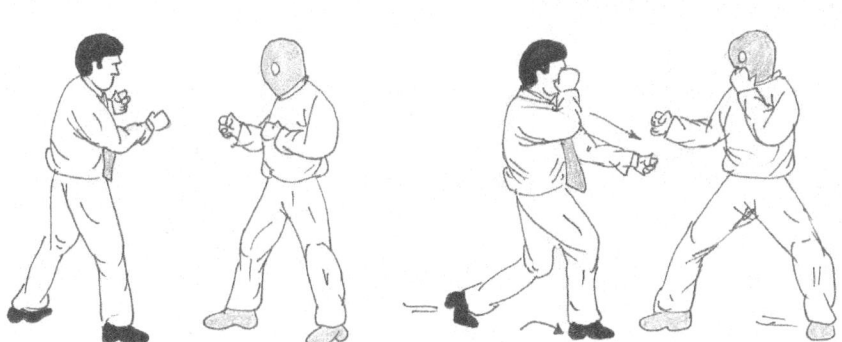

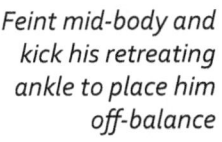

Feint mid-body and kick his retreating ankle to place him off-balance

The same technique can be executed with a **rear-leg Sweep Kick** to the outside ankle of the retreating leg. As illustrated below:

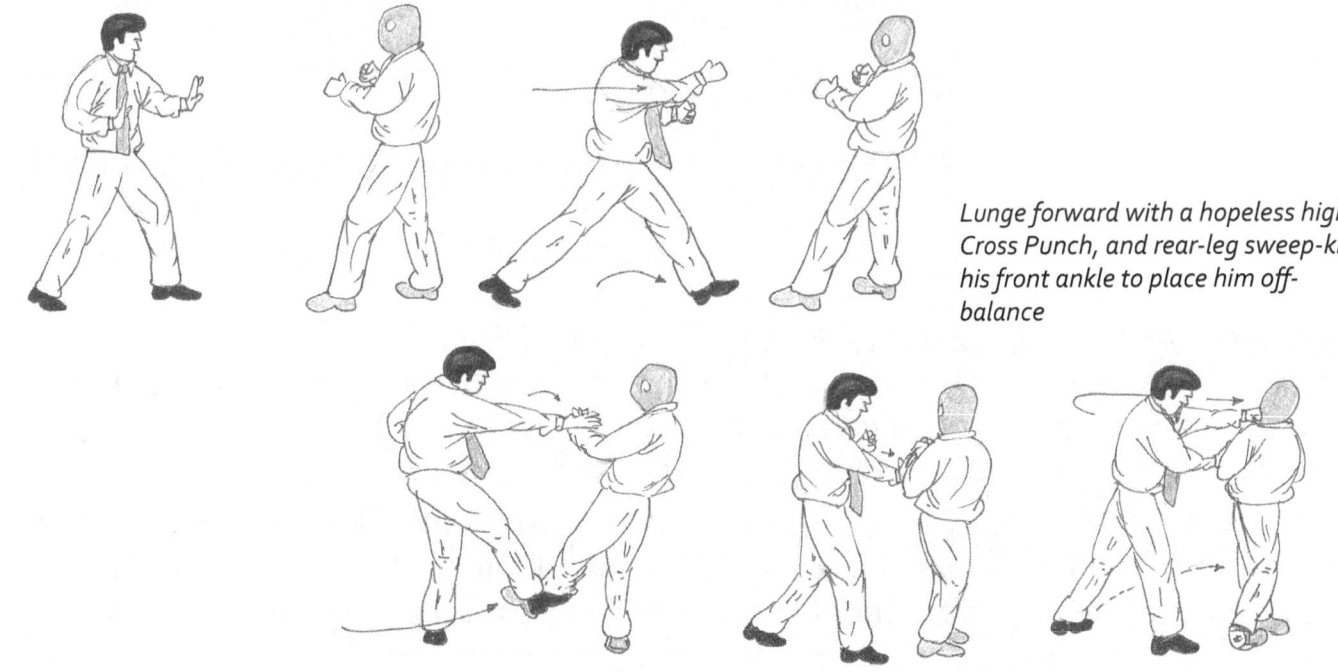

Lunge forward with a hopeless high Cross Punch, and rear-leg sweep-kick his front ankle to place him off-balance

MORE OFFENSIVE TECHNIQUES

(2) The other main type of Range Covering is in fact close to Guard Closing:

you lunge while catching his front hand to unsettle him and to neutralize his weapon closest to you. The grab is in fact a fast feint. There is no need for a serious grab: this is about being very fast and allow for the first strike to his face from your other hand. Simple and effective: the KISS principle...

Lunge explosively forward to grab his front hand, and strike his face with your other palm

It is sometimes safer to immediately **get out of the centerline** after such a technique, in case the first strike is not decisive enough. As illustrated below, you can then follow up with a Groin Roundhouse Kick.

If needed, get out of the centerline after the lunge and follow-up

(3) A last type of Range Covering is ... the Low Kick,

but it requires mastering the *non-telegraphing* principle. By keeping the upper body immobile, and especially the head height, you can step close enough for a *fast* <u>Low Front Kick to the shin</u>. The Kick is unexpected: when he'll realize you are approaching, the opponent will expect a Punch and concentrate up. The low kick is invisible. Follow up with a front-hand Palm Strike, a rear-hand Throat 'Tiger Mouth' Strike, and a Groin Knee Strike (while pulling his shoulder forward). Illustrated at the top of next page.

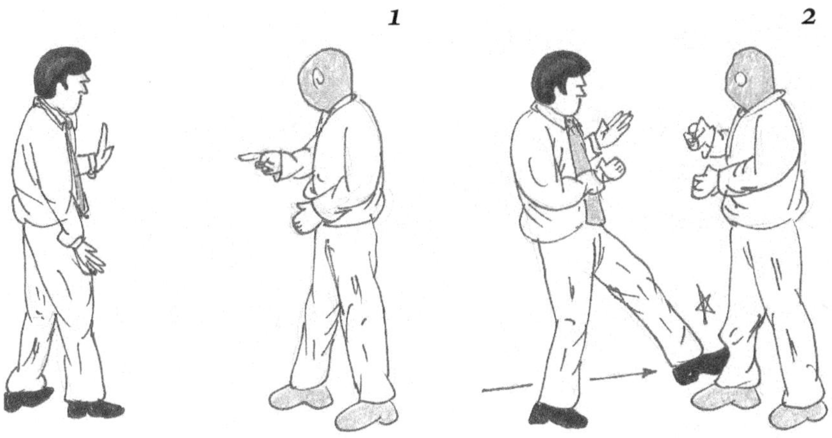

An un-telegraphed Low Front Kick to the shin is very difficult to spot and avoid; and so will be the subsequent high follow-up

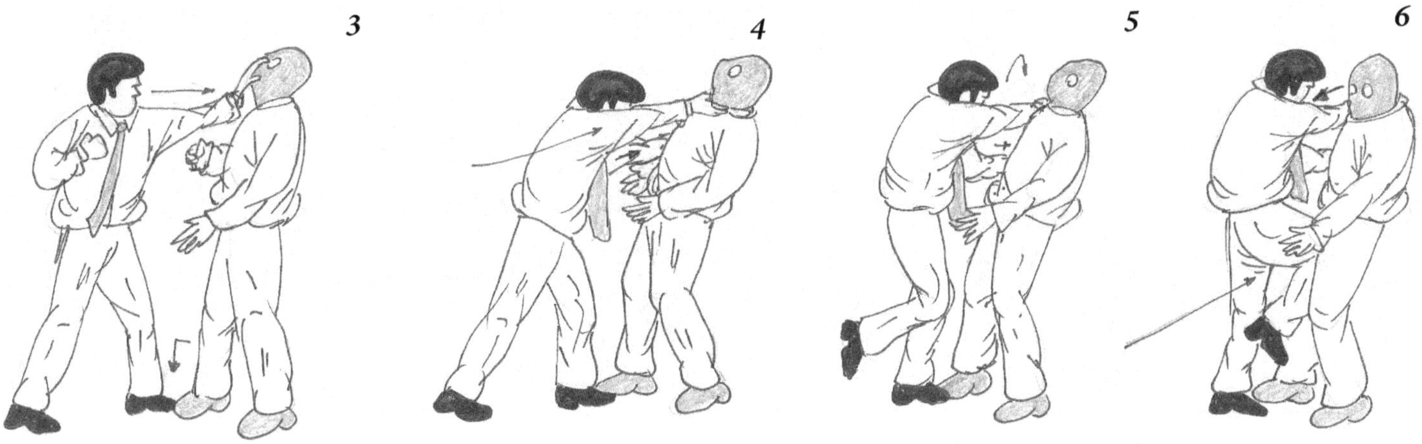

5.2   Guard Neutralization Techniques

'Closing' the opponent's tight guard will allow you to neutralize both arms *long enough to deliver your first Strike with impunity*. From then on, it is for you to keep at it. **Guard Neutralization** is, in fact, a Range Closing-type of technique, as it allows you to get closer safely. It works best with people who have a tight, tense and closed guard (like a boxer). The principle is very easy to understand and will be widely illustrated further in the book. Remember that the closing of the opponent's guard is not the purpose of the technique: <u>you must neutralize his upper limbs just long enough to allow your first strike</u>. You are not trying to tie him up or to grab him in any way; you just need to control and unsettle him for the start of your *Retzev*!

MORE OFFENSIVE TECHNIQUES

(1) _**The simplest Guard Neutralization technique is to lunge and push the opponent's guarding hands forcefully into his own face.**_

The mindset should be to dive all out and try _to strike him violently in the face with his own fists_. The principle is very simple, but the technique is fiendishly efficient if you take the time to drill it seriously. Remember: Keep It Simple, Stupid!

In the examples illustrated below, you follow up either with a Groin Kick **or** with a Twin Leg Tackle (followed by a Groin Stomp).

Crash his guard into his own face and kick the groin

Dive to push his hands in his face and tackle him before stomping his groin

90   **_ADVANCED KRAV MAGA_**

(2) The second Guard Neutralization Principle is simple too, and we have seen it sketchily in the Range Covering section.

You push his front hand _in front of his rear hand to neutralize both_, while you use your free hand to strike. From there, the _Retzev_ will start. This principle works better for lower guards, more Karate-like than Boxing-like. This is, again, both very simple and very efficient. It needs drilling though, especially the _explosive unexpected jump forward_.

In the example illustrated, you follow up with a Palm Strike to the chin (or nose), a Low Kick to the knee and a hip-driven Circular Elbow to the side of the head.

Jump explosively forward and push his front hand in front of his rear hand; strike his face with your free hand and start your Retzev

(3) The last type of Guard Neutralization is slightly more complex and requires more training:

You go _for both his guarding hands with both your hands_. This is a more sophisticated but very efficient technique. It is for more advanced 'Kravists' and requires serious drilling, but the results are worthwhile.

The technique works well against opponents with a tight high guard with fists close to one another. You lunge forward and cover both his hands with yours. And then, you push one hand down and the other one over it. When this is done you can let go of the hand controlling his lower hand: _it is his own upper hand that controls it; upper hand that is controlled by yours_. In fact, you are more or less 'tying his own hands in a knot'. The purpose is, of course, not the neutralization, but the follow-up techniques it allows against the opponent who is briefly at your mercy.

Our first example, at the top of next page, shows how you take advantage of his neutralization to simply (KISS!) palm-strike his nose and kick his groin ➤

MORE OFFENSIVE TECHNIQUES

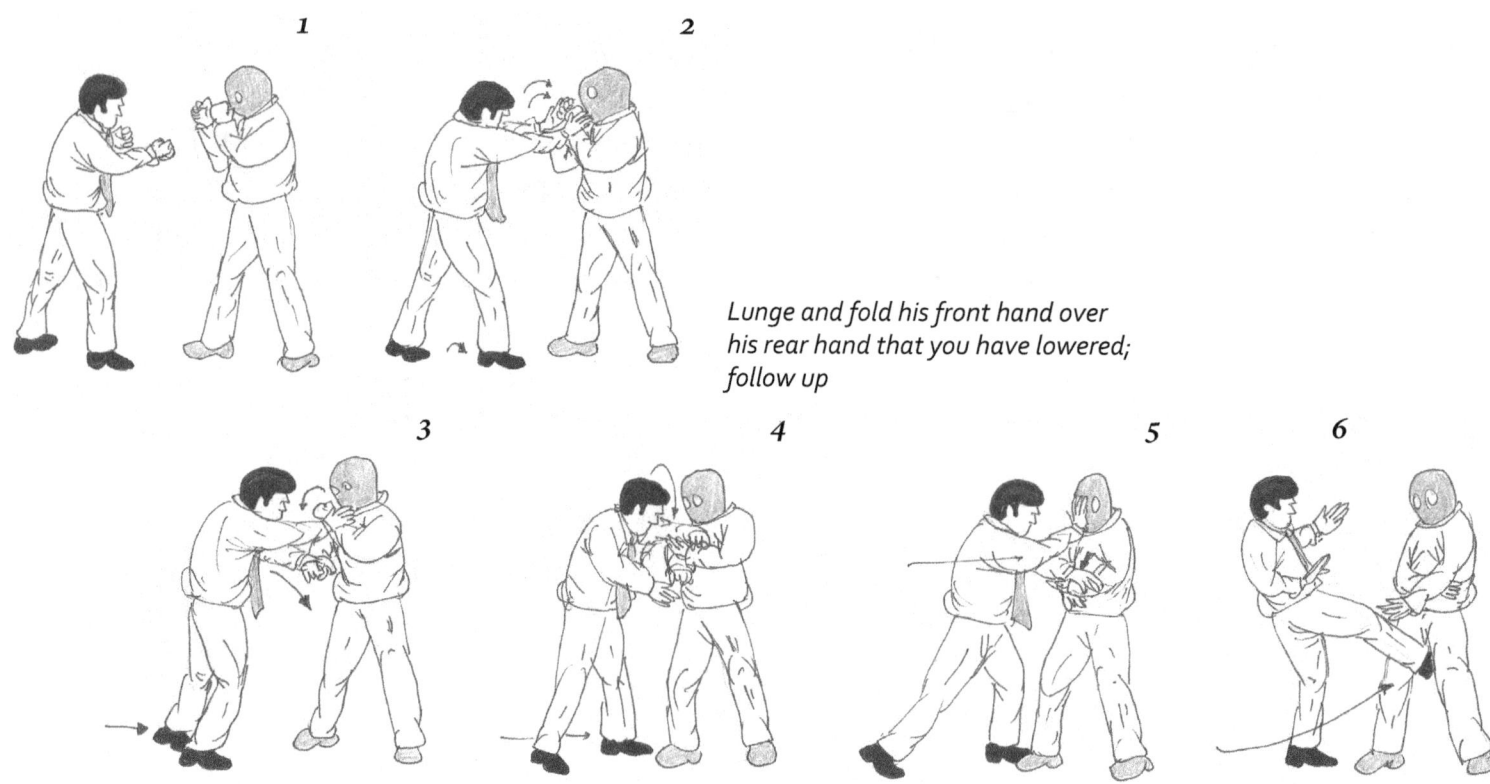

Lunge and fold his front hand over his rear hand that you have lowered; follow up

Our second example is even simpler and makes use of the momentum of your powerful forward lunge: you simply keep going for a Headbutt into his face, as his hands are neutralized.

Lunge towards him with a Headbutt while neutralizing both his guarding hands

Our last example is more complex but illustrates the fact that the neutralization is not a hold *but a dynamic transition technique*. In this example, illustrated at the top of next page, you take advantage of the neutralization to keep going forward and to overtake the opponent diagonally. You can then let go of the hands to immediately 'go' for his eyes; as you are nearly behind him, he will not see that coming. Follow up by: (1) encircling his neck and pull him back, (2) kneeing his kidneys, (3) stomping the back of his knee, and (4) hammer-fisting his face from behind.

92   **ADVANCED KRAV MAGA**

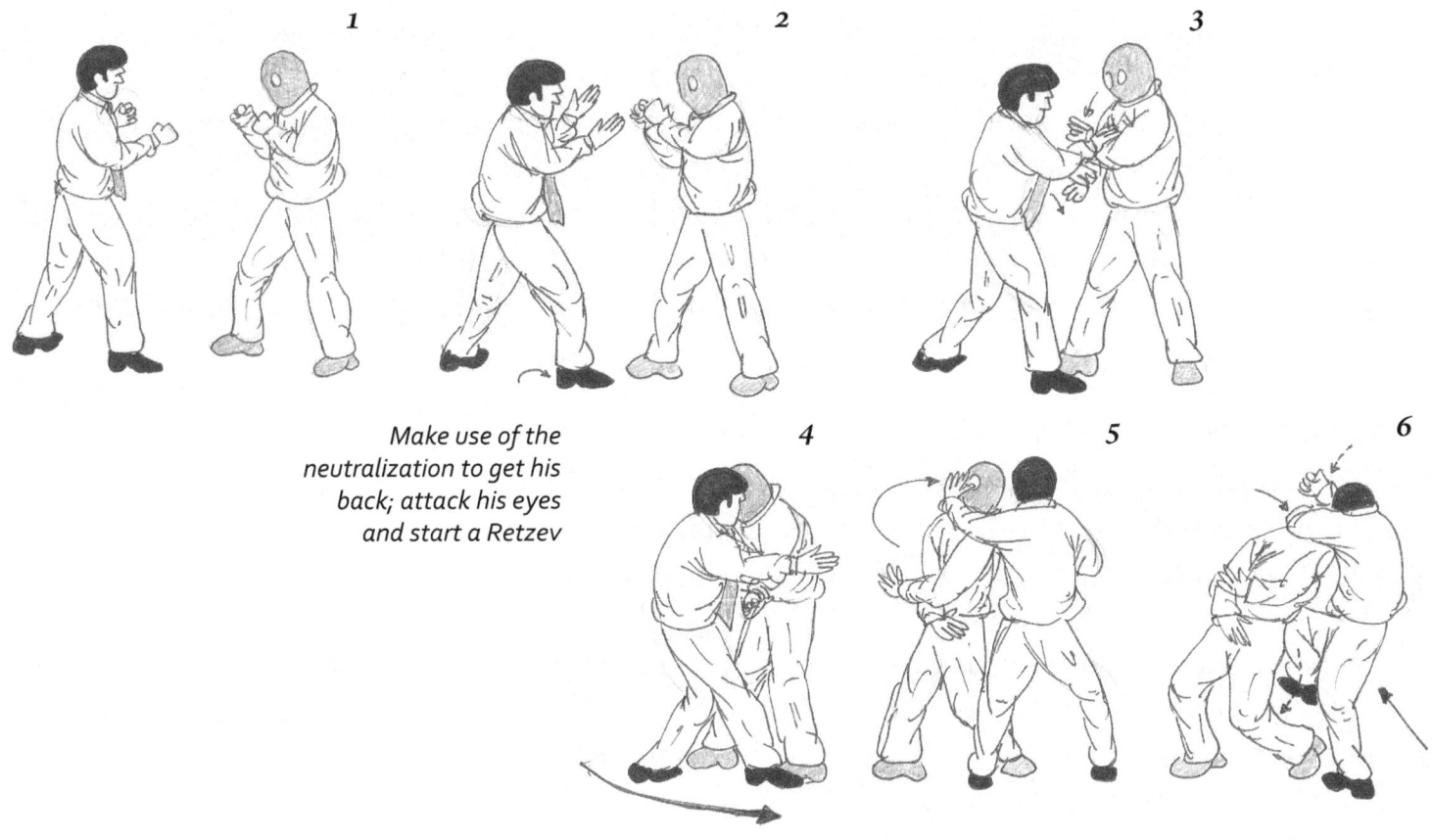

Make use of the neutralization to get his back; attack his eyes and start a Retzev

5.3 Natural Combinations

'Krav Maga Kicks' is crammed with **Natural Combinations**. The follow-up sequences after self-defense techniques are all *Retzev* based on **Natural Combinations**. The reader is invited to consult this previous book and drill the *Retzev* sequences presented independently from the techniques they are following.

But ultimately, after you have drilled all these sequences, the <u>ideal</u> **Natural Combinations** will be those <u>that work for you</u>. After lots of drilling and free fighting, patterns will emerge in your way to follow up and to link the techniques of the *Retzev*: it will be your body telling you what works best for you. Of course, that will not happen if you have not tried and drilled plenty of proven chains of techniques.

So, go for it. Drill them all, train hard and then start to develop your own preferences, most suitable to your physique and personality.

MORE OFFENSIVE TECHNIQUES

Just try to take into account **the important principle of Alternation**: try to alternate your strikes and to hit low after hitting high; and striking from the left after striking from the right. It is obvious (but still good to remind the reader) that a first strike will cause an instinctive reaction *whether it has succeeded or not*. An opponent hit in the face will lift his hands (and uncover his body and groin), and a circular attack to the left of the opponent will cause him to momentarily focus there (instead of his uncovered right side). Alternate hi and lo, in and out, straight and circular. Trivial, but remember the KISS principle...

We are just going to add a few more sequences below. Try them too and keep working hard until your intuition directs you to what is most efficient for you. Then drill those even harder and focus on them for an automatic powerful response, even under stressful conditions.

The first sequence aims at using a continuous logical move of the upper limbs, each one fading into the next *naturally*. Jab his face with your palm and follow with a Hook from the other (rear) fist. Go *through* his head with the Hook while pushing your hips forward and hit him with your Elbow by simply folding the striking arm. As you have been 'through' his head with your hip-propelled elbow, you can now go back the way you came from and go through his head again with a Hammer-fist Outward Strike. Keep the momentum to conclude with a slap (Palm Strike) to his ear with the other hand (the one from the Jab). Of course, you could keep at it if necessary. This one is about **Flow**!

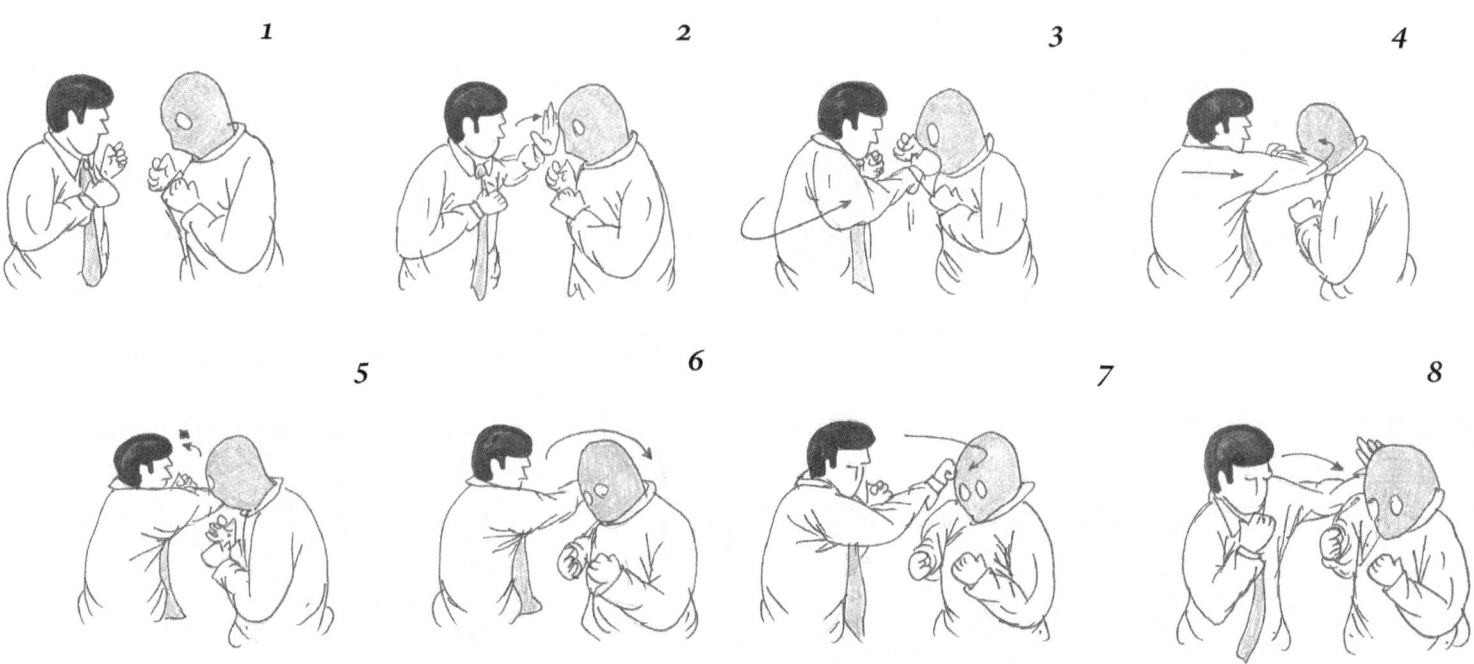

A flowing hand-striking combination starting with a simple Palm Jab

The next sequence is shorter, but can be completed in any way the reader fancies. You 'miss' a Jab by developing it beside the opponent's head, only to strike him with an **Inward Forearm Strike** to the side of the neck. The Forearm then pulls his head forward, towards your incoming hip-propelled Circular Elbow Strike. Aim for the throat, neck or nose. Follow up!

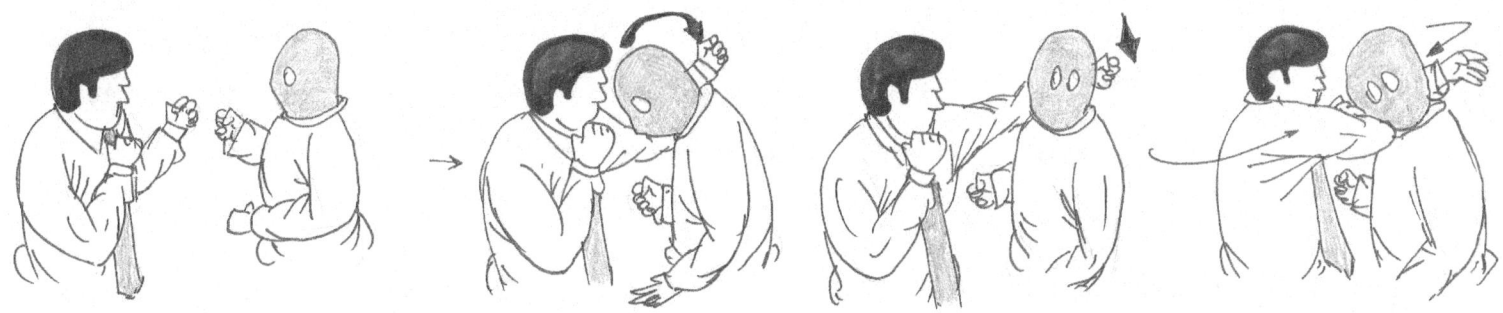

An Inward Forearm strike pulls the opponent head into a Circular Elbow

The next example starts with the simplest most classic opening. Simple but efficient! You jab with an open hand towards the opponent's eyes (**hi**) and make use of his reaction to low-kick his knee forcefully. As you have struck **low**, he will lower his hands and uncover his head for a (straight) rear-hand Palm Strike as the foot lands back and a Circular Elbow attack (**hi**). After these high strikes, why not a Knee to the groin (**lo**).

Start with a hi/lo classic; jab and low kick; then alternate high straight and circular, and back to low

The next series, illustrated at the top of next page, shows the **use of the momentum of the initial lunge**. You jab the opponent's eyes and keep going forward while bending the arm. The Eye Jab turns *naturally* into a straight Forearm Strike to his nose; if he has lifted his hands to his face, you will hit him with his own hands. Follow up with a (mildly circular) Hook to the side of his head. It is then the time to alternate to the lower gates with a Low Kick to his knee. Keep at it if necessary.

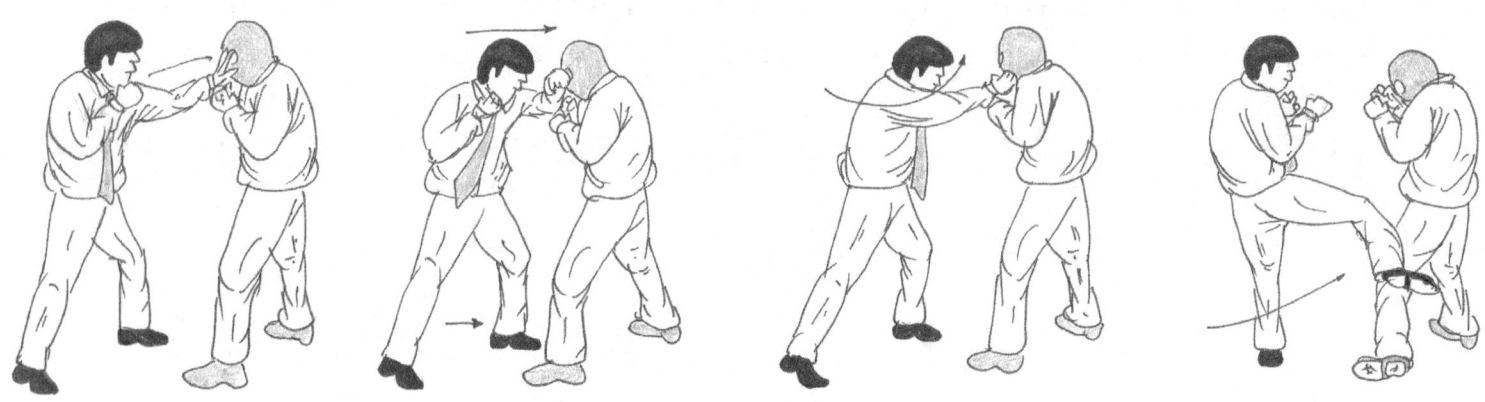

An Eye Jab turns into a straight Forearm Strike to the face, and starts a Retzev

The next example illustrates a nice **alternation flow**. It starts with the fantastic Lunging Eye Whipping technique, fast and relaxed. As the opponent cannot <u>not</u> lift his hands you reverse-punch his gut to bring them back *down*. Follow up with a (*high*) Outwards Hammer-fist Strike to the side of his head from your front hand. This strike will naturally pull your rear hand in a momentum-powered slap (Palm Strike) to the same side of his head. Should he have his hands there, they will be violently smashed into his head. The other hand then comes back *low* to hit his (certainly) uncovered groin.

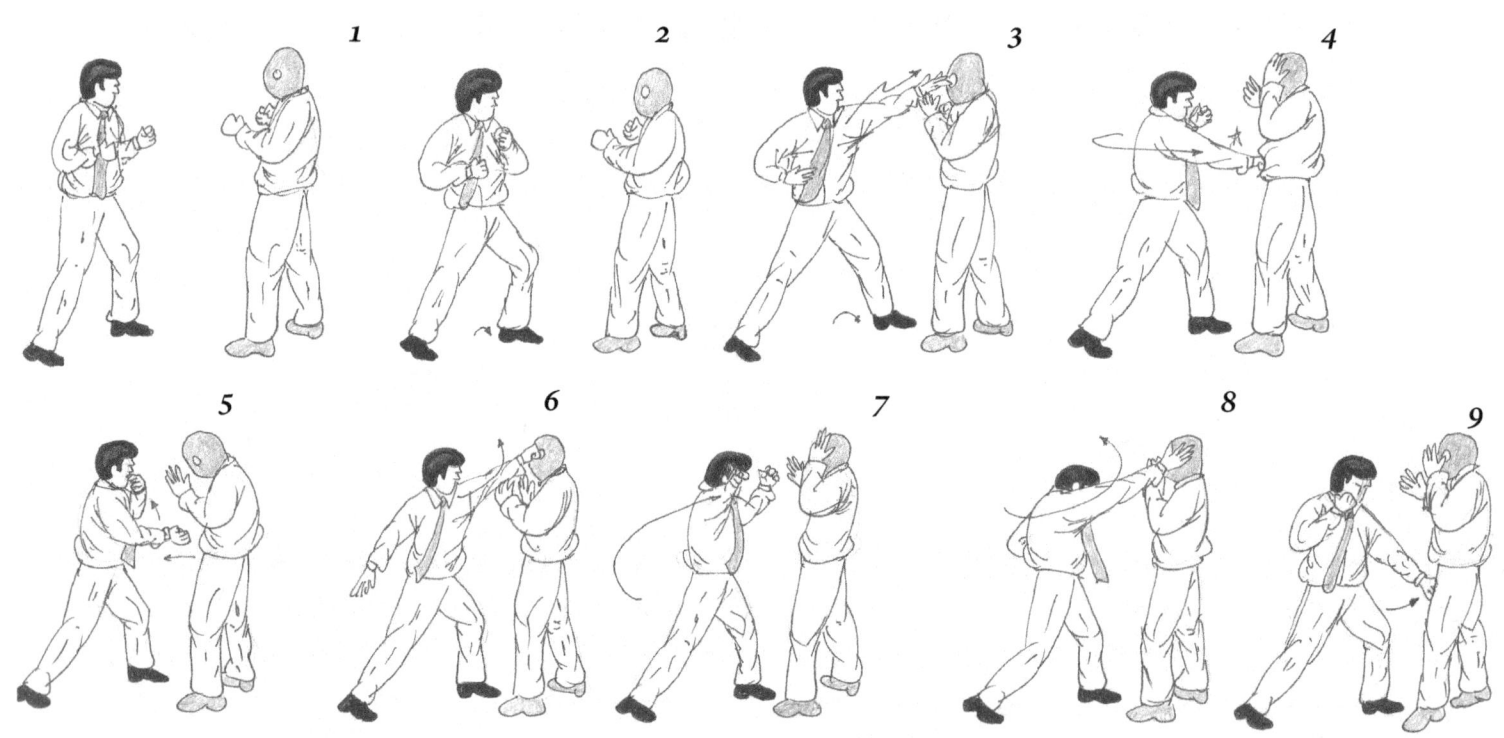

High, low, High In, High In, Low

96   **ADVANCED KRAV MAGA**

The next combination presented wants to underline the importance of the Knee Strike, and better, the **Knee Strikes in series**. In the example below, you move aside and grab the brandished front hand of a threatening assailant. You do so all the while you are striking his throat with your front hand in 'tiger mouth' configuration (the webbed part between the thumb and index finger). Keep your forward momentum and fold your striking arm, so as to naturally flow into a Forward (and slightly upward) Elbow Strike to the neck. By naturally extending your arm, you will be able to catch his head from behind to lower it for a rear-leg Knee Strike. Downward-elbow his head while lowering your foot, and conclude with a second Knee Strike from the other leg (holding his head down).

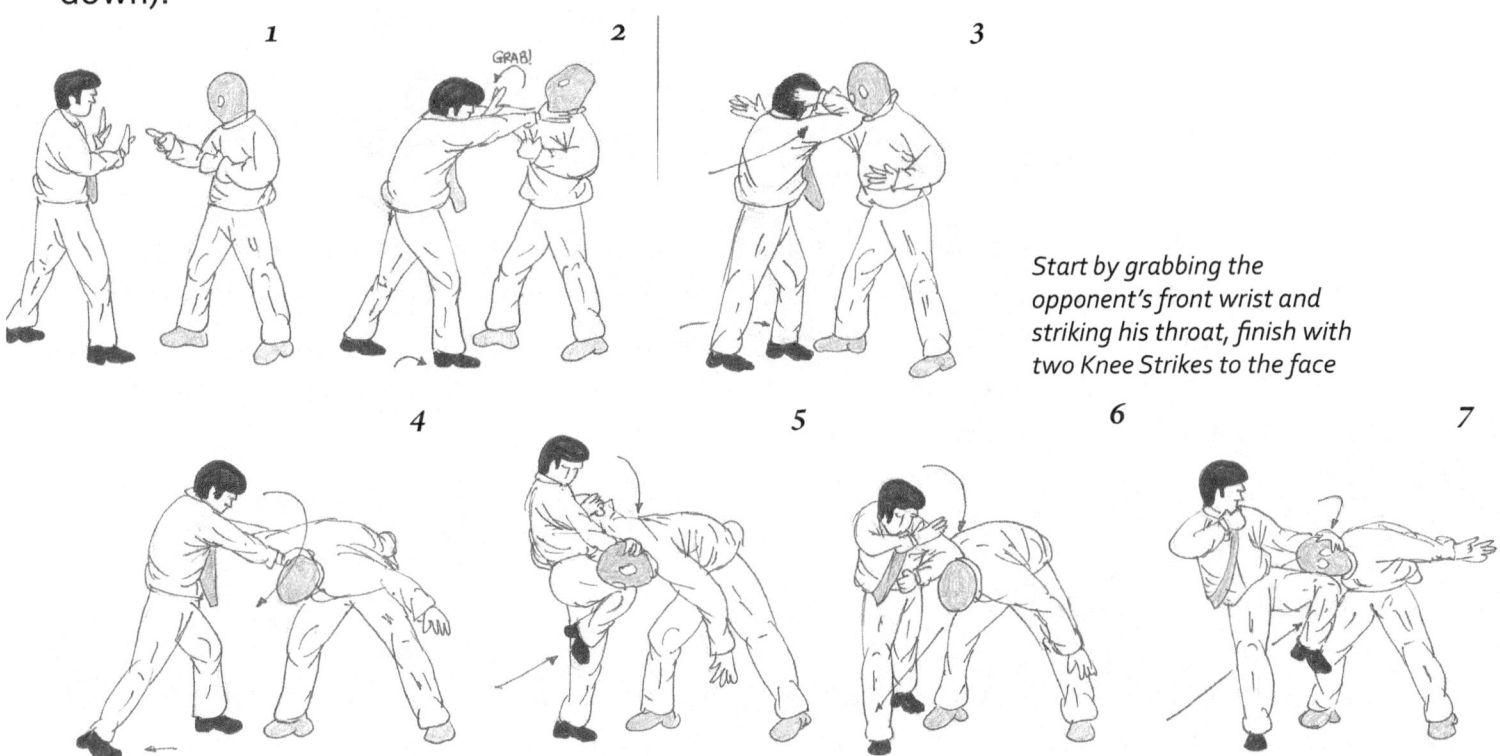

Start by grabbing the opponent's front wrist and striking his throat, finish with two Knee Strikes to the face

We shall conclude with a last example that underlines the importance of **simplicity**. The *KISS* principle and the '*Retzev*' principle are probably the most important tenets of *Krav Maga*. The Drawings at the top of next page illustrate how you lift your front leg fast towards the opponent's groin. No need for power or complicated set-ups: the purpose is to get the opponent to *lower* his hands and focus down. You then throw a long, relaxed and super-fast Eye Rake (or Eye Whip). If you are fast and committed, you cannot miss with this simple maneuver. Attacking his eyes will certainly cause him to *lift his hands back*. You can now truly go for a Groin Kick that he will not see coming.

MORE OFFENSIVE TECHNIQUES

KISS: Fake Groin Kick will allow for an easy Eye Rake; then a real Groin kick

5.4 Special Techniques

This section will deal with difficult to classify techniques, mostly offensive. These are of various types, but generally more sophisticated than the basic techniques described in the previous Chapters and in our previous book about *Krav Maga Kicks*. These techniques do require thorough drilling and free fighting experience, but being nastily efficient, they are a must for the Advanced *Kravist*.
Here they come:

5.4.1 The Elbow Strike Block

This is a sophisticated technique, not easy to execute, but very much in the spirit of *Krav Maga*: an offensive Block. Defending with an aggressive technique is what *Krav Maga* is all about!
The assailant attacks you with a punch; instead of reaching a soft target, his knuckles will connect with the tip of your elbow. This is painful and can cause serious fingers damage. Of course, you'll then follow up with your own strikes and kicks all the way to submission.
The Illustrations at the top of next page show a great way to drill the technique and make very clear what the maneuver is all about. You catch your partner's Jab on the tip of your elbow, and then his following Cross with the tip of the other elbow. Follow up with a Groin Kick. Be careful in practice and have your partner wear protecting boxing gloves.
Of course, the example presented is just a drill. In combat, you probably would not use the technique in series against a left/right punching attack. In fact, one of the primary advantages of this special technique is its effect of surprise. ➤

Have the opponent crush his own attacking fingers on your elbow tip

The principle of the technique can also work against High Kicks. The Drawings below illustrate the use of the '**Elbow Tip Block**' against the knee or shin of an incoming Roundhouse Kick. Ouch... Follow up with a Groin Kick and start a *Retzev*.

Let the kicking opponent's shin meet the tip of your elbow

In *Krav Maga*, it is always preferable to lunge to preempt an attack or to stop it in its early development. But if you are late and have to block, then this is a very fast and painful way to do it. The technique requires drilling though, and serious work is needed.

Danger, if met head on, can be nearly halved
~Winston Churchill

MORE OFFENSIVE TECHNIQUES

5.4.2 The Tying-up Guard-closing Techniques

These are sophisticated **Guard Neutralization** maneuvers *that go further* than the regular techniques presented before. In this case, you lunge and grab the opponent's guarding hands just like before, but, instead of directly going for a Strike, *you will tie his arms together* to allow for more control and a more effective follow-up. This is against, a complex technique principle, to be reserved for advanced *Kravists*. These moves require serious drilling with resisting partners to make them viable in stressful combat. But they are very effective techniques that are relatively easy to execute when mastered. In our first example, you lunge for a regular Guard Neutralization technique as

presented in the relevant section. But, once you have been able to cover his lowered front hand with his rear forearm, you keep the hold on to slip behind him. You find yourself behind him while neutralizing both his hands! Go for his eyes from behind and start your *Retzev*: he is totally at your mercy.

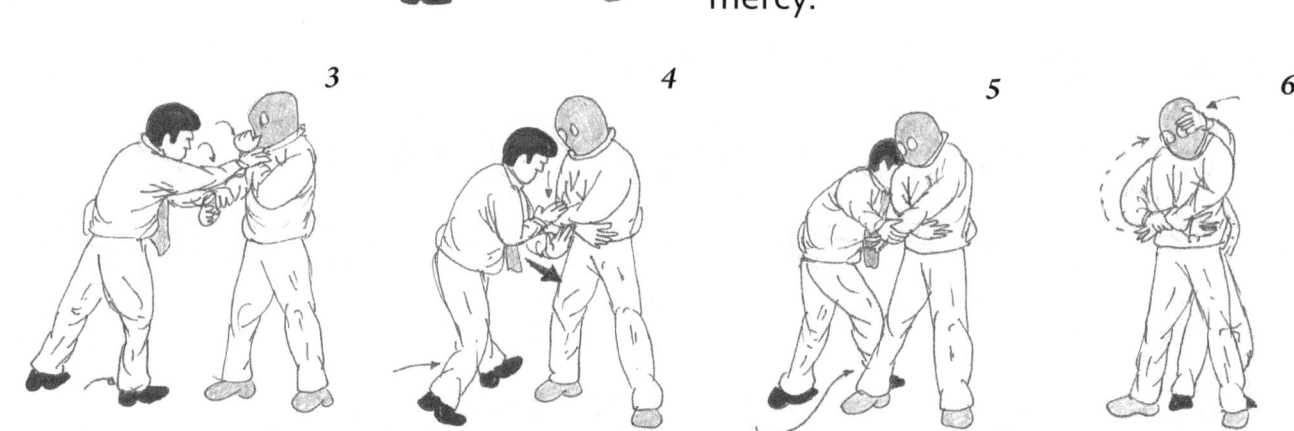

Go for his guarding hands, tie them together and get his back

The second example illustrates, at the top of next page, a **Crossed-armed Armlock** (classically coming all the way to Israel from Japanese *Aiki-jitsu*). You start like for the previous technique, but now get hold firmly of both wrists. You will then use his front arm to block the elbow of his straightened rear arm. You have him in a painful Armlock that must be applied violently and jerkily, in order to damage the joints. As you have his arms neutralized, start to kick him in the shins and, if possible, the groin. After a few kicks, you can brusquely release your hold for an immediate all-out *Retzev*.

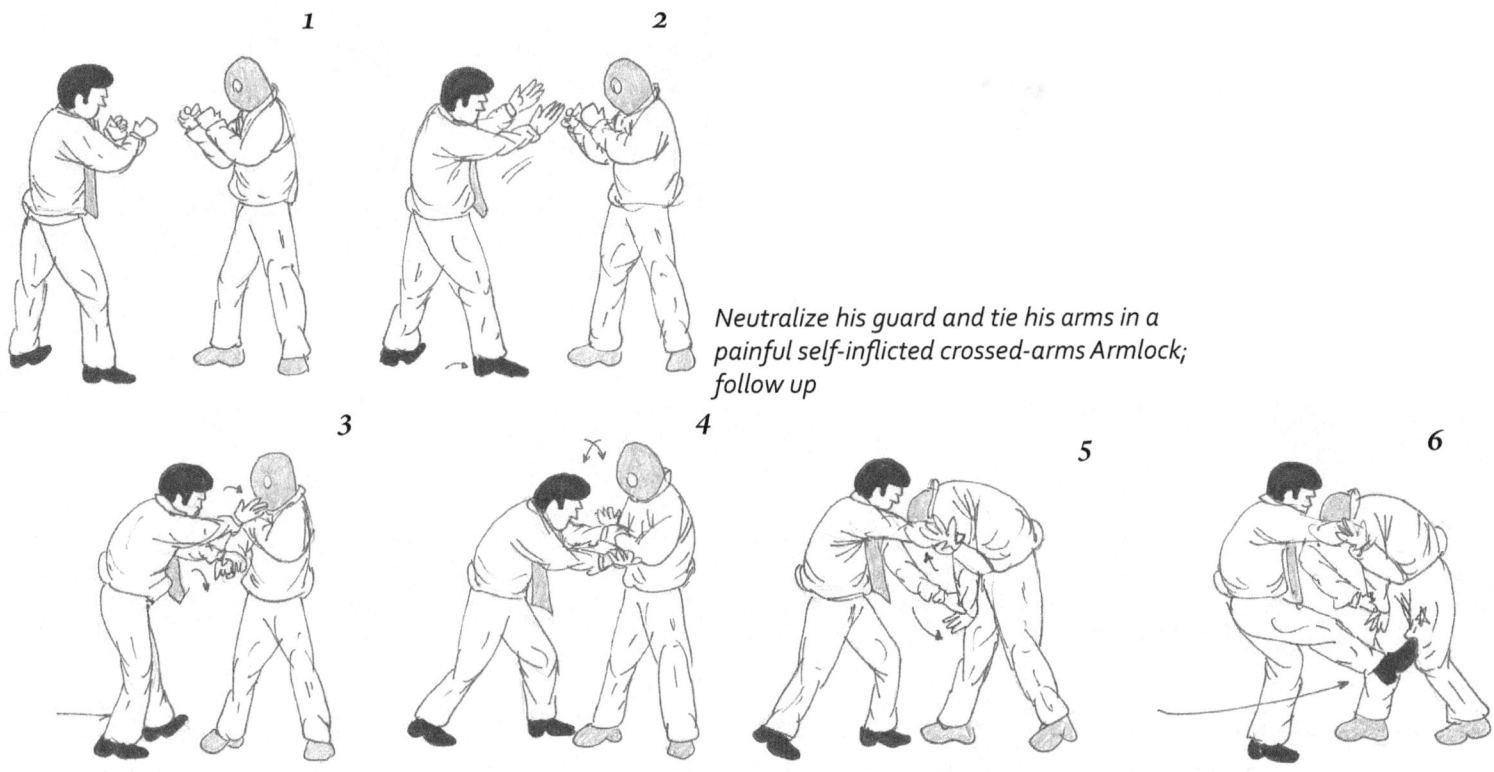

Neutralize his guard and tie his arms in a painful self-inflicted crossed-arms Armlock; follow up

5.4.3 The Jaw Lock

Mastering the **Jaw Lock** is very important for the advanced fighter: it is an important fall-back technique if you miss the set-up of a *Rear Naked Choke*. The technique is relatively easy to master. If you drill it a few times, you will get the principle and the right set-up. But what is important is to drill it enough to make it automatic in case of need.

The Drawings at the top of next page will make the maneuver very clear: you will use your Inner Wrist to crush his *Temporomandibular Joint* in an area replete with nerve endings (it is the joint connecting the jaw and the skull). This is very painful, and, done violently, can cause the joint to dislocate or at least to go into subluxation. As always in real-life *Krav Maga*, it must be executed brusquely and violently: you get into the hold as a Strike to the side of the Jaw and then use the clasping hands as a powerful vise. Searing Pain to the area radiates all the way to the ear and can also cause a lingering loss of balance.

Of course, if you can get the Rear Naked Choke instead, it still should be the preferred option...

The Jaw Lock and the targeted joint

5.4.4 Finger Locks

Finger Locks are easy to understand and to execute. Unfortunately, they are used too seldom, as people do not drill them enough to have it come out naturally in stressful combat. It is a pity, because they are sooooo easy and soooo effective. They are fast, they neutralize the opponent immediately, they cause excruciating pain, they can cause joint damage that will take the specific limb out of use for the fight and, above all, they allow for the easy start of devastating *Retzev*. What is not to like?

You simply grab one or several fingers and bend them violently, one way or another. We will show a few representative examples, but this is certainly not exhaustive. Grab one or several fingers and find a way to treat it unnaturally; simple and easy.

Of course, this is not only a mid-distance technique. If you are in close combat and get grabbed, hold or choked, you should immediately go for one finger and aim at breaking it.

Drill these techniques and try to keep in mind their effectiveness. Make sure you familiarize yourself to the idea of breaking someone's finger if he attacks you. It is not always easy to contemplate for a law-abiding normative citizen; but it is sometimes necessary...

The first example (illustrated at the top of next page) is very simple to the point of ridicule. A threatening assailant points a finger at you while assaulting you verbally. As he gets close and his intentions are clear, you simply preempt his attack by grabbing his threatening finger and bending it back towards the back of his hand. You can execute the technique gradually or brusquely according to the situation. A gradual lock will have him controlled, and a violent jerk will also break his finger and put his main arm out of commission. It is clear that the crouching position the opponent ends in, is perfect for a kick to the face and whatever will follow.

Grab a finger pointed at you and bend it back; then kick

Another devastating attack of the opponent's fingers is the **dislocation of the hand**. The purpose here is truly to place his hand out of commission for the fight. This can be required, for example, to make sure that an aggressor cannot take up a weapon to keep on fighting. Or simply to ensure that the will to fight leaves the opponent.

The principle is, again, very simple: grab the index and middle finger of the opponent with one hand; then grab the ring finger and the pinky with your other hand; then *tear them apart*!

The best way to execute the technique is to grab the opponent's wrist to allow the easy grab of the first pair of fingers. As soon as the fingers are controlled, you release the wrist to go for the other two fingers. Pull them immediately and *violently* apart, as if you want to tear the hand in two. This is not really a control technique but a destructive attack: go fast and brusque, and follow up.

We present the maneuver against an opponent extending his hand towards you, but it can easily be executed in nearly all relative positions possible.

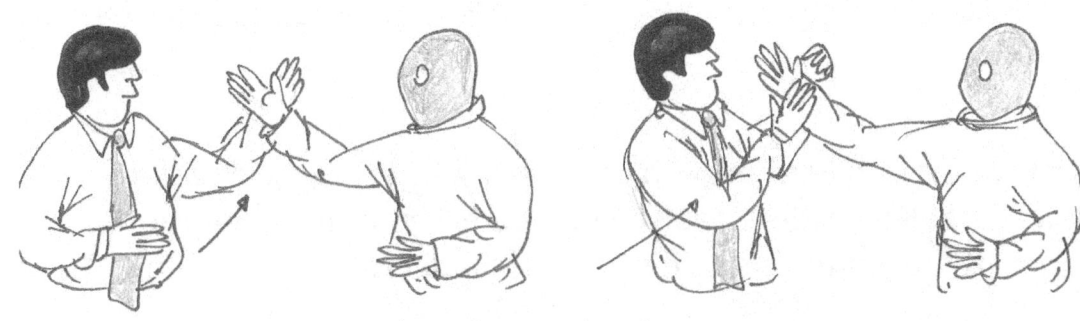

Grab two fingers with each hand and tear them apart

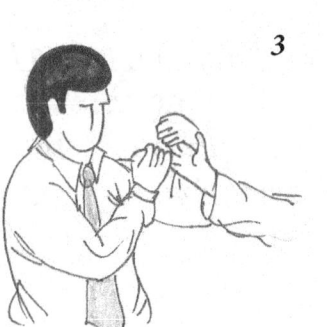

3

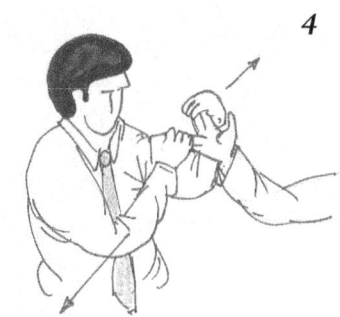

4

MORE OFFENSIVE TECHNIQUES

Our last example shows how to grab all four fingers of a hand coming towards you, twist the palm up and then lift the hand brusquely up while bending the fingers back towards the opponent. Follow up immediately with strikes to vital points (*not illustrated*).

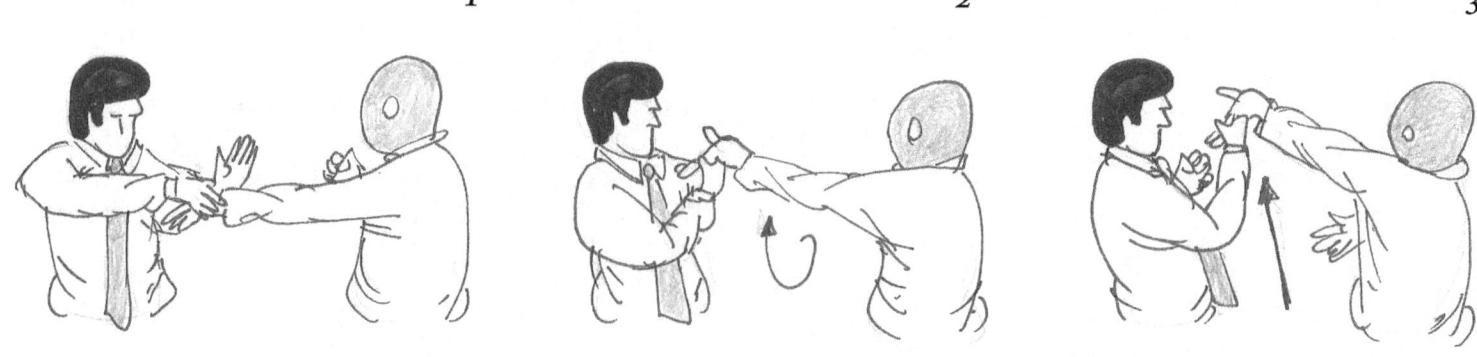

Catch fingers, twist up, bend fingers back, strike

Fingers dislocations are easy and effective, and therefore certainly *Krav Maga* material. It is always best to grab only one finger, if possible, and <u>shake it up</u>. Go for it if necessary.

5.4.5 Surprise Strikes

These techniques are basically **Feinting Strikes** with the upper limbs. They are easy to understand and exist in considerable numbers. We shall give a few examples only and let the reader develop his own feints according to his affinities and his best finishing techniques.

My personal favorite is the <u>Low Jab turning into a High Backfist</u> after causing the opponent to lower his guard. You aim the convincing Jab towards the solar plexus or (preferably) the groin according to the circumstances and gradually change the trajectory in what is called a **Progressive Indirect Attack**. See Photos at the top of next page. Follow up after the Backfist connects.

Low Jab turns gradually into a high Backfist as the guard goes down

Another simple example is the <u>'too-short' Hook Feint that turns into an Outside Forearm or Hammer-fist Strike</u>. The principle is very simple, but make sure the transition between the strikes is smooth and progressive.

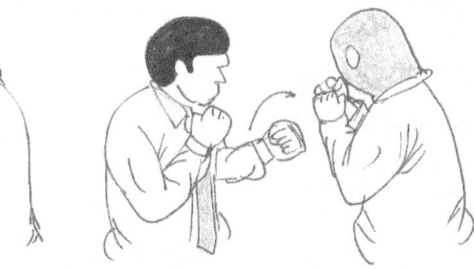

Hook Punch Feint turns into unexpected Outside Forearm Strike to the neck from the opposite direction

MORE OFFENSIVE TECHNIQUES

The next example is more compounded and aimed at showing that **all techniques are legitimate in self-defense**. The maneuver can be fully offensive or can be a 'save' if you have missed a Jab because of a lateral head movement of the opponent. You either jab outside the opponent's head on purpose, or you find yourself in this position because he has successfully moved his head sideways. The following is based on compounding two movements: (**1**) you bend the arm while hitting him with the elbow and the forearm on your way back. And (**2**) you grab his ear when your hand gets in position. As the movement is uninterrupted, you pull his ear out, which is extremely painful and places him in a very vulnerable position for your following strikes.

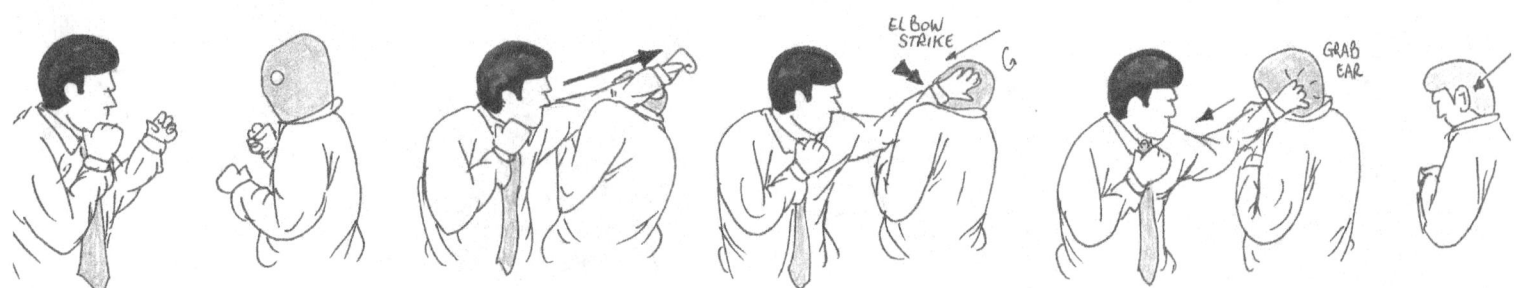

Missed Jab turns into an Elbow Strike and an Ear Grab

The next example shows how to turn what looks like a _Circular Elbow Strike into a Downward one_ that will come from above the opponent's guarding hands.

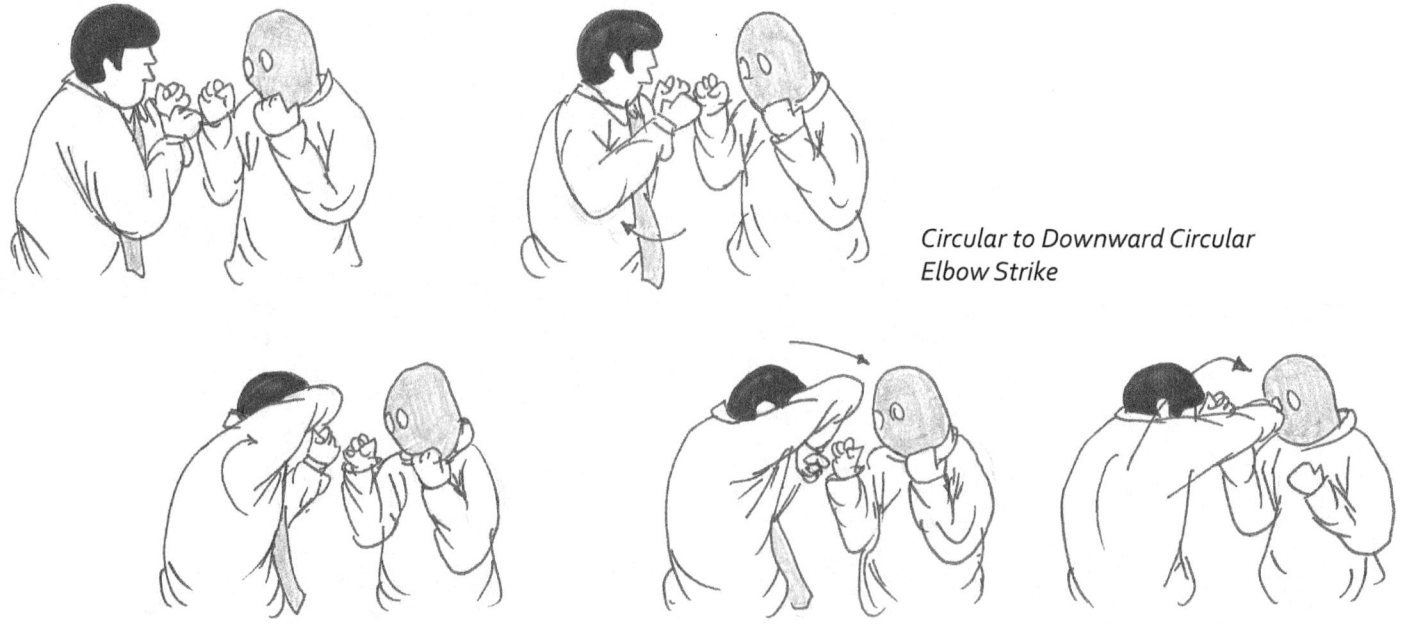

Circular to Downward Circular Elbow Strike

106   **ADVANCED KRAV MAGA**

Our last example, illustrated by the Photos below, is the simple <u>*Inward Circular Elbow Strike through the opponent's guard and head, that turns back into an Outward Elbow Strike*</u> through the offered head. You crash through the guard to come back with the power of the hips. Simple but very effective!

Circular Elbow Strike: in and back

The practicing reader will come up easily with 'Surprise Strikes' of this type that will suit his psychology, his personality and his preferred techniques. It is important to drill them thoroughly, then shadow-box them, then drill with a partner and then try them often in free-fighting.

Hard work beats talent when talent does not work hard.
~Tim Notke

5.4.6 Rear Naked Choke Set-up

The **Rear Naked Choke** is an extremely effective technique, and probably one of the few that will work against a pain-impervious attacker. In some real world situation, you can meet opponents who do not feel pain at all, no matter where and how hard you strike. This can be the result of drugs, of alcohol intoxication, of mental illness, of genetics or of very high stress levels. In these cases, your options are extremely limited: a blood choke or breaking his joints to immobilize him. The author has personally witnessed the use of a choke to control such a crazed assailant at a crowd event; the choke came after him having assaulted several people and absorbed without any problems incredible punishment from very strong security agents. Only the choke worked (It came out later that the person was in fact a Schizophrenic off his meds).

The only thing to bear in mind though, is that choking an opponent works *only if he is alone* and there is no danger to be attacked from the back by an accomplice. It is still recommended to try to bring your back to a nearby wall once you have the Choke set up. In this way, you protect your rear while having him in front of you as a shield for the few dozens of seconds needed to have him pass out. Release then immediately to prevent any permanent damage or even death. The Choke is briefly described in '*Krav Maga Kicks*', and here are a few ways to 'get to the choke' from the start.

Of course, it will be easier to set up the choke after a serious *Retzev* has mollified the opponent and placed him in the optimal relative position (behind him). But if you want to go for the choke from the start, here are two options worth drilling.

In our first example, you explode-lunge towards the opponent in a classic *Guard Neutralization* move. Go for both his guarding hands and lower them with a powerful slap.

Both your attacking hands climb then back up at shoulder level. One hand will violently slap a shoulder back while the other one will grab the other shoulder to pull it forward. This will cause the forced pivot of the opponent into a position where placing the Choke is natural and easy.

Dive towards the opponent and use his shoulders to twist him into Choke position

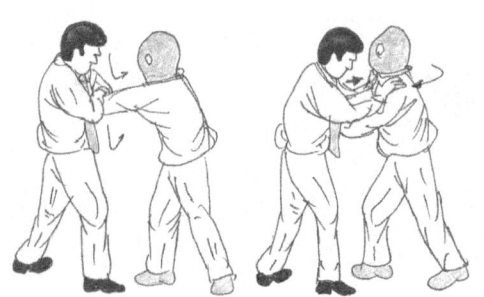  

The next technique presented is very efficient, but it does not work on bald opponents! Lunge with open hands towards the opponent's head. You can thumb his eyes or slap his ears on the way, but the real end-purpose is *to grab his hair with both hands*. Once

you have grabbed the hair, immediately pull violently while twisting his head. Once he presents his back (in a serious off-balance position), release one hand to encircle his throat while pulling his hair with the other to keep his chin up. Then, set up the Choke.

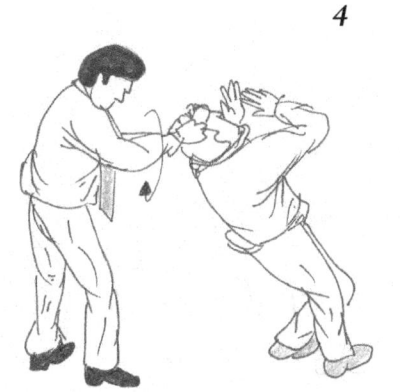

Use a hair grab to force the opponent to turn his back on you

5.4.7 Elbow Destructions

These special techniques are designed to cause joint damage in order to neutralize the assailant's arm. By doing this, you aim at preventing the aggressive use of the specific limb for the rest of the fight. This kind of technique is good to use if the opponent holds a weapon, or could do so. It is also appropriate in situation where the attacker looks non-responsive to pain (See Rear Naked Choke above). In attacking the joints violently, you will be able to prevent him to strike, to use a weapon or even to move.

The principle of this technique is simple: extend (or hyperextend) the opponent's arm, and strike the elbow while pulling the wrist. This is not to be confused for an Arm-lock which is used to inflict pain in order to *control* an assailant. Hard-core *Krav Maga* is not about control but about victory. By holding someone in an Arm-lock you place yourself at risk: from the opponent himself, if you make a mistake while being so close, or from an accomplice...

We shall present a few ways to set up the maneuver:

In the first example, you go forward to control and **encircle** a Haywire Punch (or Stick Strike). Once the opponent's forearm is under your armpit, strike violently his extended elbow from below with your inner elbow. Keep the pressure up on his locked elbow while attacking his face with the other hand; a Palm Strike to the nose or an Eye Attack will do. Start your *Retzev*, preferably by targeting his groin while he concentrates on his locked arm and his painful face.

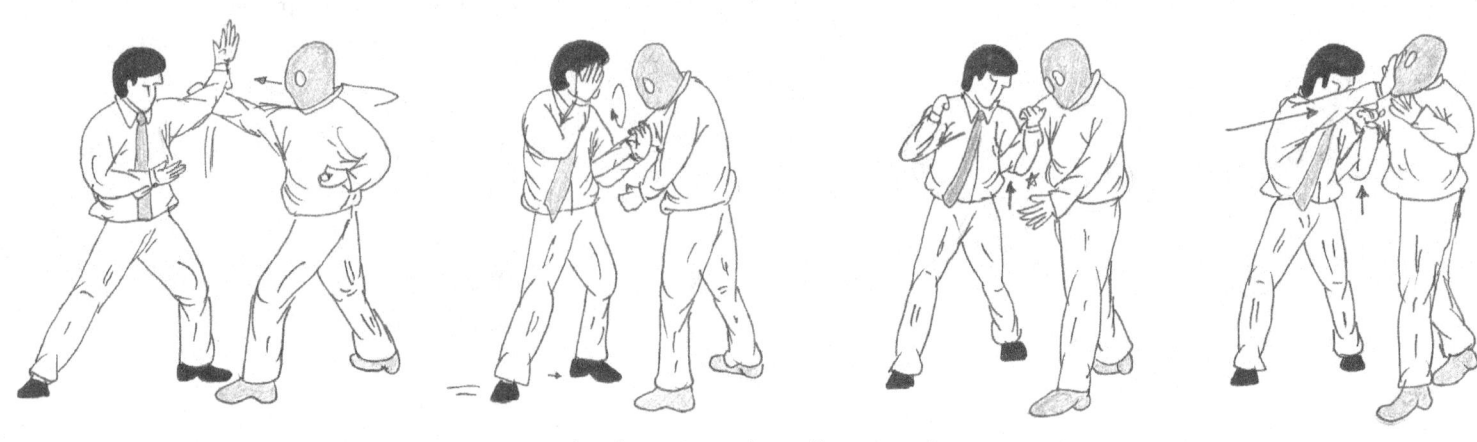

The classic Encircling Elbow Attack

The next Illustrations show the simple **Elbow Strike to the extended elbow**. You get in position by evading out of a straight punch, grabbing the wrist and striking *through* the elbow. Pull the wrist simultaneously for maximum damage, and keep the pressure to lower the assailant to the ground in classic Armlock position. Do not stay there in Arm-lock position, but start your *Retzev*, preferably with a kick to the face.

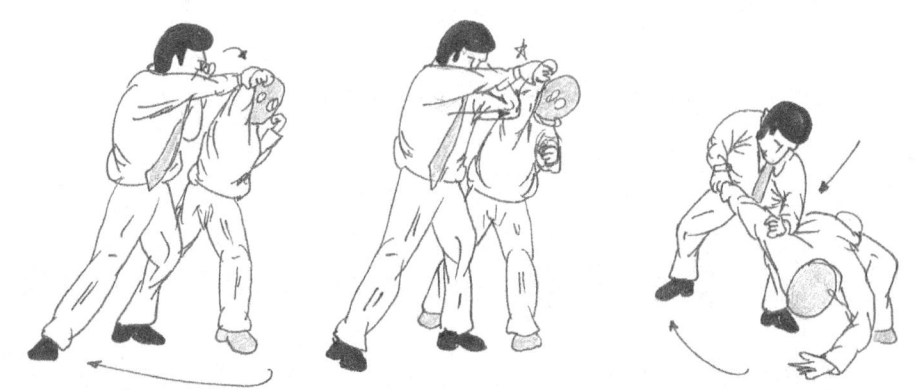

Keep It Simple, Stupid: Grab his punching wrist and strike the elbow

The next Drawings, at the top of next page, illustrate **the offensive version** of the previous technique, in opposite stances. You lunge slightly outwards to control his guard by grabbing is front hand with your rear one. Pull his wrist and strike his elbow.

Offensive Elbow Destruction from opposite guards

The next Figures show the same technique from same stances. It can be *offensive* by guard neutralization or *defensive* if the opponent starts a jab. In these relative positions, you would lunge slightly inwards.

The simple Elbow Destruction from same stances

Another way to execute the destruction is **to use the shoulder as a fulcrum**. The next example starts from a threatening lapel-grabbing attack. Grab his grabbing hand and pivot while extending his arm. Hit up simultaneously with your inner elbow; make sure you twist his wrist to present his elbow to the strike. Keep pivoting (with your back to him) to place his elbow over your shoulder while you grab his same wrist with the other hand. Pull the wrist down violently while lifting the shoulder. This is *not* a Takedown or an Armlock: do not execute this gradually. You must execute *fast and jerkily* to hurt the joint. See this as a strike. Once you have hurt his joint, follow up immediately, for example with a Rear Elbow strike and a Back Groin Kick. Do not procrastinate, as you have your back to him.

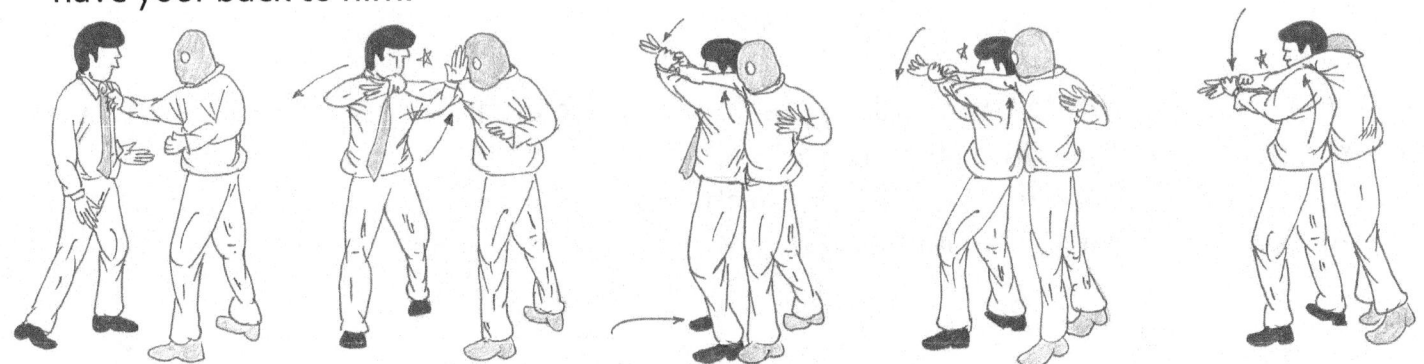

Break his elbow joint over your shoulder

MORE OFFENSIVE TECHNIQUES

5.4.8 The Side Neck Lock

The **Side Neck Lock** is fast, easy and very painful. It was one of *Master Sidney Faige* favorite techniques that he had mastered to perfection. It is kind of a Blood Choke, not as effective as the Rear Naked Choke, but easier to set up. It allows for great follow-ups. The principle is that you use your bony inner wrist to compress one carotid, and you use the opponent's own shoulder to compress the other. The general compression will also restrict the breathing, and the hacking bony press of the wrist will cause excruciating pain. The technique lends itself to a set-up in the form of a *clothesline counter* under the opponent's arm. The Figures below illustrate how you evade forward and out on a Cross Punch, while you hit his neck (clothesline-style) with the inside forearm. Clasp your hands while pushing his shoulder into his neck with your own shoulder and head. In our example, you use the Lock to throw him over your hip. Keep control of the neck as he tumbles over. His body weight will make the hold even more painful.

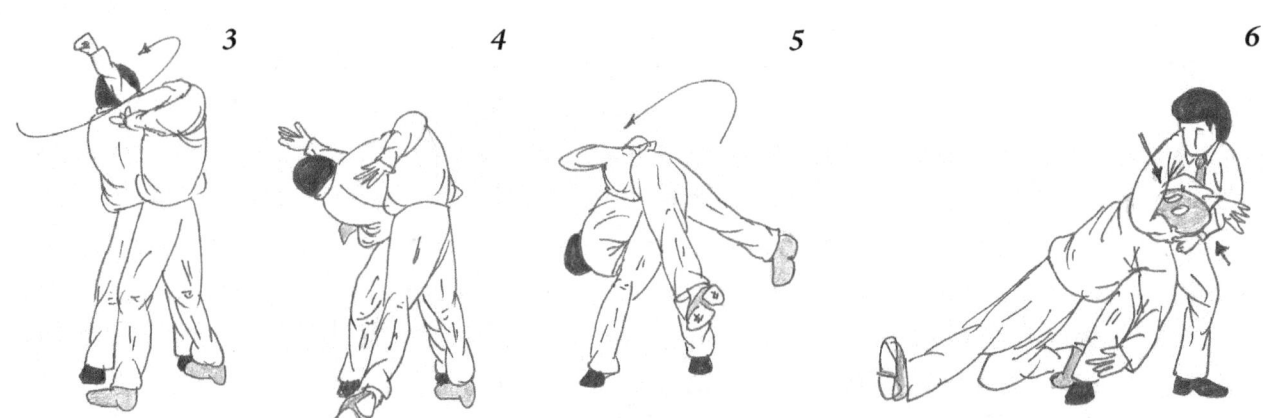

Evade a Cross Punch and set the painful Side Neck Lock for a half-takedown follow-up

The other example will deal with a Jab attack: block and encircle the attacking arm to get in position for the **Side Neck Lock**. Squeeze and use a Stomp to the back of the knee to bring him down. Go with him to the ground, if he is alone, where the side control gives you total dominance. See Drawings at the top of next page.

Circle a Jab to set up the Lock, get him to the ground with a Stomp

5.4.9 The Neck Destruction

This is a very dangerous Strike to be used only in the most severe of cases. This is an attack to the vital Neck Joints that is crippling and potentially lethal. **Training must be very cautious and its use should be only in desperate last resort.**
The example illustrated below shows the development of the technique against a Jab from opposite stances. This is didactic only, and such a technique is not relevant to such an innocuous attack. You evade forward and out while grabbing the attacking wrist. Pull his hand forward while striking the back and side of his neck with your forearm. This is a *Strike* and **not** a grab. As the violent Strike pushes his head forward, grab his chin with your encircling hand. Twist his chin back with force while releasing his hand. Hold his head in the twist by keeping pulling on the chin and use the other elbow for a hip-powered Circular Elbow Strike the exposed back of his twisted neck. Drill extremely carefully and use with extreme caution and ethics. ➡

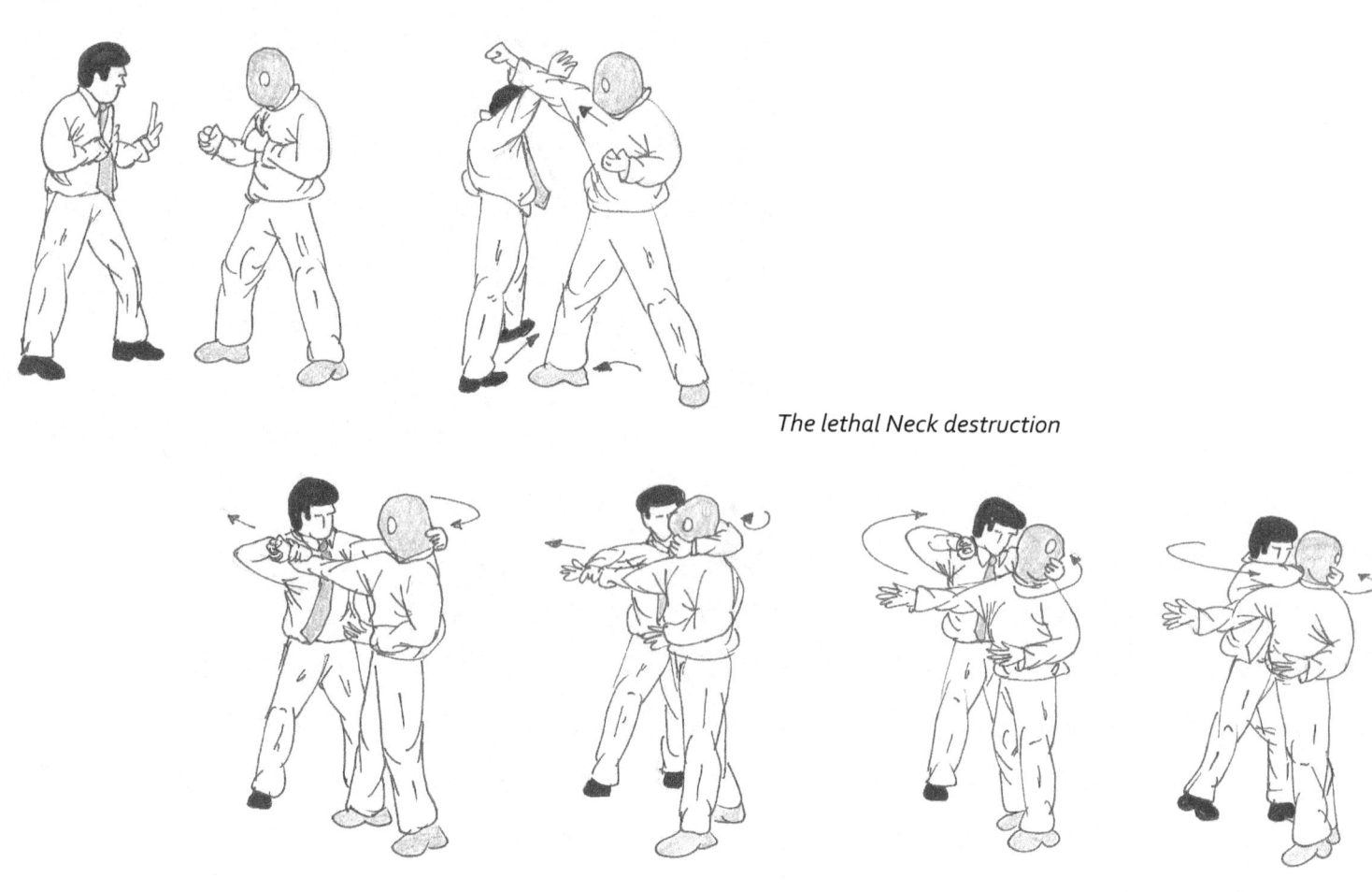

The lethal Neck destruction

5.4.10 The Eyes and Throat Finish

This is, again, a very dangerous technique to be drilled and used very carefully. It is a fantastic move, especially if your aggressor is taller than you (*which is often the case, as predators tend to prefer what looks like easier prey*). The principle is simple: you poke at the attacker's eyes, claw-like, and then attack his throat that has been 'opened' by both your push and <u>his instinctive pull back from the eye strike</u>. In fact, you poke claw-like in order to also naturally push his chin back and up with your palm. You then keep the same strong forward momentum to strike his offered throat with your forearm. When you start drilling this dangerous techniques it is a one-two move in which you even pull back the arm slightly before the forearm strike. With proficiency it becomes **one smooth move** which strength comes from the powerful forward and up surge. This is a great finishing move as a successful strike to both the eyes and throat should be enough for even the most obstinate assailant. See Photos at the top of next page.

The Eye and throat Finish in one smooth move

MORE OFFENSIVE TECHNIQUES

PART SIX

Defenses against Stick Attacks

הגנה מפני התקפות מקל

6.1 The Stick

A stick assault is a dangerous and potentially lethal attack. And it could be a truncheon, a night stick, a telescopic stick, an umbrella, a fire poke, a baseball bat, a golf club, an unbroken bottle, a pastry rolling pin, a tightly rolled magazine, and many more everyday objects ...
Remember that one powerful blow to the skull is capable of causing death or permanent damage. Although, they are potentially less dangerous than Knife Attacks, the threat of an attack with a stick must be taken very seriously and dealt with as early as possible.

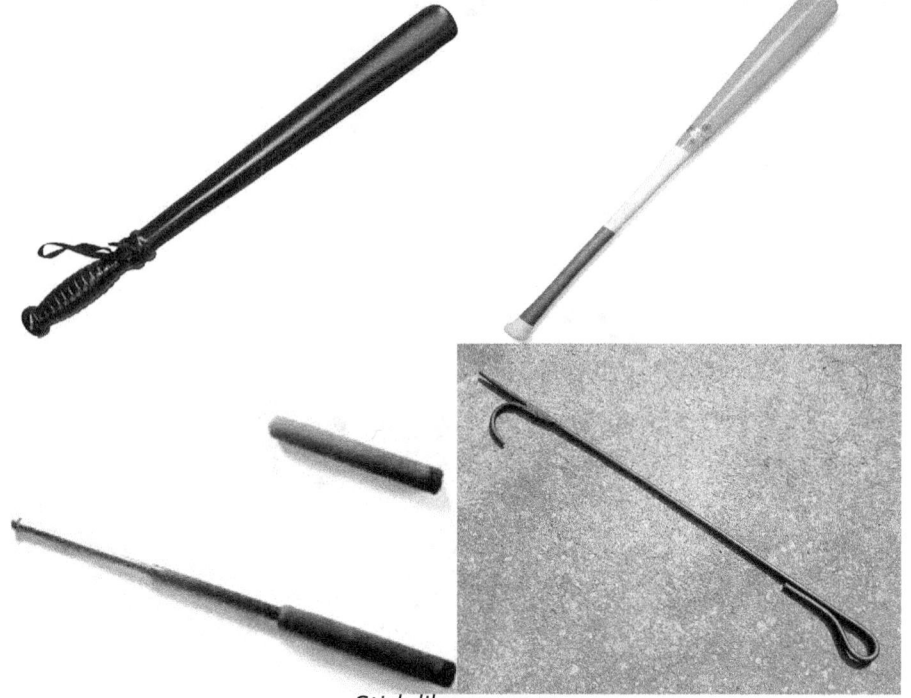
Stick-like weapons

<u>Using a stick as a weapon has several drawbacks that the defender should be aware of:</u>

6.1.a. *The stick holder is psychologically relying on his weapon that gives him confidence* (It is true for all weapons). He counts on his stick to scare you and to put you in an inferior defensive state of mind. If you attack him preemptively, you will deeply rattle him. Not only will you physically overwhelm him, but you will destroy his confidence (based on the deterrence of the stick). Do not underestimate the importance of this: a fight is won in the mind first.
If your preemptive attack is successful and you can cause him to lose his stick, the psychological damage will be even greater.

6.1.b. *A stick is effective at medium range only*: it needs momentum to gather energy, and the maximum power is at the end of the stick. This is similar to the situation with Circular Kicks. Therefore, when defending against a stick, **you should get as close as possible to your opponent**, where the stick is useless. Again: be preemptive and go forward!

6.1.c. *A stick strike is usually overhead, swinging or backhand; and these moves require <u>chambering</u>*. Only with some chambering will the strike gather enough energy to be effective. By chambering, the stick holder will 'open' himself. That is when to stop-strike him: dive in before the weapons swings back forward towards you. Again: forward and early. *Krav Maga* is all about an offensive forward-leaning attitude.

Reading these drawbacks, one can only draw the following **principles** on how to deal with a stick attack:

- Attack a stick-holder *preemptively* as soon as possible. Do not wait for an attack to crystallize.
- If you are attacked, *dive in as soon as the assailant chambers*: attack the opening created by the move.
- If you are too late, *go forward anyway*, eventually diagonally.

Forward, offensive, early, and keep going. That's *Krav Maga*…

Should you be able to disarm the assailant and get hold of the stick yourself, you should be aware of the drawbacks mentioned before for the stick holder. And therefore:

- Be dynamic and *strike immediately as you get control of the stick*. Keep going until you win the fight with no hiatus.
- *Do not rely on the stick* for your defense; use kicks and other strikes in *Retzev*.
- If you have a stick and are not in a dynamic situation, it is better to *poke* with it than to swing. *Poke at sensitive targets* like the eyes, the throat, the ears, the mouth, the floating ribs, and more; this way, no need to chamber.

6.2. Preemption

If you are suddenly confronted by an individual holding a stick, **go immediately on the offensive**. Forget the hindrance of your social upbringing: this is what gives predators an edge. Do not overthink the situation: holding a threatening weapon while confronting you does not leave any doubts about his intentions. This is a dangerous physical threat, and waiting gives the advantage to the assailant. Someone threatening you, directly or indirectly, with a weapon, has most probably the intention to use it.

Preemption is always to be preferred in *Krav Maga*. Explode into a forward diving attack *while your opponent is still gearing himself up to attack* and is still gloating in his supposedly advantageous situation. You will rattle him psychologically and physically, and you will probably be able to start a *Retzev* that will conclude the fight before the attack could even materialize.

Your preemptive attack can be one of the following:
- **Simply an offensive move that completely ignores the stick**. Our previous book (*Krav Maga Kicks*) presents many examples, and so does this one in the various sections of Chapter Five (mostly 'Range Covering'). We will not repeat these examples here. So, drill the unarmed techniques presented with a partner simply holding a stick menacingly. And also drill the additional techniques presented below.
- **An attack that neutralizes the stick hand** while striking sensitive targets. These are basically the 'Guard Neutralization Techniques' of same Chapter Five. Use them as they are: go for the hand as if it is a guarding limb and ignore the fact that it holds a stick.
- **A dive to grab the stick** while striking sensitive targets with the other hand. You are not trying to disarm him, but just to neutralize the stick for the few seconds necessary to start your *Retzev*. Examples will be shown.
- **A Stop-strike as the opponent starts to chamber** by lifting or wielding his stick. You can then kick or strike the parts of his body uncovered by the chambering move.

6.2.1 Ignore the Stick

The first set of Illustrations how to 'stop the step' of an assailant approaching. **Ignore the stick and stop-side-kick his advancing knee**. Remember to strike forcefully *through* the knee with the power of the hips. We have illustrated that the ensuing *Retzev* starts with a 'Low Kick' through the other knee. And do not stop there.

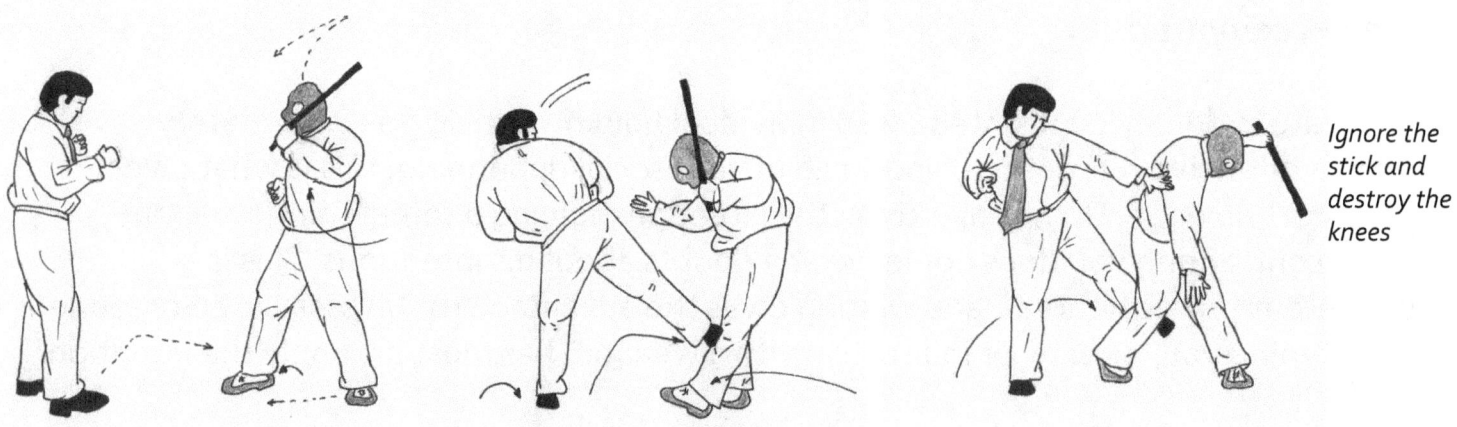

Ignore the stick and destroy the knees

You can also 'stop the step' of the approaching opponent **with a fast and low Roundhouse** to the front knee or better, **to the groin**. Land close and control the stick hand while punching the floating ribs forcefully. Grab his head for a Knee Strike and push him away for a full-powered Groin Front Kick. Keep going. See Figures below.

Stop the step with a fast Roundhouse and start a Retzev; ignore the stick

In the next example, **you simply kick his shin** as he is still in threatening mode. Remember to be *stealthy* (upper body does not move) and to kick harshly *through* the shin surface. While you lower the foot, attack his face with a Palm Strike, over his armed hand (in order to hinder any reaction with the stick). Start your *Retzev* with a 'Low Kick' *through* the knee joint, and a Roundhouse of the other leg to his groin. And keep striking...

Preempt any stick strike with a painful Shin Kick that is the start of a series of uninterrupted attacks

STICK ATTACKS

Another way to follow up on the previous **Shin Kick preemptive attack** is presented in the Photos below. The retracting Low Front Shin Kick turns *naturally* into a Side kick Chamber. Kick powerfully to the groin or the floating ribs area. You can then start your *Retzev*, for example with a crushing Low Side Kick to the front knee.

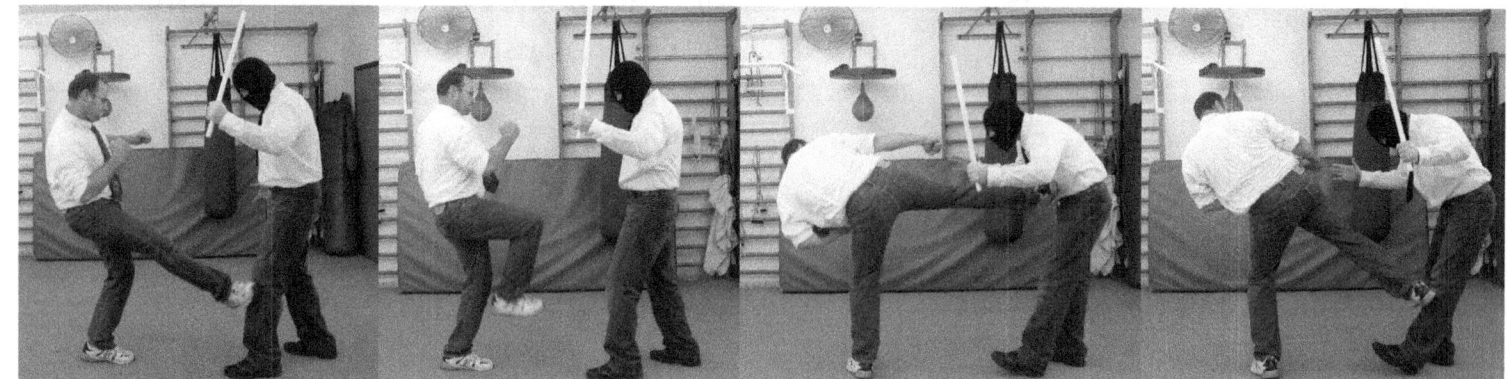

Attack with a Shin Kick that turns into a powerful Side kick, and follow up

We conclude this section with a more *sophisticated* approach, recommended for advanced trainees only: **crescent-kick the arm holding the stick**. If you are proficient and flexible, it is a very aggressive maneuver that will rattle the opponent's confidence. Hopefully you will also hurt his elbow joint and destabilize him. Follow up in stride with a naturally-flowing Side Kick to the floating ribs. You can then side-elbow his head as you land the kicking foot forward, and take him down with a classic Outer Reaping Throw.

Initiate a preemptive attack targeting the elbow of the stick-wielding arm

122   **ADVANCED KRAV MAGA**

6.2.2 Neutralize the Stick Hand

Please refer to the previous section about 'Guard Neutralization Techniques'. Drill the same techniques with the partner holding a stick. You also *ignore the stick* and go for the temporary neutralization of the hand (that happens to hold the stick).

6.2.3 Neutralize the Stick

The same techniques used *to neutralize the hand and the guard* can be used here. Instead of moving and controlling the hand, you move or grab the stick, just for the time necessary to attack sensitive points. It is easier because the stick is longer and usually more in range.
Do not grab the stick in the spirit of trying to disarm him or gain control of it. You grab or move the stick just to neutralize it temporarily, while your other hand attacks his eyes or his throat. Grabbing the stick has also the advantage of diverting the assailant's attention from the incoming strikes.
Drill all the previously presented 'Range closing' and 'Guard Neutralization' Techniques, but with the stick in mind instead of the opponent's hands. It is pretty easy: just dive in aggressively.

Here come a few new and specific examples.

The first set of Drawings, at the top of next page, illustrates how to **dive and grab the brandished stick, while attacking the opponent's throat**. Keep your forward momentum as the Finger Jab becomes an Elbow Strike. All the while, you are keeping hold of the stick, but do not concentrate on it and do not try to take it off him; let him worry about that. Straighten the elbowing arm behind his neck to pull his head down into a first Knee Strike. Follow up with a Downward hips-driven Elbow Strike to the back of his neck. The *Retzev* can go on with another Knee Strike to the face, a grab that applies pressure to the eyes and a Groin Kick.

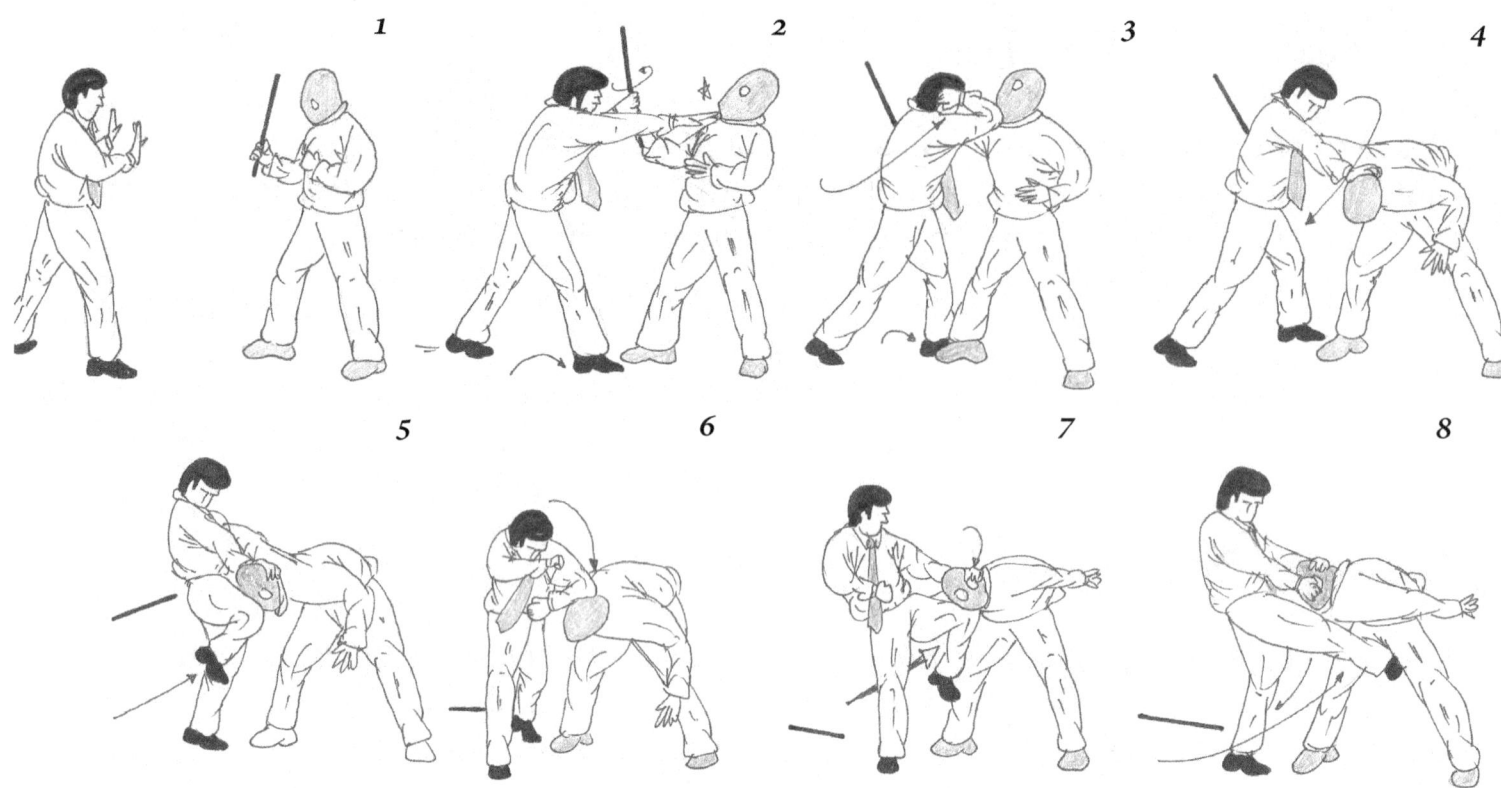

Dive in for the stick while, in fact, attacking the throat; start an implacable Retzev

You can also simply **dive for the stick to attack the eyes**. Then start your own following-up series.

Go for the stick and poke the eyes with the other hand

Or you could **kick his groin after grabbing the stick**. Attack his eyes when your kicking foot lands. He will certainly release the stick at this stage, but you are already attacking his knee joint with a circular 'Low Kick'. Kick *through* and keep attacking until he is fully vanquished. See Illustrations at the top of next page.

Dive for the stick and kick his groin; follow up by poking his eyes and more

6.2.4 Stop-strike the Chambering of the Stick Attack

The idea is pretty simple, but it requires timing and speed that only strenuous drilling can achieve. The obvious chambering is usually up for a haywire downward strike and it tends to really 'open' the whole body and leave it unprotected. The target of choice will usually be his groin, which ensures that the chambering stick strike will not mature to completion…

The first series of Drawings, at the top of next page, will make this amply clear.
As the assailant lifts his stick to gather energy for the strike (or simply to threaten and intimidate you), you hop forward with a *front-leg fast Roundhouse Kick to the unprotected groin*. Simple, easy, clean. Start your *Retzev*, for example with a Low Kick through the knee joint.

STICK ATTACKS

Fast and stealthy Groin Roundhouse as he lifts his armed hand

There are, of course many ways to follow up on the Groin Kick. You could, for example, insert a Forearm Strike to the side of the assailant's neck before the Low Kick to the knee. Do what is natural to you and do not stop until full victory.

The Groin Stop kick can be followed by your own version of the Retzev

Of course, **a straight Front Kick to the groin** will do as well to stop the developing stick strike. The Photos at the top of next page show how to kick as he chambers up (The stick has to be imagined by the reader, as it is a make-believe drill). You can naturally follow up by attacking the back of his neck, offered by his crouching in pain. Keep pounding him until the fight is clearly won.

126   **ADVANCED KRAV MAGA**

Front Stop Kick to the groin as he lifts his stick hand

The assailant could also be **grabbing your wrist or lapel as he prepares to strike**. That should not make any difference: kick his groin, brutally. And then follow up, for example by grabbing his head for a Knee Strike to the face.

If he tries to grab you while chambering, forget about it just kick the groin

STICK ATTACKS

Other Kicks can be used to stop the developing stick strike at the chambering stage. **The Penetrating Side Kick to the floating ribs** is a good example, because the lifting of the arm opens the ribs to make them much more vulnerable. Remember to kick *into* the target, at least a few inches. *Do not push*, but kick fast and chamber back.

Stop the chambering with a well-timed Side kick into the floating ribs; follow up with a strike to the back of his neck

Another possibility is the use of the **Upward Back Kick to the groin** in its Spin-forward or Spin-back version. The advantage of this Kick is in its stealthiness and the fact that your presenting your back will embolden him to lift his stick and chamber his strike. The natural follow-up of a Side Elbow Strike will stun him for the rest of the *Retzev*: a Knee Strike to the face and a Low kick through the knee after a violent push-away. Keep at it!

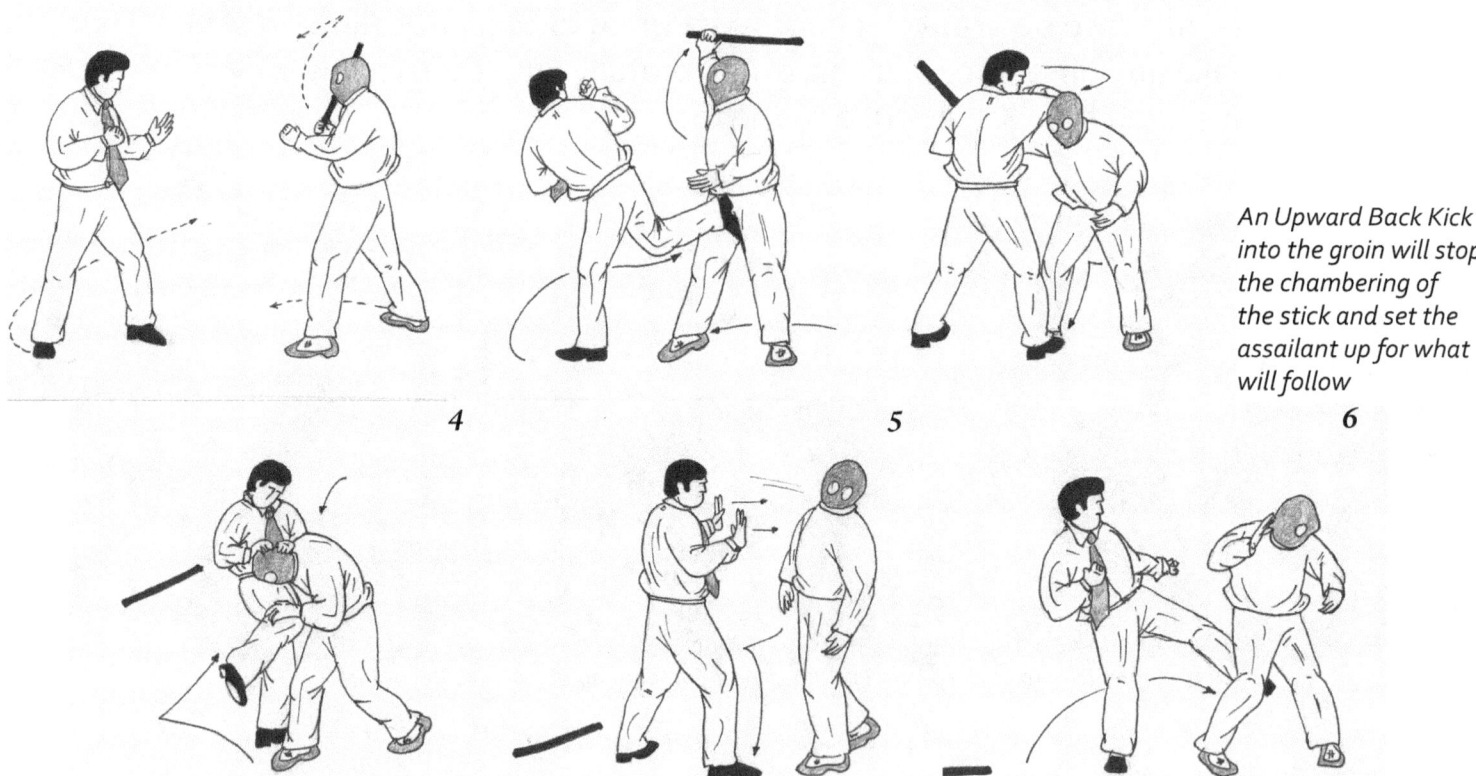

An Upward Back Kick into the groin will stop the chambering of the stick and set the assailant up for what will follow

If the assailant holds his stick (a baseball bat) **with both hands and lifts it high up for an all-out attack**, dive immediately forward into his move to attack him with an early Palm Strike to the chin. Strike up and through. This is a very dangerous strike that hurts the neck joint and adds its momentum to the forward momentum of the assailant. Follow up until you are sure he is neutralized.

Against the chambering of a downward baseball bat strike, jump forward with a powerful Palm Strike to the chin

6.3 Defense against a Downward Stick Strike

The Downward Stick Strike is the most common; it can have a straight or a diagonal trajectory. This attack is atavistic: it unconsciously tries to bash your skull like on ancient battlefields. It requires a good chamber in order to gather the energy necessary to hit your head forcefully, and therefore is easy to spot. Such a strike, if successful, is potentially lethal: it can crack your skull. It can also break your orbital bone, your clavicle, your nose, your mandibular joint, and many more. This is a very serious aggression that requires a swift and violent response.

Of course, *preemption* is preferable, closely followed by *attacking the chamber*, as seen before. But if you have been taken unawares, you'll have to deal with the attack in more traditional ways. But remember the Golden Rule: always go forward! The closest you are to him, the less he can hurt you. The maximum power is at the tip of the stick; so, dive in! *Krav Maga* is about aggressive defense. And this has the additional advantage of unsettling the assailant, both psychologically and physically.

There are basically **2** ways to deal with a Downward Overhead Stick Strike: (1) Block or (2) Evade. And then comes what is generally happening: a Blocking Evasion which a mixture of the 2 responses. Most commonly you will go forward diagonally to evade the general momentum of the opponent, while blocking or at least controlling the stick arm.

Blocking is pretty basic. But it is important to avoid the orthodox 'elbow vs elbow' Upward Block of some traditional Martial arts. In *Krav Maga*, the blocking elbow goes up *diagonally*, and it goes *forward*. Its purpose is to deviate mildly the stick trajectory without stopping it by force. At the moment of contact the elbow is about 45 degrees from perpendicular and keeps extending towards straight. It also goes forward towards the strike. And, as mentioned, the block is generally executed while getting slightly out of the way of the strike (forward of course). The coming figures illustrate clearly the diagonal and forward characteristics of the effective Deviating Block.

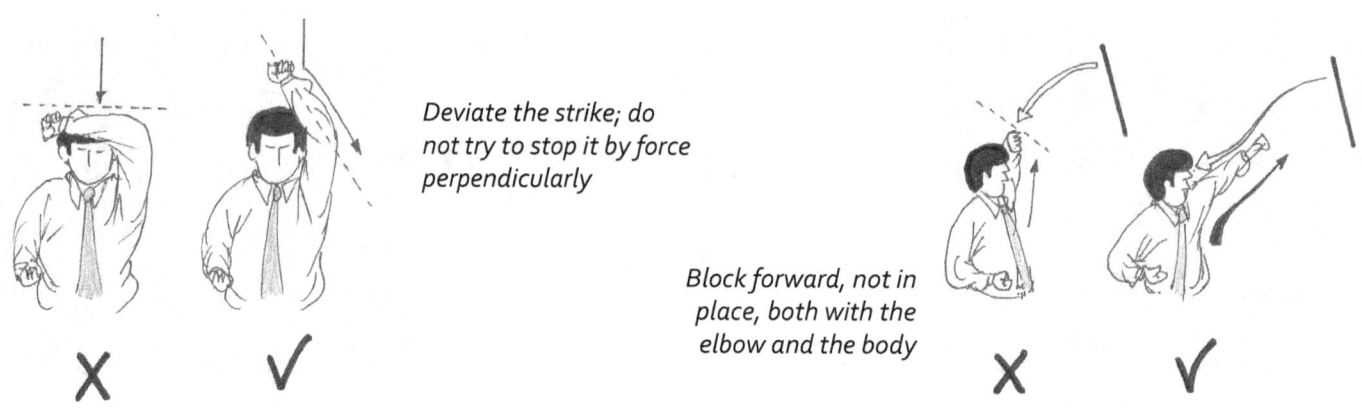

Deviate the strike; do not try to stop it by force perpendicularly

Block forward, not in place, both with the elbow and the body

The typical and refreshingly simple way to deal with a **Downward Overhead Stick Strike** is therefore a Diving-forward Block with a quasi-simultaneous Eye Poke. The Block has the advantage of covering your head partially to protect it. As illustrated below, you should follow up with a Groin Kick, a Knee Strike to the face and a Hammer-fist Strike to the back of the neck. Simple, offensive, forward-going... in other words: *Krav Maga*!

Dive forward with a Deviating Block while attacking the eyes

3   4   5

130   ***ADVANCED KRAV MAGA***

Evading is also, in principle, very simple. But, as you are jumping forward, it is generally best accompanied with at least some control, if not even a 'security' Block. But a possible 'clean' Evasion is presented in the Photos below: you dive forward and out, without blocking or controling, and lean away while chambering a powerful Side Kick. Go for the exposed floating ribs and start a *Retzev*.

Evade forward and out for a Side Stop Kick to the ribs

Of course, **some control of the attacking arm is always welcome** and makes for a safer evasion, as illustrated by the coming Photos. Evade out and forward while keeping tabs with the stick arm, and kick fast towards the ribs (or the groin if you can). The Kick is a hybrid between a Front and a Roundhouse Kick, fast and surprising. You can follow up by striking the exposed neck and start a full *Retzev*.

Evade forward and out while deviating the attack; kick and follow up

The advantage of keeping some control of the attacking arm, is that you can evade deeper forward while staying close to him. The next Photos show how to **evade deep forward and out while keeping the stick hand in check**. You then are in position for a devastating Stomp to the back of his knee.

Dive forward and out, very close to the opponent, and keep control of the attacking arm; stomp-crush the back of his knee

At the end of the day, the most common way to deal with an Overhead Strike that is underway, is <u>**the Evading Block**</u>. This can be more of a *Block* or more of an *Evasion* according to the circumstances and your temperament. Scores of examples will be presented, but the simplest and most classic application is the "Clothesline" counter. As illustrated by the Drawings coming at the top of next page, you evade *forward and out* while blocking/deviating the attack. It is important to keep the forward momentum of the assailant alive. Grab his attacking wrist and pull him forward to accentuate his forward move. Let go and strike his throat and/or face with your whole arm going back forward with full bodyweight backing. This is the typical 'clothesline' maneuver that makes maximum use of the forward energy of the attacker.

➡

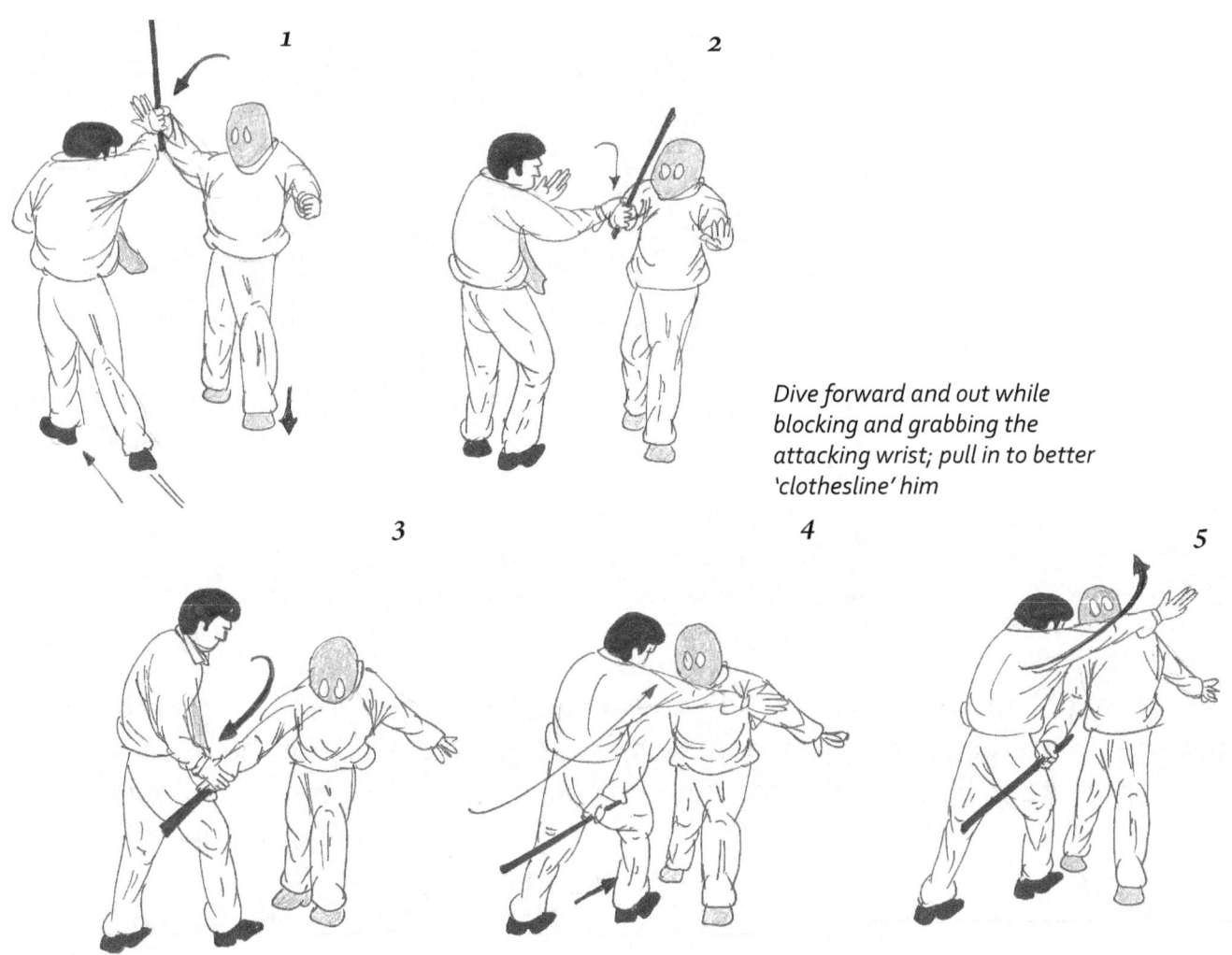

Dive forward and out while blocking and grabbing the attacking wrist; pull in to better 'clothesline' him

We shall now present a few more examples of **Overhead Stick Defenses**, falling more or less into the different categories described.

We will start with a few illustrations of the more 'blocking' dive forward, *with less evasion*. This is the classic aggressive *Krav Maga* reaction that is often to be preferred, if you are well trained and confident. In the first set of Drawings at the top of next page, you see how to dive forward while blocking/deviating the Strike. You then get so near the attacker that you can easily encircle his striking arm going down and control him from very close. From this position, several *Retzev* will be presented.

The ***first*** set will show how to kick his groin and pivot to throw him to the ground. Keep his armed elbow encircled when taking him down! You can then grab the stick and stomp his wrist to disarm him; make sure to stomp through the joint as if to crush everything into the ground.

➡

STICK ATTACKS 133

Dive in and deviate the strike to encircle the attacking limb; follow up with a groin kick, a throw and a stomping disarm

The **second** set of Illustrations shows how to execute the same defense and follow up with an Outer Reap Takedown and a Hammer-fist Strike to the side of the head. You can then hyperextend his elbow by crushing it against your thigh, before throwing the arm violently towards the ground. Stomp the wrist as it lands on the ground and follow with a Stomp of his face that crashes his head to the ground.

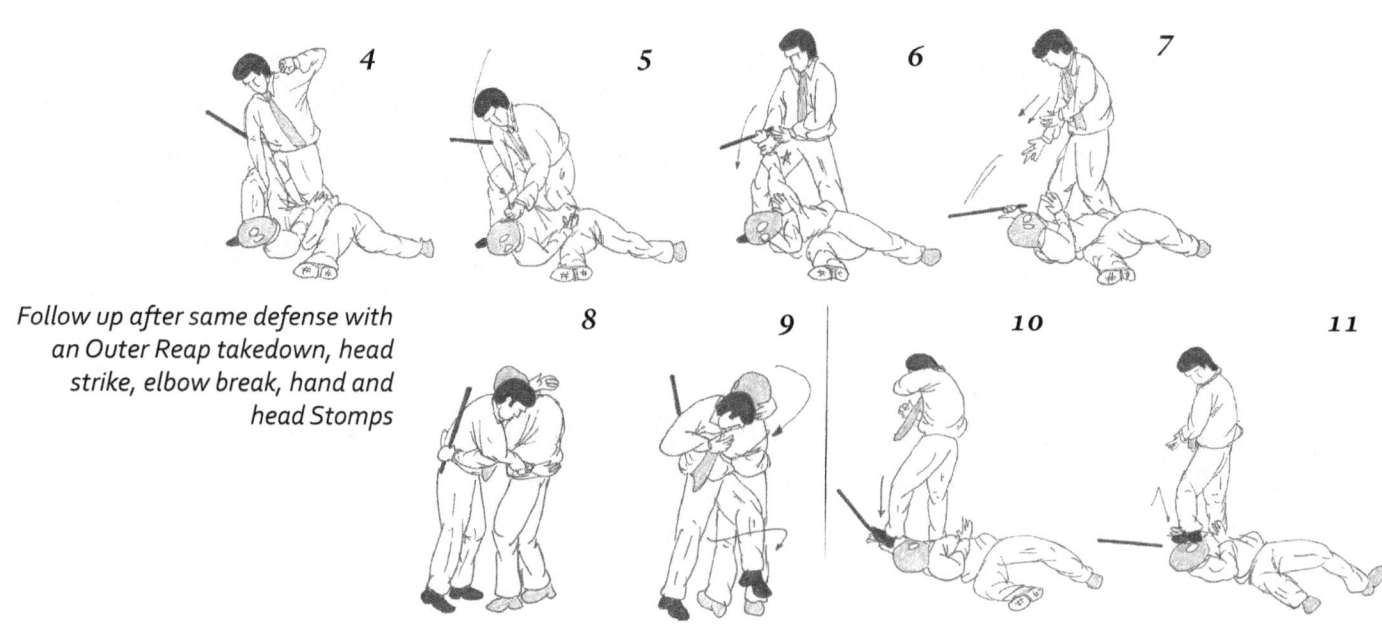

Follow up after same defense with an Outer Reap takedown, head strike, elbow break, hand and head Stomps

ADVANCED KRAV MAGA

Our last possible *Retzev* after the same diving defense will consist of a **Forearm Strike to the neck** with the arm that has controlled and lowered the stick strike. The same arm then extends to lower his head down for a powerful and body-driven (other) Forearm (Inside Elbow) Strike to the back of his neck. Grab his head, preferably with your fingers in his eyes, for a switch in pivots: lift and twist his head up and then down to his rear, all the way to the ground. A Palm Strike should slam his head in the ground, if warranted, and could be followed by a Stomp Kick to same head.

Follow up the same defense with Forearm Strikes and a vicious Head Twist Takedown

STICK ATTACKS

Blocking while evading gives you the option **to grab the attacking wrist,** which is great for control and for an easier counter towards a sensitive point. But grabbing also allows for most sophisticated techniques ending up in a **<u>Disarm</u>** and in you having a stick to conclude the fight.

<u>Our first example</u> illustrates the classic blocking move with a clear forward-out evasion. The Evading Block turns easily into a wrist grab with your non-blocking hand (which can grab momentarily for a better control).
Once you have completed the grab, your blocking hand goes immediately to attack the eyes; and then to grab the end of the stick. Your opponent is hurt in the eyes and you make use of his despondency by disarming him: keep his wrist in place and lower the stick violently for half a circle, as per a fulcrum, before pulling the stick free. Use the stick to immediately poke him deeply into the throat or the eye. Start your *Retzev*; I would start with a Groin Kick. You can then (but do not have to) use the stick to hit sensitive targets but *do not become reliant on it*.

Evade and Block can become a 'Grab and Disarm'

ADVANCED KRAV MAGA

Another Disarm from the same basic 'Evade forward and Block' is presented in the coming Drawings. This is a more sophisticated technique, easy to execute but requiring drilling in order to become automatic in stress situations (*Muscle memory requires training and hard work*). In this example, you encircle the arm to do a full circle before grabbing the wrist in a classical move. You grab the end of the stick, for a long fulcrum, just as you grab the wrist. All this has been very fast, and you only have to lift the end of the stick (violently) while keeping the wrist in place, in order to disarm the assailant.

Pull the stick back to immediately <u>poke</u> deep into his exposed floating ribs; you keep his grabbed arm up and pull him into the strike. Follow seamlessly with a Groin Kick and strike his offered skull with his own stick. Keep at it if necessary.

Dive, evade, Block, Grab and Disarm; then kick and use his own stick against him

The last two examples will illustrate that **the Blocking Evasion needs not be exclusively to the outside**.

The *first* set of Photos, at the top of next page, shows an <u>Evading Block to the Inside</u>, followed by a simple Knife-hand Strike to the side of the head or neck. Of course, that is only the beginning of a *Retzev*! Your inside position to a rattled opponent is perfect for a Knee to the groin as a starting move.

STICK ATTACKS 137

Block while evading on the inside and strike naturally to the head or neck

The last set of Photos will show the same **Inside Evasion that makes use of the opponent's momentum to take him down**. This is a classic *Ju-jitsu* move and principle, that is very much in need to be drilled. If you are skilled, the Takedown can be a real slamming throw, *Judo*-style. If your grappling is not yet to par, it will still be easy to get him to fall to the ground, or at least to fly into the nearest wall (or into his accomplice). This important move is all about *using his momentum without blocking it*.

Evade in and grab his arm for a takedown by the energy of his own momentum

138   **ADVANCED KRAV MAGA**

6.4 Defense against an Horizontal Inwards Stick Strike

This kind of attack is rarer, but possible, especially from a more proficient opponent, with maybe training in *Arnis* or *French Cane Fighting*. The principle stays identical: *go in where the stick is less effective*. And for this type of attack: go towards the inside of the attacking arm, because the closer you are, the less momentum has the arm has had. The best blocking maneuver is the **full side protection** also used against Circular Kicks, because you are not exactly sure at which height he is truly aiming. So, your forward arm is down for protection from shoulder level to mid-thigh, and your rear hand guards the head in an Outside Block Position.

Of course, with enough training and confidence, you can also dive in with a simple Block while attacking his eyes or throat, in true *Krav Maga* spirit. Both options will be illustrated.

In the first set of Illustrations, you see how to jump forward in a protected way to block the strike very close to the assailant. Bend you low-guarding arm to control his armed limb while using your forward momentum for a full-powered Elbow Strike to the head. Then naturally knee his groin. You can then keep with a *Retzev* of vicious Strikes, or go to the Disarm presented: Grab the stick-holding wrist and keep his arm in place with your own; grab the end of the stick, fulcrum-style, and pull it down violently. The Disarm is also an Inner Elbow Strike executed with all your body weight onto his own elbow. You can now use his own stick for a Backhand Downward hit on his skull, using the natural twist-back move of the hips. Kick his groin and keep at it...

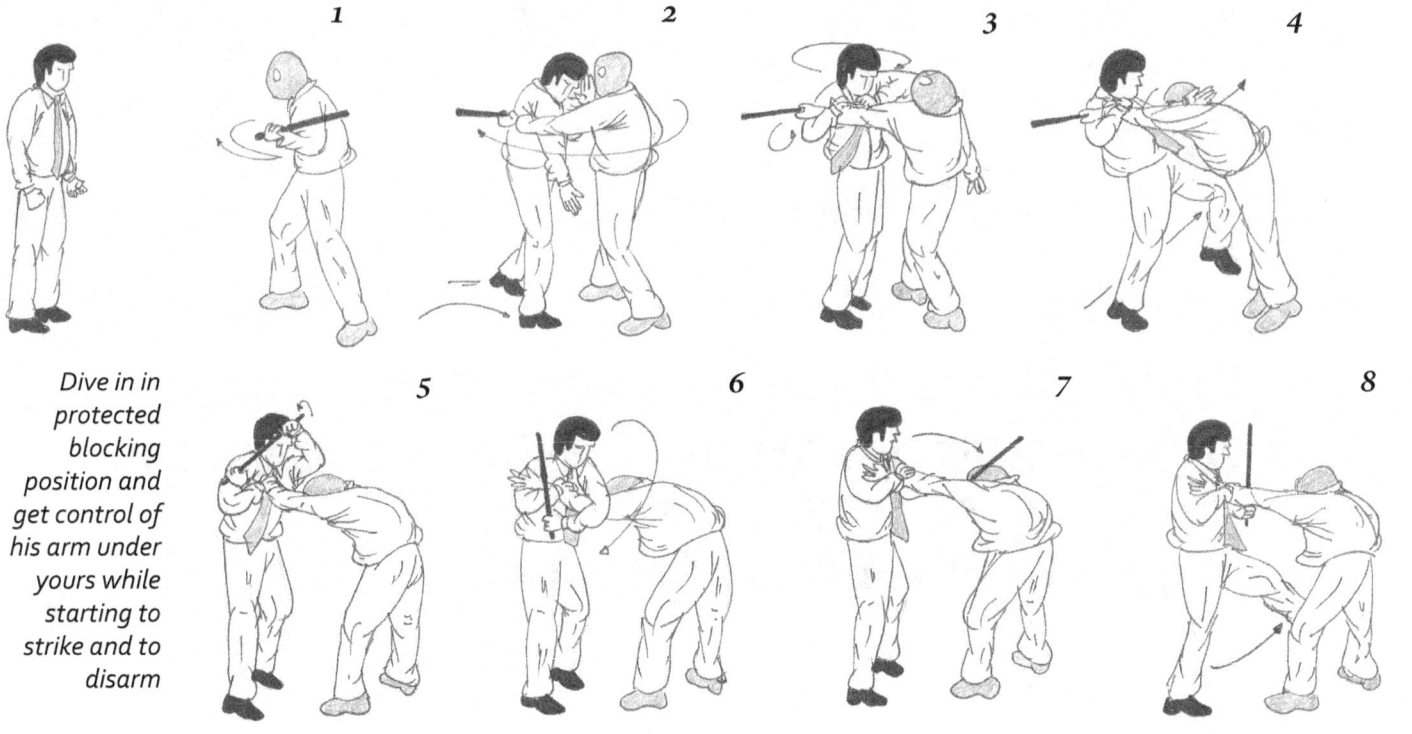

Dive in in protected blocking position and get control of his arm under yours while starting to strike and to disarm

STICK ATTACKS

The second set of Illustrations shows a simpler Dive forward with simultaneous Block and Eye Attack. This is the ideal *Krav Maga* move (but not always possible). You can then start a classic series of strikes to sensitive points, like we already know how to deliver. But the Drawings will, instead, illustrate a more sophisticated (but easy) Disarm. The reader is invited to drill both options: his own naturally flowing *Retzev*, and the *Disarm* (followed by a *Retzev* as well).

The Disarm comes from a very natural encircling of the striking arm, while the opponent is rattled by the eye strike. At the end of the encirclement, the stick is immobilized under your armpit. Strike his wrist powerfully with a Forearm/Hammer-fist Strike of your other arm. Simultaneously, you use your body to pull the stick out of his grab. Then use the Twist-back forward for a powerful Groin Kick that starts a relentless *Retzev*.

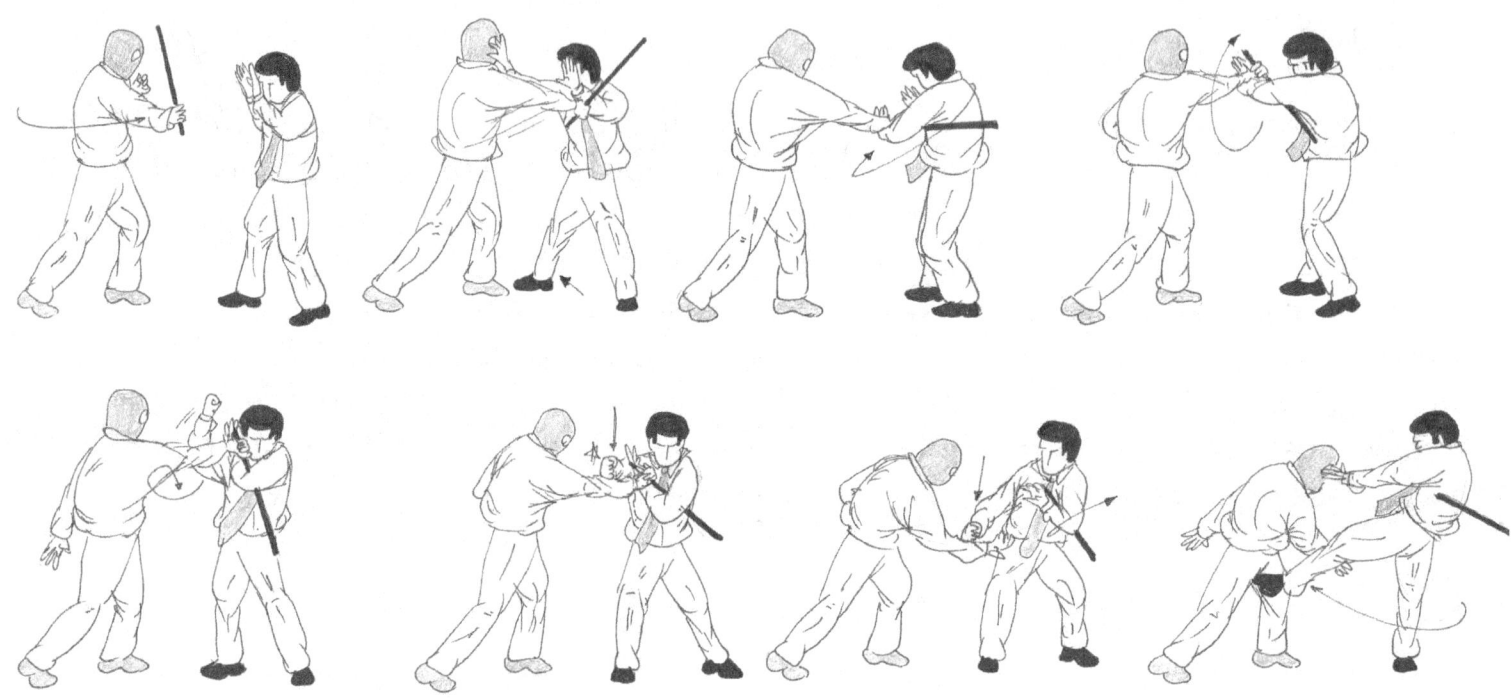

Dive, Block and Attack the eyes; then Disarm and follow up

However beautiful the strategy, you should occasionally look at the results.
~Sir Winston Churchill

6.5 Defense against a Backhand Stick Strike

This is a more common attack, and even more it is a natural follow-up strike after a horizontal or diagonal inside strike: the attacker simply goes back into position with the backhand strike. It is quite a powerful strike, as it allows for the use of the hips, and it is imperative again to dive forward and early, before the attack has developed.
We are giving a few examples, of various levels of sophistication, but they all have the opening move in common: <u>Jump forward diagonally and attack the assailant eyes while blocking or controlling the armed arm</u>.

In the first example, you will follow the Eye Strike with a full encirclement of the arm that should end in a natural wrist grab. During the circular move, you will grab the end of the stick and lift it fulcrum-like for an easy disarm. You then immediately use his own stick for a hard strike *through* his elbow. Start a *Retzev*; I would suggest an Eye Poke with the stick followed by a Groin Kick, but it is all up to you.

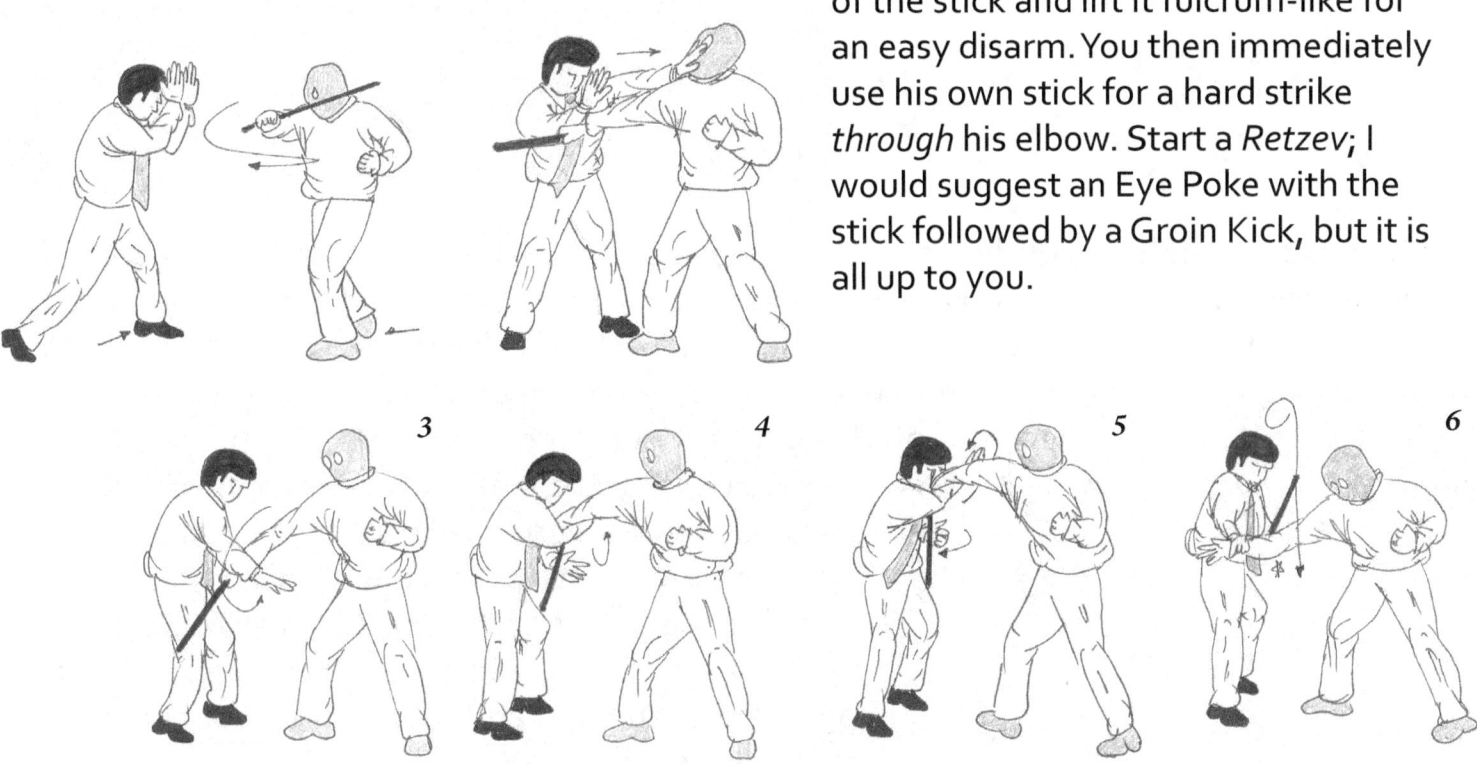

Dive in and out with an Eye Strike and a blocking control; disarm and start a Retzev

The second set of Drawings, at the top of next page, illustrates a Dive *forward and out* with a Double Block that turns into a simultaneous Grab and Eye Attack. As you are deeper inside, you can use your body to lock his weapon arm: pivot *brusquely* to hurt the joint. As he starts to bend forward, strike his shoulder with your elbow and hammer-fist his head. From there, you are on your own. You could push him all the way to the floor and stomp his elbow or hand. You could push him away and kick his face. Follow up according to the situation and your temperament.

*Dive and Block, Grab and Strike the eyes;
Arm-lock and Hit*

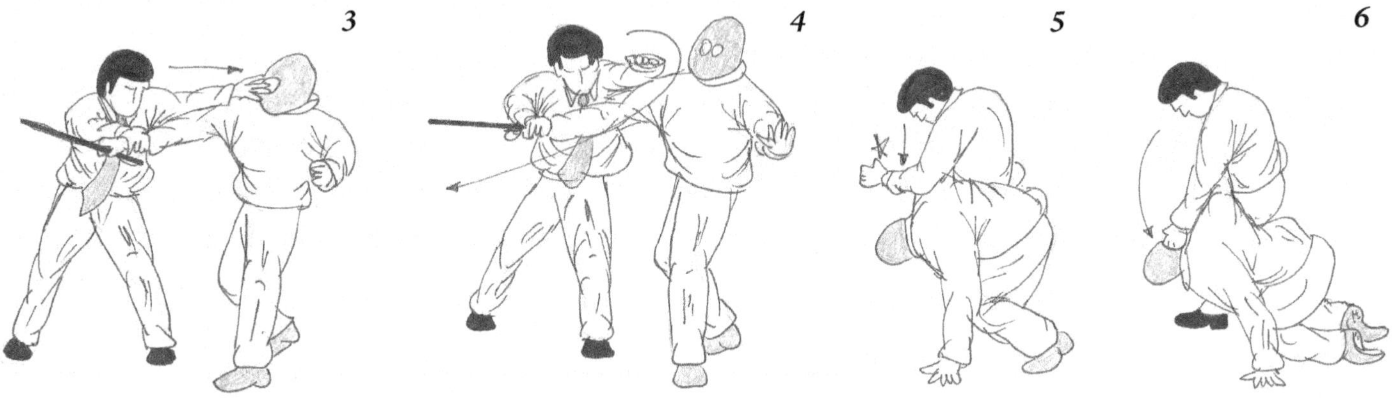

The next example is slightly more complex and therefore requires more drilling, but it is very efficient. You dive in with the Eye Attack, like always. Grab the attacking wrist and twist it so the stick points down. Your other hand will come below his arm to disarm him by pushing up and out of his immobilized hand. It is much easier than these imperfect words. Try it, it is easy and natural. This Disarm does not give you the stick but lets it fall to the floor. But the disarm movement lends itself naturally to a Forearm Strike *through* his elbow, that smoothly turns into an outside Hammer-fist Strike to the throat or the side of his neck. Start a *Retzev* with a Circular Elbow Strike *through* the head powered by the hips and that pulls up your knee towards his groin. Keep at it.

Dive, Strike, Grab, Disarm, Attack the joint and keep striking relentlessly

142   **ADVANCED KRAV MAGA**

Our last example will show how to get the assailant to the ground for control, as can sometimes be required. [*The reader is reminded that submission of an assailant is relevant only in a controlled situation in which there is no danger of an accomplice jumping you from the back*].

The Illustrations show, again, how to dive, block and attack the eyes. You will then use your eye-striking arm to encircle his weapon arm from the outside up. As soon as the way is clear, you attack his face with your elbow, in order to mellow him for the setting of your Arm-lock. Your Elbow Strike turns into a *violent* lowering of his head towards your upcoming knee. Pull him down brusquely to the ground with the Arm-lock (more precisely shoulder lock) and place your knee onto the back of his neck. You can either place the knee for control, or strike down with the knee with force (*dangerous*!) according to the circumstances. In this position, you hold the assailant down with the Armlock control and you can easily disarm him.

After the forward evasion and Eye Strike, set up an arm-lock and take him to the ground for control

"Difficulties strengthen the mind, as labor does the body"
Seneca

STICK ATTACKS

6.6 Defenses against Baseball Bat Attacks

The use of **Baseball Bats** for aggression is pretty common, even in countries where Baseball is not a thing. It is because the baseball bat is thicker at its extremity and delivers more energy at impact than a regular stick (This is the principle of the '*Masse d'Arme*' of the Middle Ages). The bat is also manipulated with both arms which gives it even more power, power that can be further boosted by the use of a body twist.
A bat is therefore a very dangerous weapon, not to be taken lightly. It usually targets the head to bash the skull and cause brain concussion.
These were the bad news. The good news in turn, are the fact that it requires large and noticeable chambering; and that, requiring both arms, it neutralizes the opponent's arms and prevents their use for blocking or feinting or...
Again, dealing with a Baseball Bat will require going *towards the attack*, and not back. The closer you will be to the opponent, the less in danger you will be. So, dive in diagonally *as early as possible*, and fearlessly. He will not be expecting you to come towards the danger, and it will rattle him. Of course, the earlier is the better: preferably preemptively, before he is even set to start his attack. If you miss that opportunity, then you must strive to use his chambering move to attack as he is fully opening himself (just like in the section of the Overhead Stick Strike).

Jump diagonally forward as early as possible

144   **ADVANCED KRAV MAGA**

The fact that the attacker has to use *both hands* to attack is going to be of good use in the follow-ups: both arms are together and can be dealt with in that way, without him being able to block or grab anything. The coming examples will make that clear.

The first set of Drawings illustrates the diagonal dive forward and the *deviating of the opponent's arms*. It is not a 'hard' block, but the inflection of the trajectory without stopping its momentum. You lower his hands, and, from this position, come back up and forward with a violent '**Clothesline**' move. Connect hard with your forearm into his throat or face and go forward and through. This will get him to the ground. Stomp his face while pulling the bat out of his hands. Follow up.

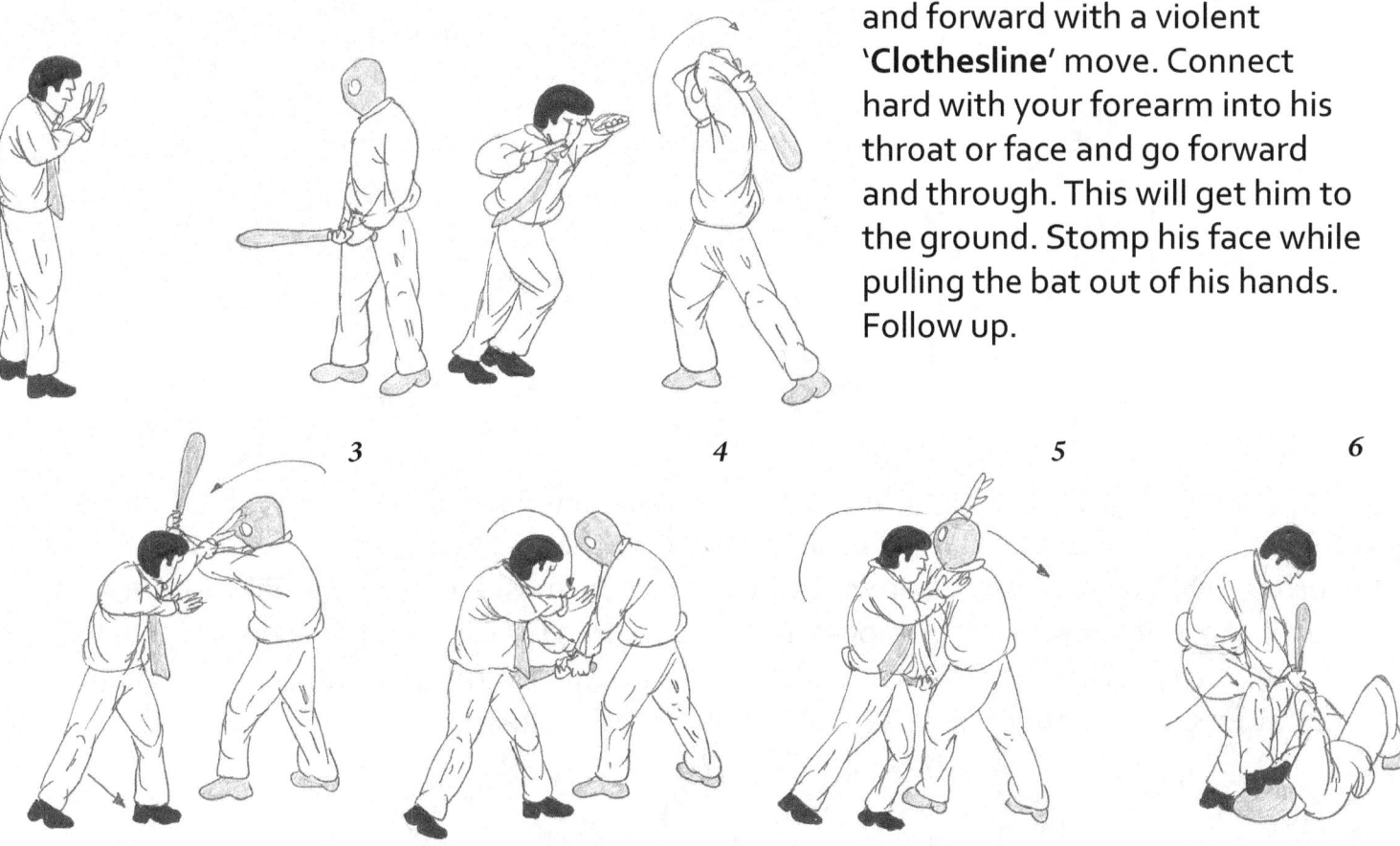

Dive diagonally forward as early as possible and 'clothesline' him

The **horizontal** (or diagonally downward) **attack** is pretty common with the Baseball Bat, because of the skull bashing intention. All principles remain identical to what we have already seen.

In the Figures at the top of next page, you see how to dive forward in the protected position already encountered. Simple. Attack the eyes immediately with your upper hand, and follow with a Groin Slap with the lower hand. You could keep the fingers into his eyes while slapping if you want. Start a *Retzev* and let the strikes rain until he is fully vanquished. This move his easy and simple, what is not to like?

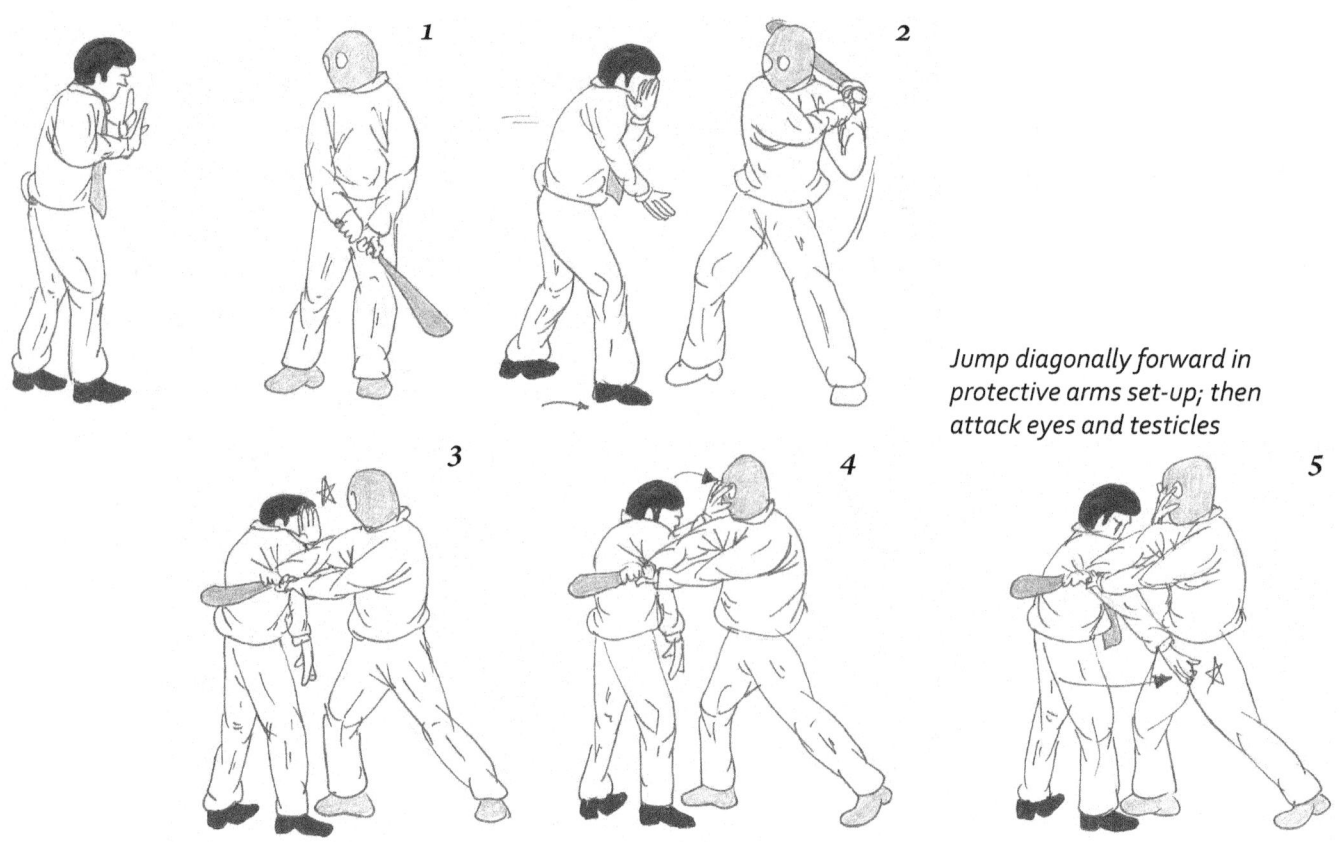

Jump diagonally forward in protective arms set-up; then attack eyes and testicles

One of the things that can be done about a diagonal bat strike is to use its big momentum **to send the assailant to the ground**. The Photos below illustrate how to evade forward in order to blend into the opponent's effort in order to use his energy against him. As per the principle of 'breaking an unlocked door' you hold him in Shoulder Throw position and 'help' him to keep going forward and down. As he falls on the ground, you can go after him and stomp his fingers, wrist, elbow, ankle or even head.

Use the assailant's momentum to throw him to the ground with an easy Shoulder Throw

ADVANCED KRAV MAGA

Of course, if you prefer striking to grappling, the coming Photos show you another way to go. You will start, as always, with a forward jump and control/block as he prepares to strike. Your rear hand is already on its way for a **Forearm Strike through the back of his neck**. Follow up immediately with a Palm Strike to his face and a Low Kick to the back of his knee to bend him backwards. Finish him with a Knife-hand Strike to the exposed throat.

Go forward and block; begin a series of strikes to sensitive targets

The two coming examples will illustrate your advantage of having the assailant holding the bat with two hands: it will make the **Disarm** easy!

The first Drawings at the top of next page, show, again, the forward Dive and Eye attack. You can then encircle both his arms together with your rear arm, in a large body-driven move. Strike his caught elbow with your palm, while pulling back with your body the bat that is stuck under your armpit. The Palm Strike must both hurt the joint and push his arms back: Strike *through*! Follow up with a naturally flowing 'Low Kick' and keep striking.

→

STICK ATTACKS

Dive and Strike the eyes, before encircling both his arms for a Disarm

The next and last example is nearly identical to the previous one, but the Strike to the elbow is different and allows for a **Disarm in which you get control of the bat** for a mean Counterstrike.

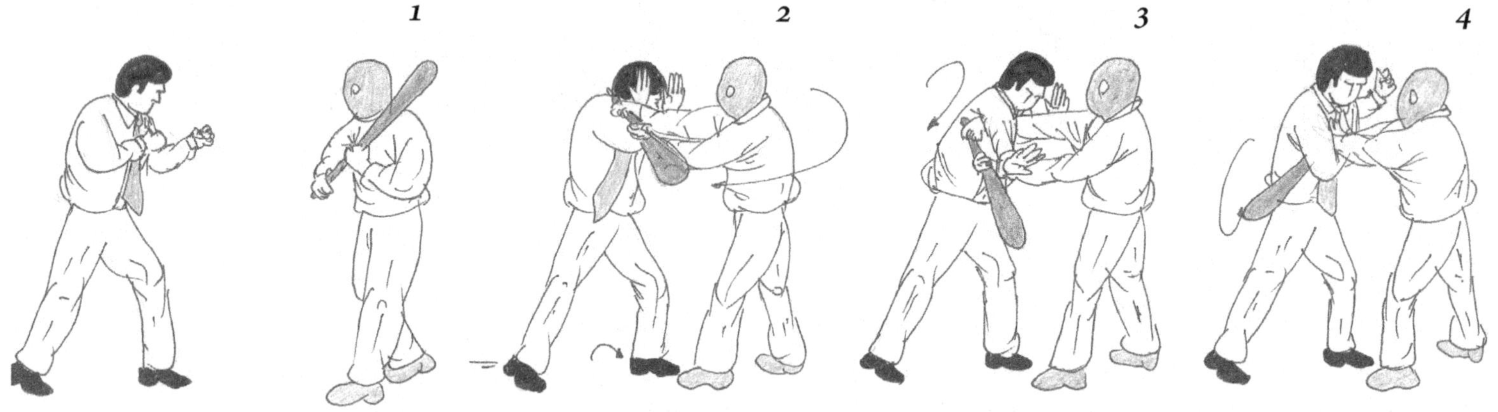

Disarm and hit him with his own bat

148 **ADVANCED KRAV MAGA**

PART SEVEN

Defenses against Knife Attacks

הגנה מפני התקפות סכין

7.1 The Knife

A **Knife** is a lethal weapon! Simple.

Do not let Hollywood make you believe that handling a knife-wielding attacker is easy. It is extremely difficult and dangerous, and nearly impossible against a well-trained attacker (Thankfully, predators and muggers are not into the discipline and hard training work required).

This simple fact leads to a very important conclusion: **avoid fighting against a knife at all costs!** There is no shame in running away or in giving up your wallet; or both. If you can, run away (towards light, crowds, security forces, ...) while shouting for help. If it is appropriate, throw something towards your assailant before starting the sprint of your life: dirt, coins, your wallet, your purse, your coffee or anything else at hand. **There is no shame to running away from an extremely unfair fight or from a life-threatening situation**.

It is important to understand that a sharpened knife does not require force to hurt or kill: it cuts and penetrates literally like into butter. A simple cut can completely freeze your psychological ability to fight; think of suddenly seeing your own blood flowing out in quantity. A compromised artery will have you dead in a matter of minutes. Even a small poke can cause irreparable damage to internal organs. An easy slash can severe tendons and blood vessels, causing loss of control on limbs and huge flows of blood. Do not underestimate how easy it is to win a fight with a knife!

You should also realize that **you have no idea how you will react to even a minor cut**. The best trained individual could undergo a severe psychological shock at seeing his own blood in a fight and even freeze totally. This is not a sign of weakness, but simply physiological. Training gradually towards using a real knife should help prepare coping for such things, but there is no guarantees (see next section). Therefore, **always run if you can!**

Of course, there are situations where there is no escape: when it is clear that giving up your wallet will not save you, when the escape route is closed, when a loved one is being attacked, when your physical or sexual integrity is being threatened, when the knife is used to force you to change your location with your assailant, and in the case of amok stabbing by a terrorist. Then you fight! Then you fight the *Krav Maga* way: aggressively forward and targeting the eyes and throat of the opponent, all the way.

Knife is here used as a generic term for anything short that can cause cuts and stabs: it could be a screwdriver, a cutter, a broken bottle, a pair of scissors, ... The previous warnings, the handling principles and the techniques stay the same.

And all this brings us to another point: against a knife, **try to make use of any suitable everyday object at hand,** either to protect yourself or to attack. Examples will be given in the last Chapter of the book. But think of throwing coins, dirt or hot beverage towards the assailant's eyes. Think of using a chair, a suitcase or a bag as a shield. Think of using your umbrella as a poking weapon (eyes), a screwdriver as a knife for you, anything that can help goes...

7.2 Training for Knife Defenses

The previous section has made clear that Knife Defenses will require serious training, which importance cannot be minimized. Training must be intensive, repetitive, realistic and brushed off regularly. It is a trivial statement, but important to understand and apply. Anything else would be wasted time.

1. **Use a rubber knife and drill the techniques as they are presented**; start slowly and increase speed gradually. It is imperative that your partner attacks realistically: a poke to the belly targets the center of the belly with force, and not sideways 'in-order-to-help-you'. Your partner must understand that helping you is executing the most realistic attack possible.
2. **Once the technique is mastered, it should be drilled at full speed and power.** Your partner attacks you at random time intervals and tries to score with his knife.
3. **You can then add a few other possible attacks to the repertoire that can be chosen from by your partner.** He will attack you, with no warning with a stab, or a downward strike, or a slash. You will have to defend yourself accordingly. At that stage, you should let your own *Retzev* take over (if you feel it is appropriate) after the basic defense.
4. The next stage of training will require an **additional partner whose role is to increase your level of stress**. During your drilling, he will suddenly shout at you, move around, distract you, touch you, and even push you around. Of course, this must be all done gradually. But make no mistake, this is a very important phase of the training.

5. The next stage will be to prepare you psychologically for a real encounter: **the knife you are confronting should gradually become real**. It is extremely important, because of the possible 'freezing' reaction that can happen to anybody in real life: seeing a real sharpened knife aimed at you could completely stress you out and cause you to lose your ability to react as drilled. This is not cowardice or anything to be ashamed of, but an atavistic unconscious reaction to stress. Therefore, you will repeat all the phases of training covered, but with a <u>wooden</u> knife which will cause hurt and pain when it will connect. Start drilling seriously and prepare some analgesic ointments for after-training.

6. The last stage of training is to repeat all the training stages with **a real metal knife, but <u>blunted</u>**. You should never use a sharp knife for training: the simplest mistake could be fatal. Even then, this kind of training *is only to be done under the supervision of an accredited Krav Maga or Martial Arts instructor*. For added safety, the trainee should wear protection like a body shield and padded clothing. The training should start very slowly and carefully; speed and force should be increased very *gradually*. The only thing that must not change is the realistic trajectory of the attack, without which the drilling is meaningless. This stage is for advanced and well trained *Kravists* only. Be exceedingly careful.

7.3 Training Progression

We shall present a whole array of defenses against all sorts of knife attacks, classified by the general type of attack. These defenses will be explained **in the order in which they should be practiced and mastered**. And ultimately used...

<u>It is important to work on the simplest defenses first</u> and fully master them before progressing to the more sophisticated ones. It is not important to know many techniques, but it is vital to totally master them and to ingrain them into your muscle memory. In stress situations, your body will be on autopilot and use the most appropriate mastered maneuver. Mastering a technique requires a long time and hard training, and it should go through all the stages of training presented in section 7.2.

Starting with the simplest defenses will first make you ready for any encounter; it will also prepare you psychologically and physically to progressing to a more sophisticated technique that is also possible and maybe better adapted to your psychology. Once the next stage is mastered, your body will instinctively choose between the response most suitable to the situation, to your personality and to your physiology.

Here come the different levels of defense techniques against a knife threat or a knife attack: ➔

7.3.1 RUN.

You should work on your sprinting skills! This is no joke. As mentioned, always flee a confrontation against a knife if you can; there truly is no shame. Running should be your first option. You can start running after a fake body move or after distracting the would-be attacker by calling out to an imaginary friend behind him. Maybe you can push him aside and start running, or you can throw something towards his eyes first. You get the idea.

7.3.2 Attack preemptively.

If you cannot run away because it is too late, because the way is blocked or because you have to protect your loved ones, then an aggressive preemptive attack can change the situation. It can make the assailant rethink his intentions and maybe go and look for an easier victim. It can rattle him psychologically and make your further moves easier. It can open the way for you and/or you loved ones to start running. If you attack someone who expects you to cower, and if you do so before he even has concretized his own attack, you definitely hold the psychological upper end. Use it for further fighting or to disappear. It is the famous *Bruce Lee* who said: "**There's only one basic principle of self-defense: you must apply the most effective weapon, as soon as possible, to the most vulnerable target."**
Attacking preemptively can mean the use of Kicks, of Body-bent Kicks or of Guard-neutralizing techniques already presented in this book. Whatever suits your personality.

7.3.3 Block & Strike.

The next stage of defense, if you have not been able to flee or attack preemptively, is to block whatever is on its way to you and to strike vital points nearly-simultaneously. This is a basic *Krav Maga* principle, and it means <u>blocking aggressively forward.</u> By going forward, you muddle your opponent's range calculations and expectations, and you also attack him psychologically. The simultaneous or nearly-simultaneous strike should target vital points only, usually the eyes or the throat. Then kicks in the most important *Krav Maga* principle: **Retzev**! Do not stop striking until the assailant is neutralized, and keep attacking vital points, if possible only primary (groin) and secondary. A neutralized assailant should then be fully taken out with stomping joints strikes: fingers, wrist, elbow, knee and/or feet.
You should not proceed to more sophisticated defenses before you have totally mastered the preemptive and 'block & strike' level!

7.3.4 Wrist and Arm Locks.

Krav Maga do not use Armlocks and Wristlocks like *Ju Jitsu* and *Aikido*. In *Krav Maga*, a lock is not something to strive for, but something to use briefly in order to place the assailant in a certain position. *Krav Maga* is about survival and not about control. That is why the Locks of Krav Maga are executed **fast and violently** in order to *seriously damage the joints.* Moreover, *Krav Maga* Locks are never to be used before having 'mollified' the opponent with preparatory aggressive strikes to vital points.

It is important to understand that, in a life and death situation, you should not get into a meaningless grappling strength challenge about the control of the armed wrist or about succeeding the setting of a Lock. This is unnecessary and exceedingly dangerous. It is much more difficult to set a Wrist Lock in real life than it seems from practice with a partner: your opponent will instinctively react with all his power to avoid it and you will find yourself in a tug-of-war about it. Doing so makes you lose the *Retzev*, and puts you at risk of losing control of the knife as you are very close.

To sum it up: **Lock-like moves must come immediately after a successful attack of a vital point, they must be short and violent, and they must be followed by more aggressive strikes.**

And it should be clear that these techniques require a lot of realistic training, going to all the necessary stages of training presented.

7.3.5 Disarmament.

Disarming an aggressor should not be the purpose of your defense; do not obsess about it. Disarming will come naturally if you have already inflicted enough damage to make it safe. Basically, you disarm him because you can and you have already won the fight.

It is important to understand that disarming an adrenalin-laden opponent is not as easy as it seems. Even if he is hurt, his body will instinctively hold the knife as hard as possible; and he will not let go. It is totally unnecessary to get into a tug-of-war about getting his weapon; much better will be to keep striking his vital points and keep destroying his joints. When adequate, you conclude the fight by releasing him of his weapon hold.

An illustration of the 'holding on' phenomenon in fighting, and the inability to think straight used to be given by *Jigoro Kano* when presenting his well-thought *Ju-jitsu*-style in early times. [*It would be strongly condemned nowadays by Animal-cruelty activists, and rightfully so, but these were very different times*] He had someone hold up a dog by his tail, head down; the poor dog was always trashing around to try to attack the hand holding his tail, when in fact it would have been easier for it to claw or even bite the body of the guy holding it. Forget stubborn holding in a fight, and condition your body to concentrate on the real targets...

...The techniques themselves for peeling off the knife from his fingers are pretty simple and will be presented in the relevant examples.

7.3.6 Using his own knife against him.

These techniques are iconic of *Krav Maga*, but it should be understood that they are **the last stage** and require a lot of work and total mastery. On top of the obvious irony, these maneuvers have the advantage to be extremely aggressive, for a fast neutralization of an attacker. It can be important to deal with an attacker fast and decisively; a stabbing 'amok' terrorist attack comes to mind. An interesting side benefit of such techniques is that your prints should nowhere be on the stabbing knife, which could help avoid lots of serious complications, even if your reaction is clearly legally justified...
Do not attempt these defenses before you have mastered all previous stages. Then work hard at them in the most possible realistic way.

7.4 Minimizing damage

Before we start, there are two drills that are important to do at the start of all training sessions about Knife Self-defense. Anyone training seriously for the possibility of a knife fight should expect the possibility of being wounded. An important skill to acquire is the instinctive reaction to knife contact in order to minimize the damage inflicted. The basic idea is simply of going with the knife strike in order to dissipate its energy and remove the straight-on target. Like everything else in self-defense training, it is about lots of drilling to make it automatic; if you have to think about it, it will be too late anyway. Therefore, purposeful and serious drilling with a partner is imperative.
The two drills are presented on next page. Start by having a partner poking or slashing you *slowly* with a knife and you reacting just before full contact. Gradually increase speed, and then have your partner to poke fast at random. Then have him target closer and closer to your centerline, which will force you to instinctively evade more.
The first set of Drawings, at the top of next page, illustrates how to instinctively deal with a **poke**: "go" with the strike by pivoting in place. Your shoulders power the twist, with one shoulder pulling the target away, and the other coming in with the arm to deviate (block) the poking trajectory. It is simple to understand and to execute, but it should be drilled endlessly.

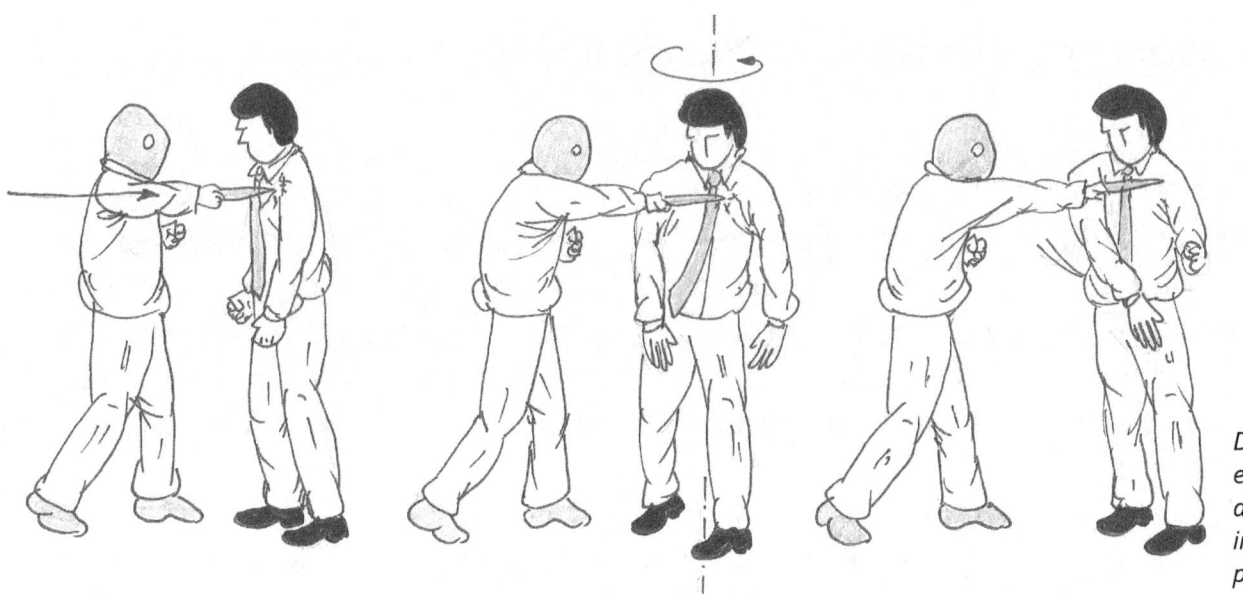

Drill the twisting evasion to dissipate the impact of a poking attack

The second set of Illustrations shows how to 'accompany' a **slashing blow** by twisting and pulling back. The shoulder will again pull the 'outside' arm to strike the slashing arm out of trajectory, in kind of a block. Again, the principle is easy to understand, but practice makes perfect!

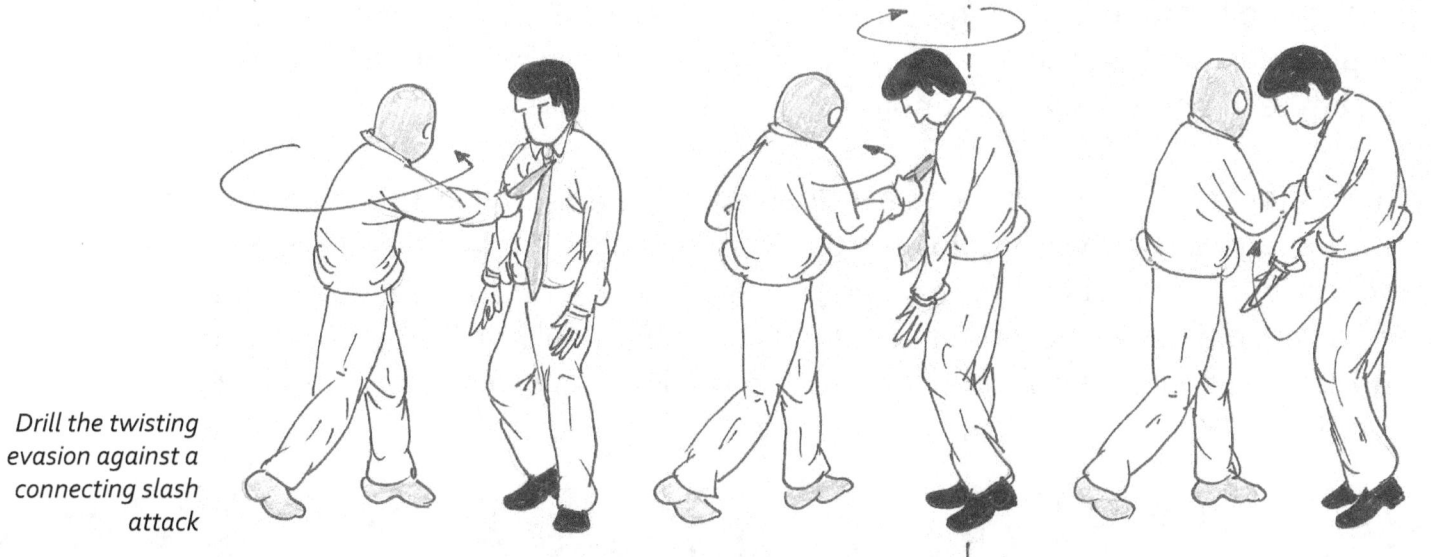

Drill the twisting evasion against a connecting slash attack

These exercises will only be of help if they are regularly drilled, in spite of lacking 'sexiness'.
So, drill, drill, drill.

No plan of action ever survives contact with the enemy.
~Helmuth von Moltke the Elder

7.5 Preemptive attacks against a knife-wielding attacker

Needless to repeat ourselves again about the advantages of preemptive attacks. The success will be highly dependent upon the effect of surprise, the aggressiveness and the speed of closing the gap. In other words: **explode forward with everything you have!** Trust your gut instinct if someone approaches you while holding something hidden away; let your sixth sense do the work. Strike as soon as there is the hint of a threat or of getting in too close a range. Even a knife held down in a non-threatening manner is a threat and a real danger. Take the initiative.

The reader is invited to refer to Chapter Five and consult the sections about 'Range Covering' and 'Guard Closing'. Most techniques presented can be used against a knife-wielding assailant, and they should be drilled so. We shall not re-present them here. Of course, remember the *Retzev*!
Another way to deal with an approaching threat is the 'Body-bent' Kick: you kick the would-be attacker in the knees or groin while keeping your upper body away from a possible knife strike. Your aggressive surge forward will surprise him and allow you to keep kicking until he backs off or is vanquished. You can also follow-up with a Guard Closing technique before continuing your *Retzev*.

The first set of Photos illustrates a kicking combination that stops an advancing attacker and will allow for following up. Side-kick his front knee while bending away and let your foot rebound for a higher Side Kick to the ribs or lower belly that will keep him away. Make sure you kick hard *through* the knee to stop him and cause damage. And follow up after the second kick, with more kicks, groin attacks, guard closing techniques ,…

Stop a threatening assailant with Body-bent Side Kicks

Another example is presented in the next Photos. This time, the first **Body-bent Kick** is a fast Hopping-forward groin Roundhouse, followed by a knee Side Kick. You can then close the distance aggressively to control his armed hand and start your *Retzev*.

Stop an approaching knife-wielding assailant with a groin Body-bent Roundhouse and follow up

Of course, the preemptive kicks need not be Body-bent if this is not a technique that you 'feel' is good for you. The simple straight **Penetrating Front Kick** is just as good. Drill all and see what comes out for you in free-fighting drills.

The coming set of Drawings illustrates the simplicity of this approach: a guy comes towards you with a knife, kick him in the general *groin* area as soon as he gets in range. You can follow up by getting control of his brandished armed hand while poking his eyes. Then, keep at it…

A simple Front Stop Kick will allow you to take the initiative from an approaching threat

The next set of Illustrations, at the top of next page, shows that you should start your kicking as early as relevant from your technical point of view. **Attack as early as possible**, especially if you have mastered a *long forward-going Penetrating Front Kick*. Target the general lower belly/groin area and follow up, in this example with a short Front Upward 'real' groin Kick, and a joint-destroying Stomping Side kick to the knee.

KNIFE ATTACKS

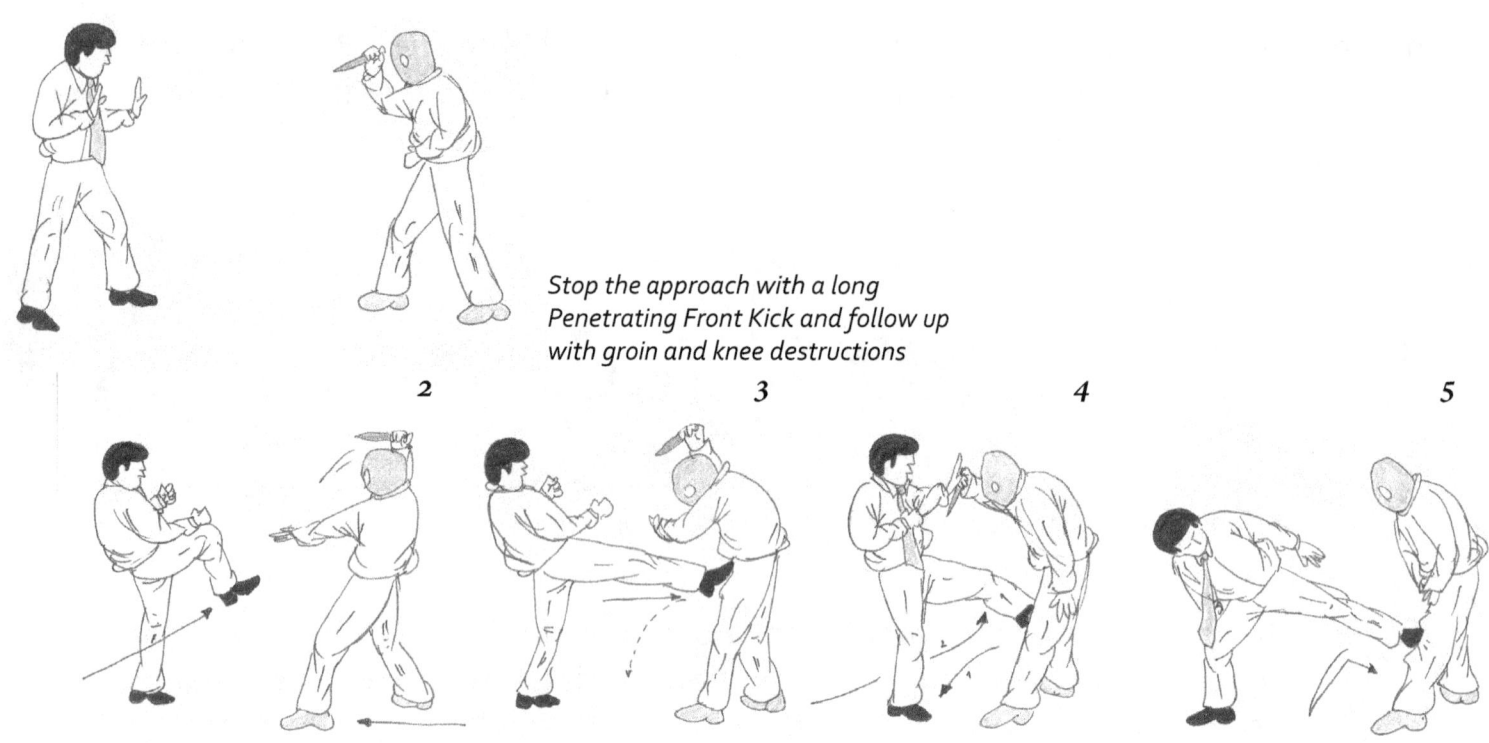

Stop the approach with a long Penetrating Front Kick and follow up with groin and knee destructions

The coming Figures will now illustrate that a Front Kick or any other Stop Kick, can be followed by other techniques than simply kicks or eye strikes. In our example, a threatening attacker approaches and expects you to frightfully wait for him. But a successful **Groin Front Stop Kick** will stop him and place him at the mercy of a Double Ear Slap to catch his head and take him down with a vigorous Neck Twist. Bang his head on the ground and maintain it there for further strikes, uninterrupted of course.

A Groin Front Stop Kick will have your would-be assailant crouch down in pain and offer himself for a hard Neck Twisting Takedow

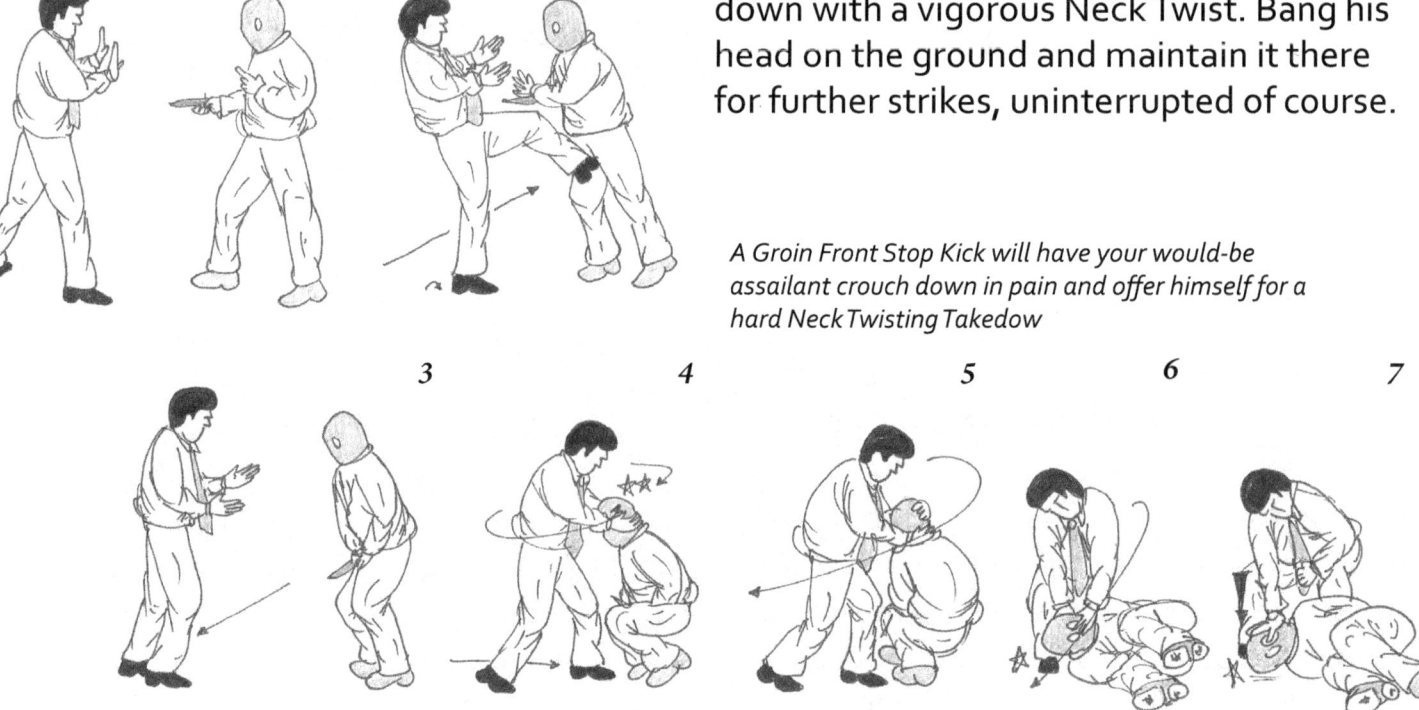

ADVANCED KRAV MAGA

Our last set of Drawings presents a maneuver related to the 'Range Covering' section. We present it here last because it is *a sophisticated Disarming Technique for advanced Kravists only*. The first part is a regular diving forward and getting control of the opponent's armed wrist. But the rest of the technique is more sophisticated and relevant to an attacker holding the knife up in an icepick grip. It is to be drilled *only* after you have mastered all other Knife Defenses, with kicks and strikes.

In our example, you dive forward to catch the opponent's wrist from the inside while poking his eyes. Use the eye pain to twist his wrist and bring the knife blade up. It is now easy, if you are well-trained, to push away the blade with your forearm. If you do this while twisting his wrist further, you will cause his fingers to open and the knife to fall down. To make sure you can do this disarming maneuver, you have used your eye-poking hand to strike and then grab & squeeze his throat. As soon as he starts releasing the knife, you encircle his arm and grab your throat-squeezing arm in a Figure-Four Lock. Now, remember that Locks in *Krav Maga* are transitions and joint damagers. Use your body and arms to brusquely hurt his elbow joint and then to take him down. Help the Takedown with your fingers (previously at his throat) into his eyes. When he is on the floor, you could stomp his ankle to neutralize him, and kick the knife away.

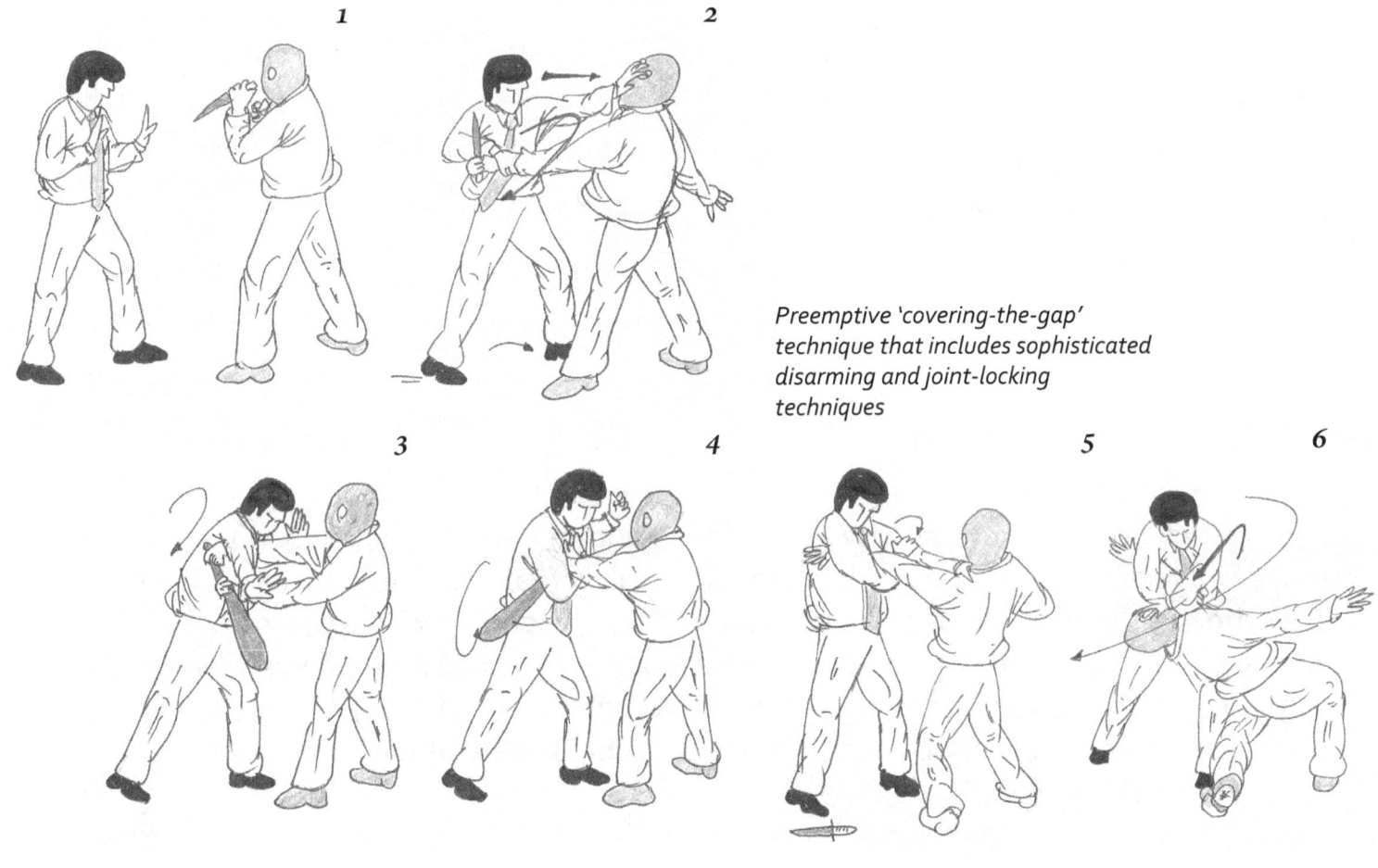

Preemptive 'covering-the-gap' technique that includes sophisticated disarming and joint-locking techniques

KNIFE ATTACKS

7.6 Disarming Principles

Disarming techniques should *not* be attempted before the trainee has fully mastered the 'Striking' Knife Defenses. Locks and Disarmaments are sophisticated techniques that require a good understanding of fighting dynamics and a lot of training. Fighting with an opponent to set a Lock or to take away his knife is not something you want to get in. You have to stun him first and then damage his joints or take his knife, because you then can.
The principle of **Knife Disarming** is pretty simple, but it is easy to forget that it is much more difficult to do in real life than with a partner, even a resisting one. Your opponent will put everything he has into not-relinquishing his weapon.
So, once you feel advanced enough you should start to familiarize yourself with the basic Wrist lock that allows disarmament. The basic version is presented below, and the Drawings are clear. Drill this gradually faster and mark both the twist and the downward push. In real life, you will have to twist and push *violently* and *with the help of your whole body*, not only your arms.

The basic Wrist Lock

Now you will notice that this Wrist Lock has the additional effect *to cause a straightening of the fingers*; this will be the **disarming** feature. Once you have mastered the setting of the basic Wrist Lock, you should start practicing with a partner holding the knife. Once in position, you can use the second hand to push the fingers down. From there it will be very easy to 'peel' the knife-handle out of his hand. Practice carefully, but remember that in real life you **twist brusquely and strike down** rather that pushing gently down.

➤

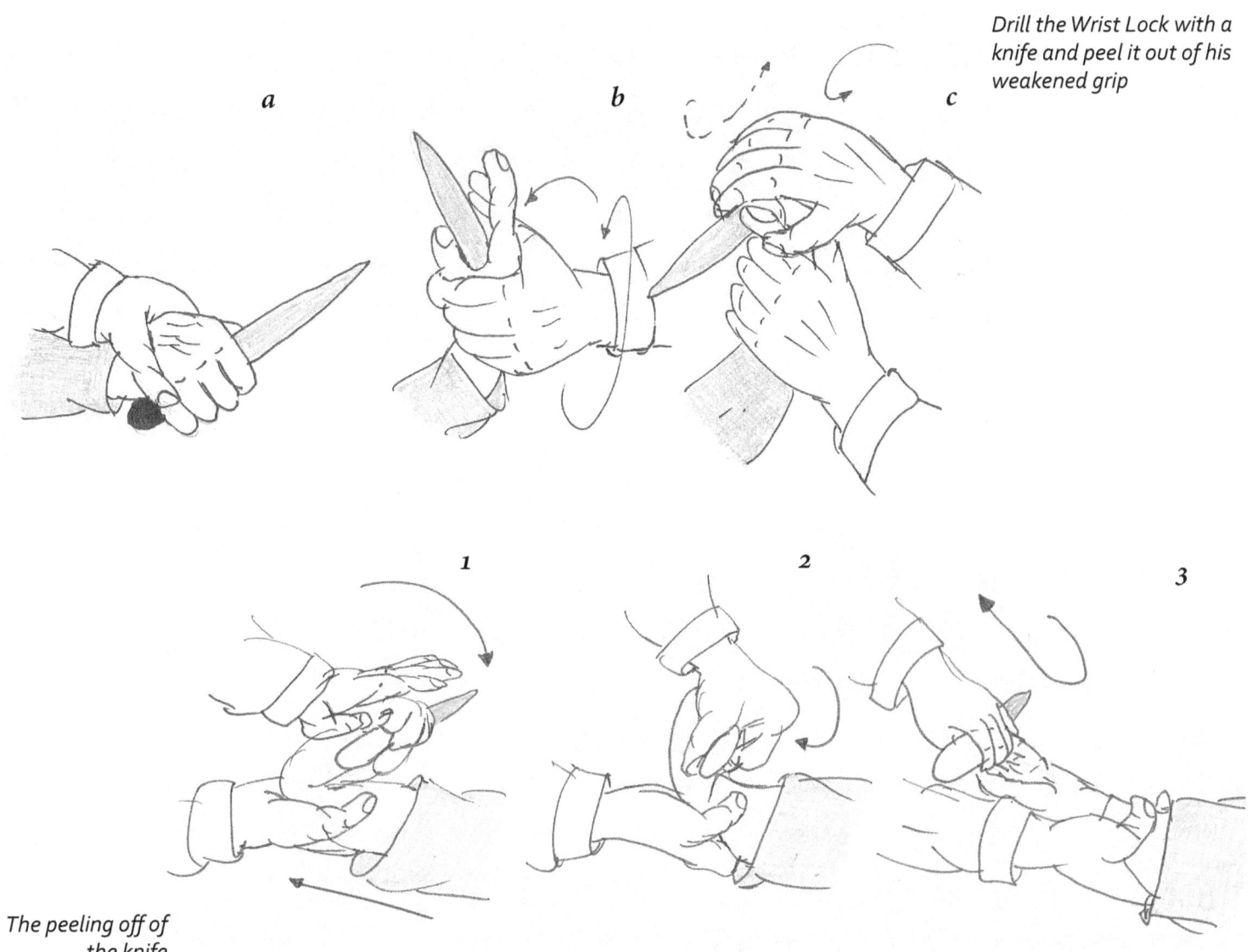

Drill the Wrist Lock with a knife and peel it out of his weakened grip

The peeling off of the knife

To conclude this section, we shall present a classic *Aiki Jitsu* series to drill in order to understand the <u>principles</u> behind these kind of wristlock maneuvers. It also teaches you evasion principles and the use of the whole body in order to set Locks. This is an important <u>exercise,</u> but it is not *Krav Maga*. Drill it regularly until you 'feel' the natural setting of a Wrist Lock, then have your partner resist more and more. It will help you much in your further progress with Disarming and Locking techniques.

The Figures at the top of next page show clearly how to evade-out a body stab, get control of the stabbing wrist and set up the Lock. You pass in front of him to use your body to set up the Lock without blocking the general forward momentum of the attacker. You keep your twisting motion and push down to take him down while causing the release of the knife. If you keep twisting, he will fall on his back besides you, and you will be able to kick his extended elbow and stomp his face.

KNIFE ATTACKS

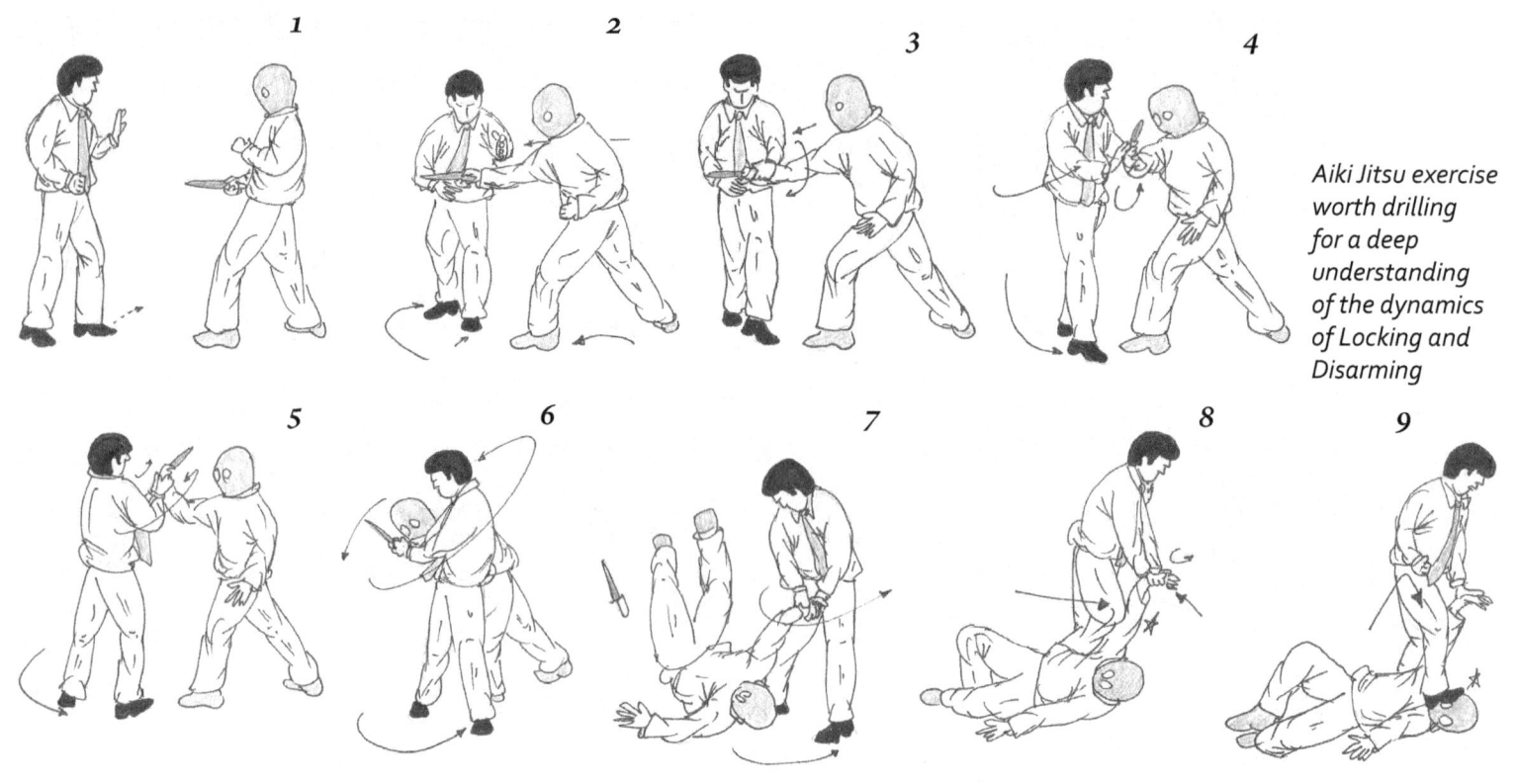

Aiki Jitsu exercise worth drilling for a deep understanding of the dynamics of Locking and Disarming

7.7 Close proximity Knife Threats

The good news is that a threatening opponent wants something for you and is not attacking you (yet). The bad news is that he is probably already too close. You therefore have to react explosively and aggressively *as soon as possible*, before he decides to attack himself. It can be productive to first look as if you will be caving to his demands, even pointing to your wallet pocket; and then **explode**.

7.7.1 Close but non-touching knife threats
The assailant is close *but there is no contact of the knife blade with your body*. He is threatening you or making demands while brandishing his knife forward. Lift your hands in a non-threatening submissive way; that allows you to defuse the situation while getting out of inertia. Explode in a powerful slap to his armed wrist in order to throw it to his in-side. Immediately **kick his groin**...

... The slap removes the knife from the dangerous central axis and places him in a position that prevents the use of his other arm as well. Lower your kicking leg and get close to him to knee his groin with the other leg while slapping his ears and grab his head. His armed arm is still neutralized between your two bodies. Grab his shoulder and arm in its position and push him violently away. Go after him with a powerful long Penetrating Front Kick (hopping if necessary) as he stumbles backwards. From there you should either pursue him with kicks, or you should turn around to run away.

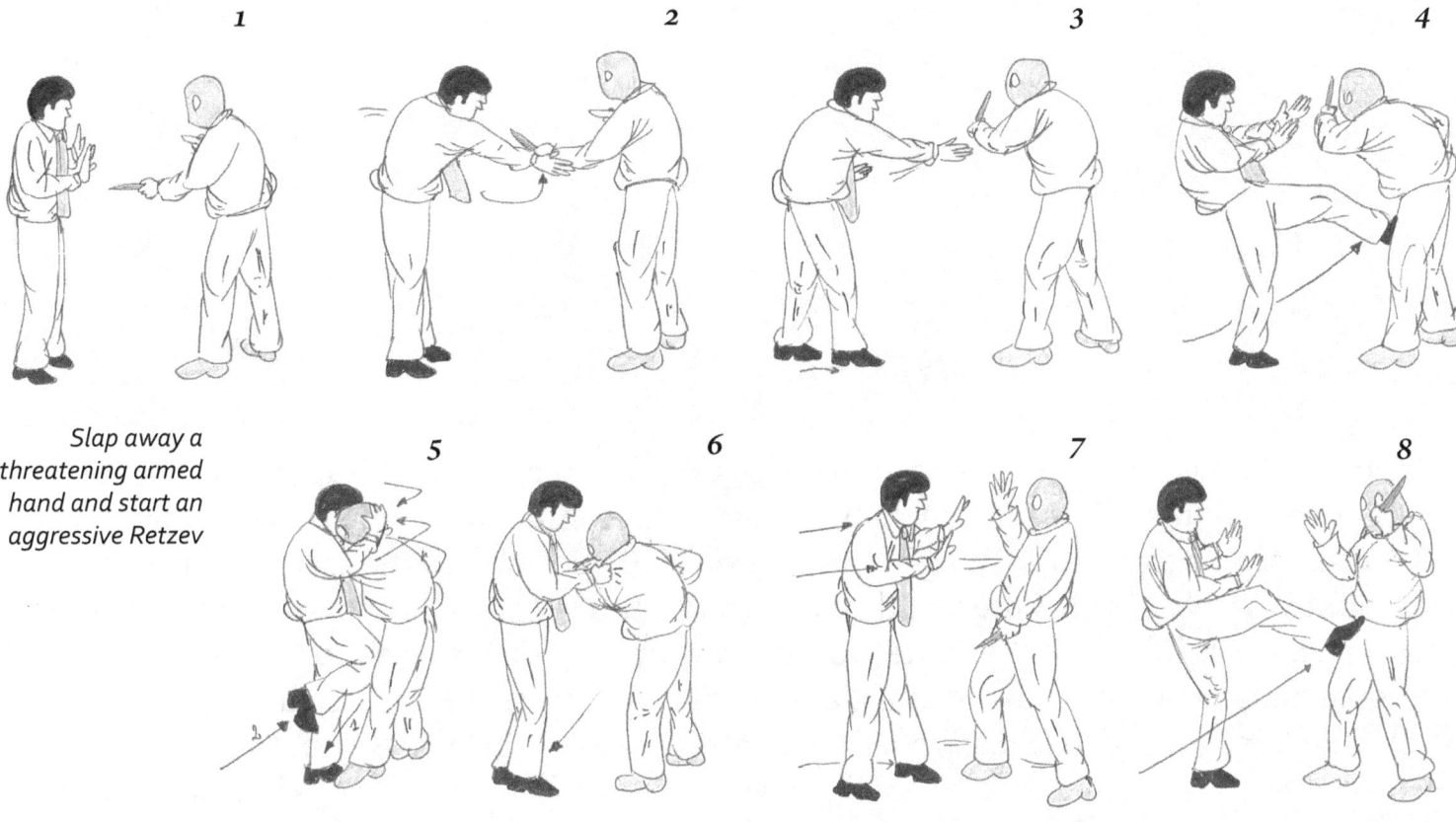

Slap away a threatening armed hand and start an aggressive Retzev

If the assailant is **closer** than in the previous example, you have to react before he can approach further. The Drawings at the top of next page illustrate how to **lunge forward** and out while striking the armed forearm to the attacker's in-side. Keep going forward, so as to make the use of his knife irrelevant and strike his eyes with the blocking hand. You keep on your forward momentum and twist his head (with your fingers in eyes for better control) all the way down. You keep control of his armed arm under your armpit while slamming his head on the floor and then immediately stand up while grabbing his wrist with both hands. You can then stomp-kick his extended elbow all the way to the floor. Crush the elbow *into* the floor and stomp his head to conclude. *The starting forward lunge is the key to the success of this series.*

KNIFE ATTACKS

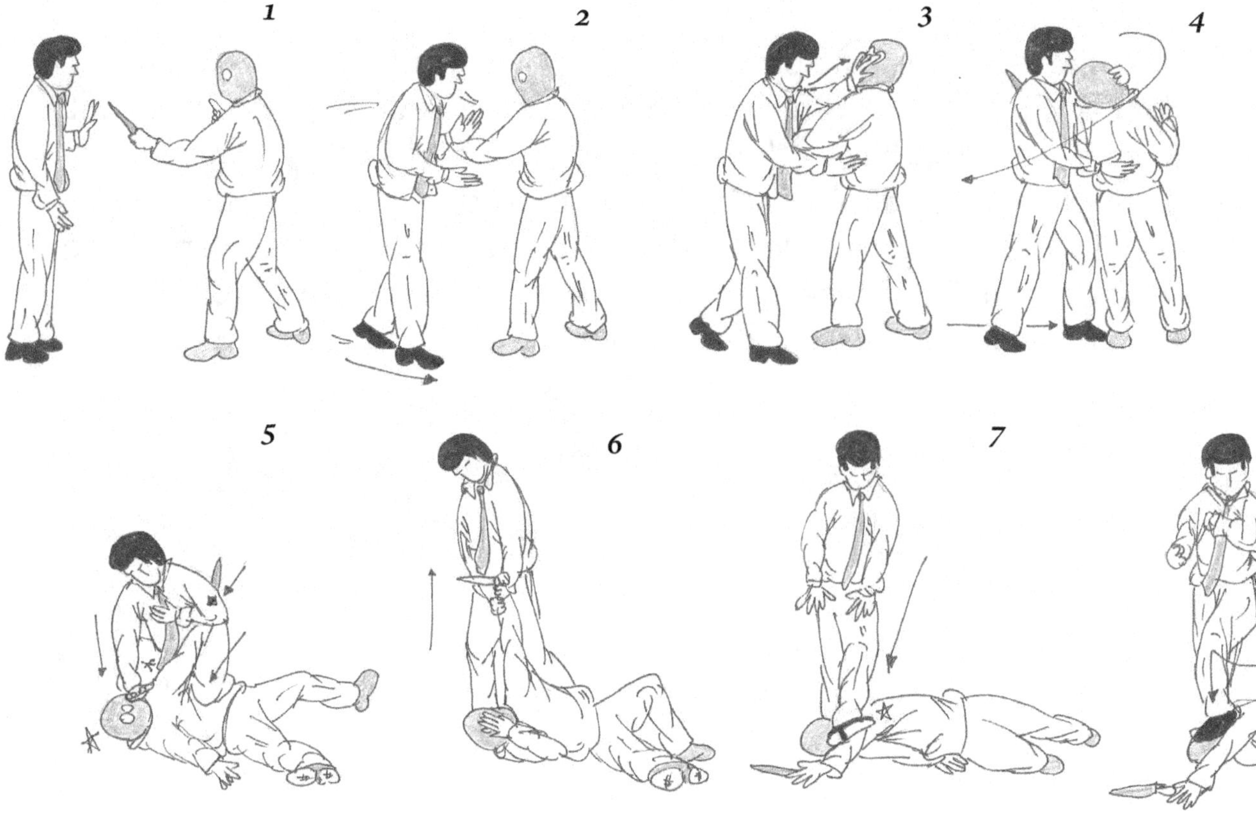

1 2 3 4

Strike the armed hand aside while lunging with an eye strike; follow up with a Head Twist Takedown and more

5 6 7 8

If the assailant is even **closer** than in the previous example, and is still approaching, you have to react before the blade can come into threatening contact with your body. Immediately grab and push his armed wrist from the outside; explode into the move and push with all your body weight. Immediately add your second hand to the push and force his hand onto his own belly. While he concentrates to resist the move, you kick his groin. Use the pain and surprise to take his armed hand into classic Wrist Lock position, and repeat the Groin Kick. You should now be able to disarm him as described earlier. In any case, pull away, with the knife or without.

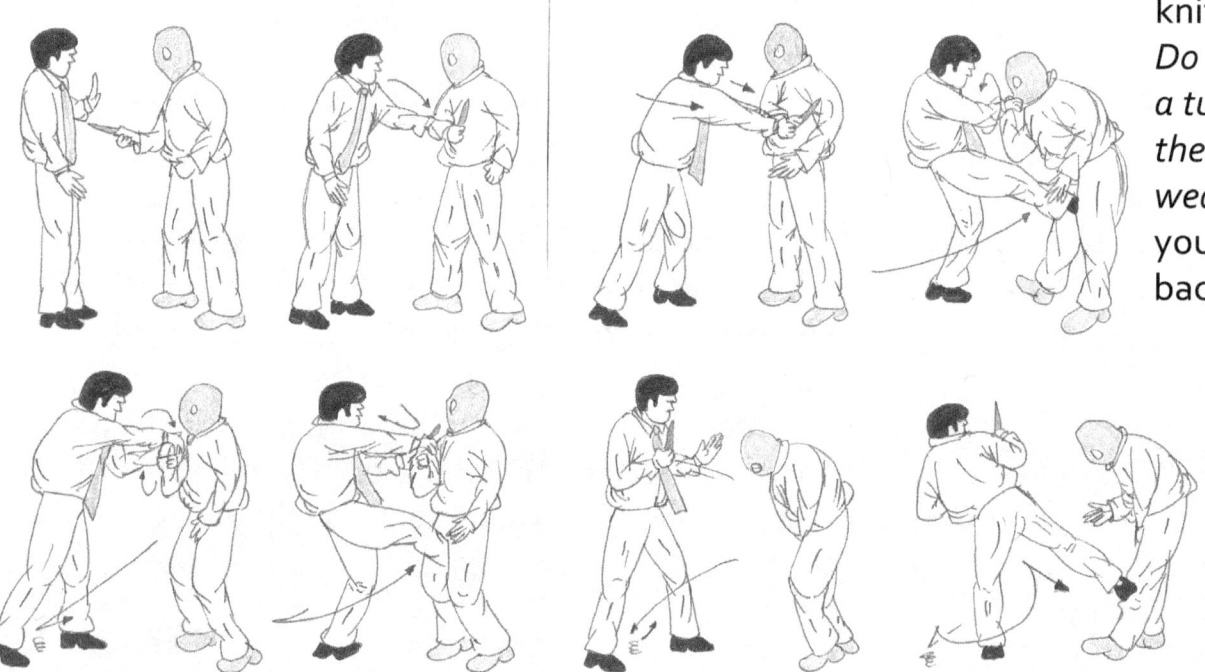

Do not ever get into a tug-of-war about the possession of the weapon. As soon as you are away, come back with a Body-bent Side Kick through his knee. Keep kicking.

Grab the threatening hand and push it with all your body towards the opponent's trunk; start kicking

166   **ADVANCED KRAV MAGA**

We shall now present an **Armlock Disarming defense** against a more dangerous threatening attack, in which your assailant uses little stabs towards your face to intimidate you and submit you to his will. Block one of the stabs while going *forward and out* and simultaneously attack his eyes from the inside. This is classical *Krav Maga*, but it needs serious drilling. Grab his armed wrist and strike his inside elbow to bend his arm. You can now release his wrist to place him into the Armlock. Remember that armlocks in *Krav Maga* are about joint damage: pull him forward while twisting *violently* to damage both shoulder and elbow. You can now easily pull him to the ground. Change your hold to the Figure Four Armlock illustrated and set it *violently* to disarm the attacker.

Block/Evade/Counter a threatening stab, attack the eyes and start a sophisticated and joint destroying defense

We shall conclude this section with an **Armlock defense** against a low knife threat from very close. Holding the knife hidden on his side will allow your assailant to get close without showing his weapon. The subsequent strike or threatening hold will be an upward low stab, which is a very dangerous eviscerating attack. As soon as you see the low knife holding, you must react to avoid it getting in contact with your body. Attack the armed wrist with a classic *Downward X Block* and start the Armlock set up. You are surging forward with power! Set the Armlock by twisting *violently* to cause harm; this is not about control. Stomp his toes and shake him by lowering yourself with a shock to his locked shoulder. Then strike his extended elbow with both hands for elbow damage. You can follow up with an Upward Front Kick to his face as the start of your *Retzev*. See Illustrations at the top of next page.

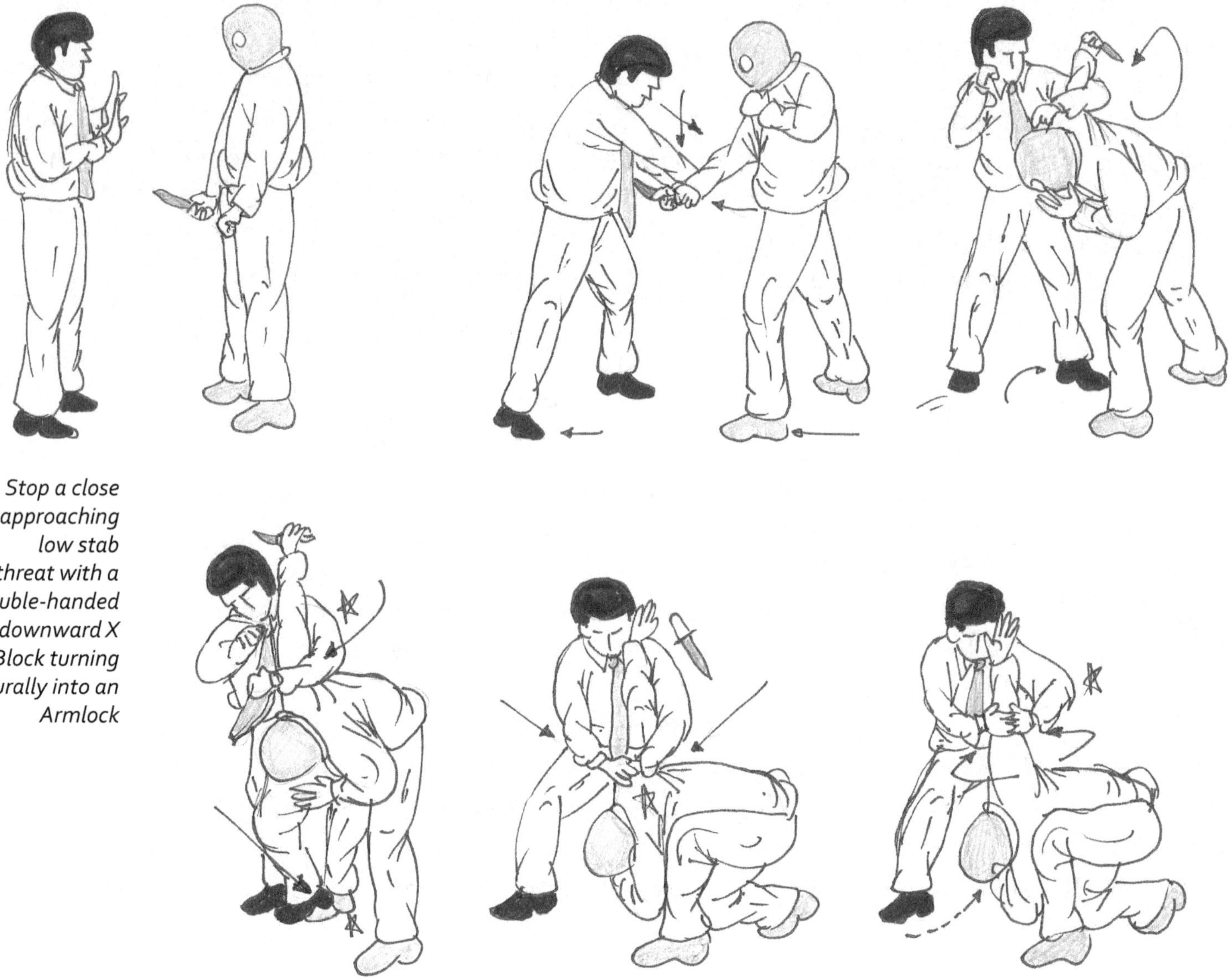

Stop a close approaching low stab threat with a double-handed downward X Block turning naturally into an Armlock

7.7.2 Front threats with blade contact

In theory, blade contact makes a potential strike less powerful. But remember that the opponent can push with all his body and a sharp knife will cut or penetrate easily. The good news is that a *threat* is not an attack: the assailant wants something and gives you time to react. Do it fast and viciously.

The first set of Illustrations shows a "**use his own knife against him**" technique against a knife-on-the-belly threat. Pull your belly back while slapping and pushing his armed hand towards his own body, with all your (body) power. Keep the momentum and headbutt his face while your second hand comes to help control his armed wrist pushed to his own belly. Kick his shin or knee forcefully, and then suddenly invert your momentum while pulling the kicking leg back. You have pushed with all your might, and suddenly you go with his instinctive resistance and pull him forcefully while extending his arm. He will again naturally react to counter your pull, and you can then go back to pushing while bending his arm and setting up the hold that will allow to stab him with his own knife. Use the power of your hips to push the knife towards his ribs and you can then knee his groin to lower his resistance and push it further.

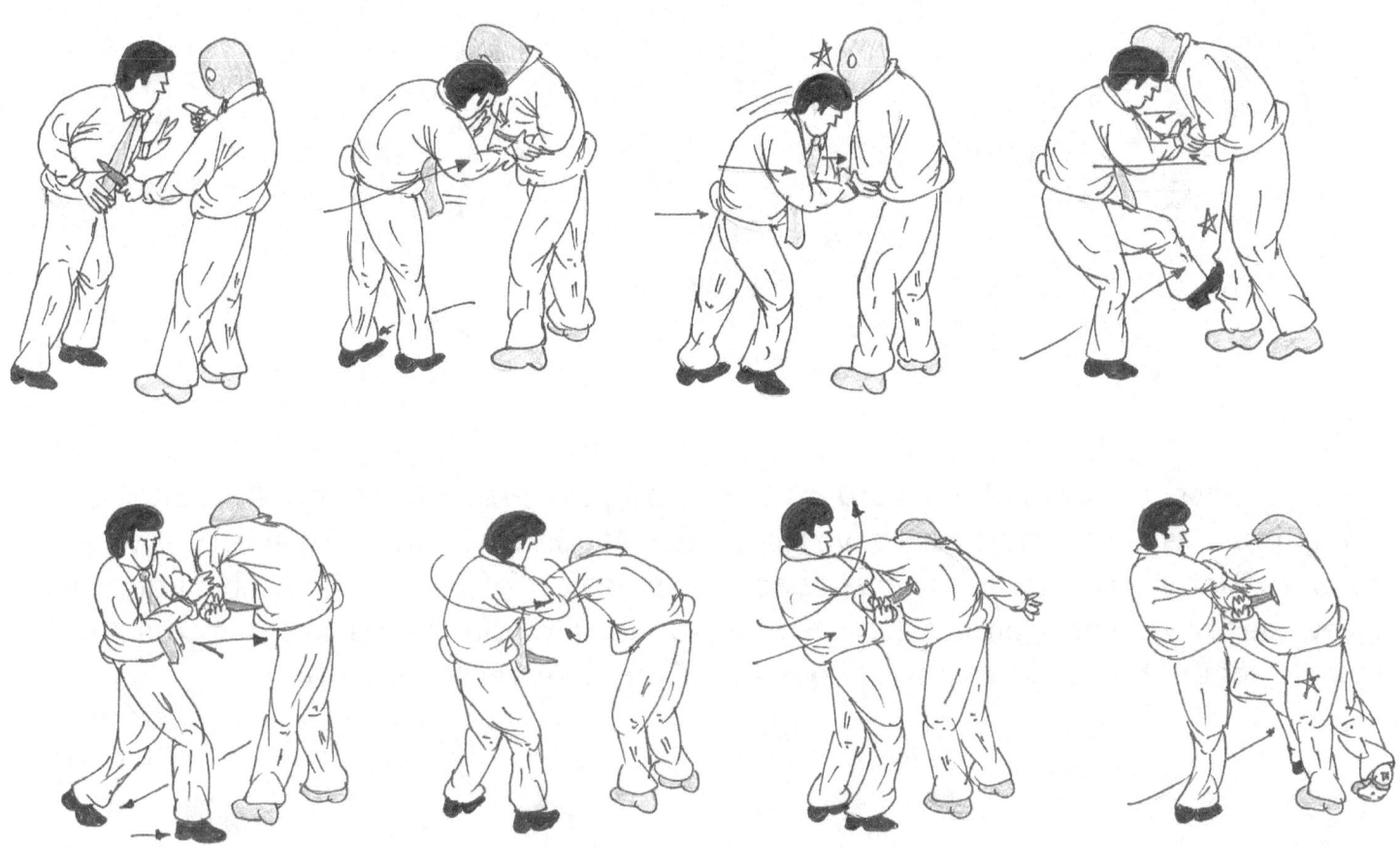

Glue his armed wrist to his body with all you have and headbutt him to allow for the set-up of the stabbing defense; use his natural reactions to push and pull to keep him off-balance

A more dangerous front threat is **blade contact with your throat**. A sharp knife can go through that area like butter and you are in clear and present danger. Make sure the assailant believes that you are wielding to all his demands; if you can divert his attention just before exploding into the technique, go for it.

In the **first** set of Drawings, you can see how to remove the knife on your carotid by striking inside out (and grabbing the wrist). Nearly simultaneously, you are striking his throat that you will further pinch [*You could also strike the eyes and then go down to grab the throat*]. Kick his groin with everything you have and strike his neck as he bends in pain. Pull his head down into a knee strike from the other leg. All the while, you have kept hold of his armed wrist. From here, you can keep striking or you can push him away and run...

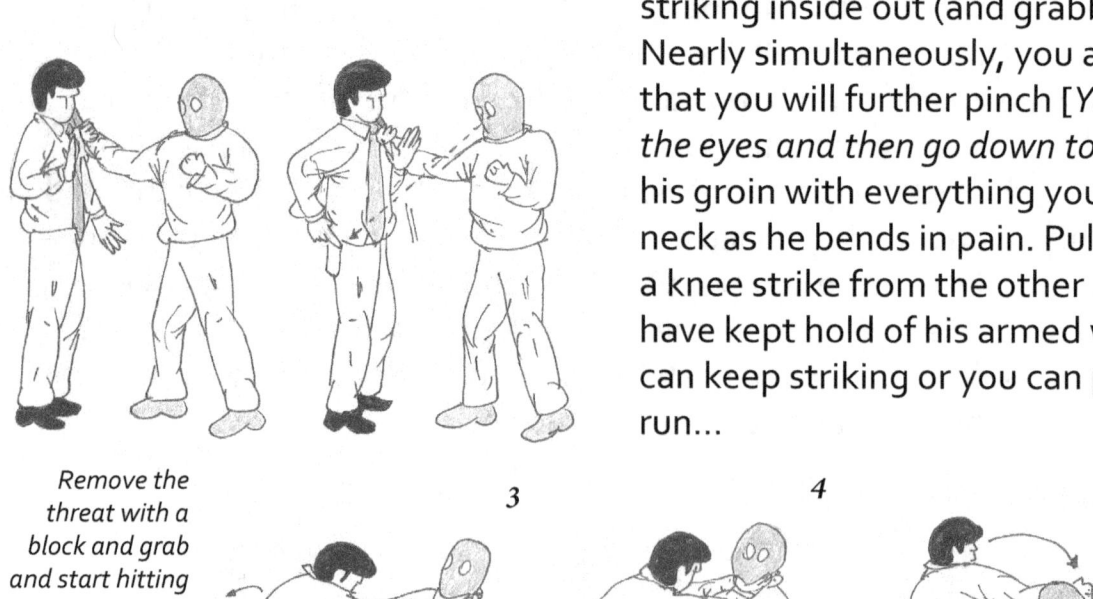

Remove the threat with a block and grab and start hitting

If the aggressor holds his knife **across your throat**, the situation is more difficult and dangerous. As illustrated, you'll have to push his hand to his body with an *explosive* forward momentum (move the head back and sideways of course and push diagonally). Keep the forward momentum and grab the armed with both hands. Kick his groin in order to help set up the classic Wrist Lock position. Start a *Retzev* from there.

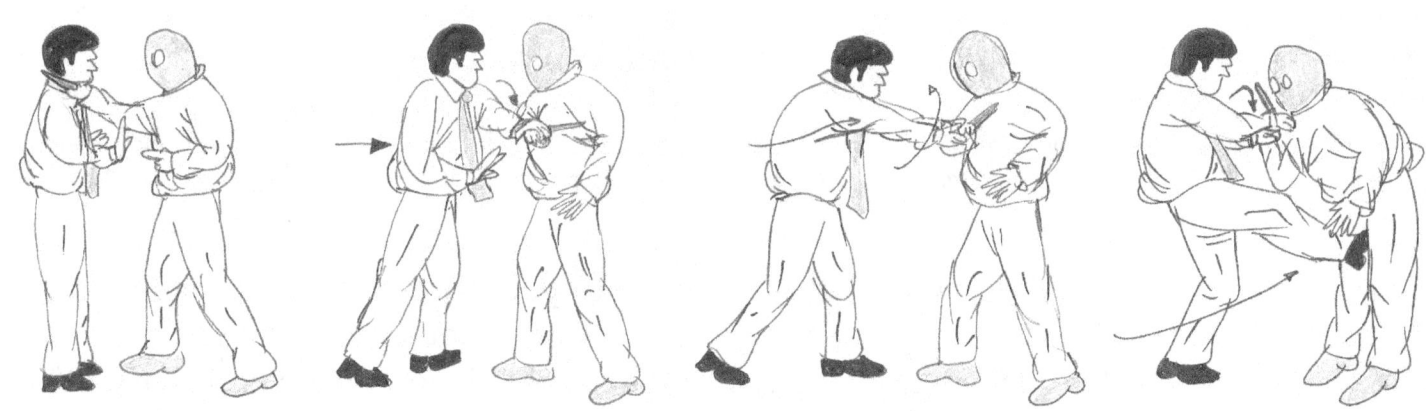

Push the threatening hand to the assailant's chest, kick his groin and follow up

ADVANCED KRAV MAGA

The next example will illustrate clearly the **classic Wrist Lock to disarming sequence**, of course after a well-deserved groin kick. The knife threat is a straight carotid hold, but the slap/grab move is different than in the previous handling of this threat. The 'slap and grab' comes from the *same side* hand and slaps the armed wrist *inside out*. At the same time, you go forward diagonally away from the threat but towards him. Grab the wrist with your other hand in the Wrist Lock position and then adjust the other hand for

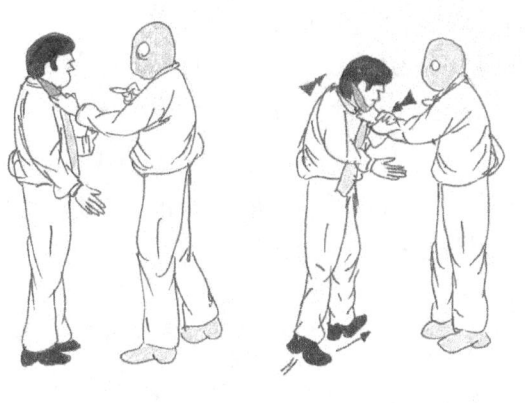

the classic hold. This will only be possible if you are pushing aggressively forward and *if you use your body power* to get into position. As he concentrates on his grabbed wrist, kick his groin with all you have. You can now push his hand in Wrist Lock and peel the knife out of his straightening fingers. And now is the time to kick him again in the groin or in the floating ribs. Keep at it.

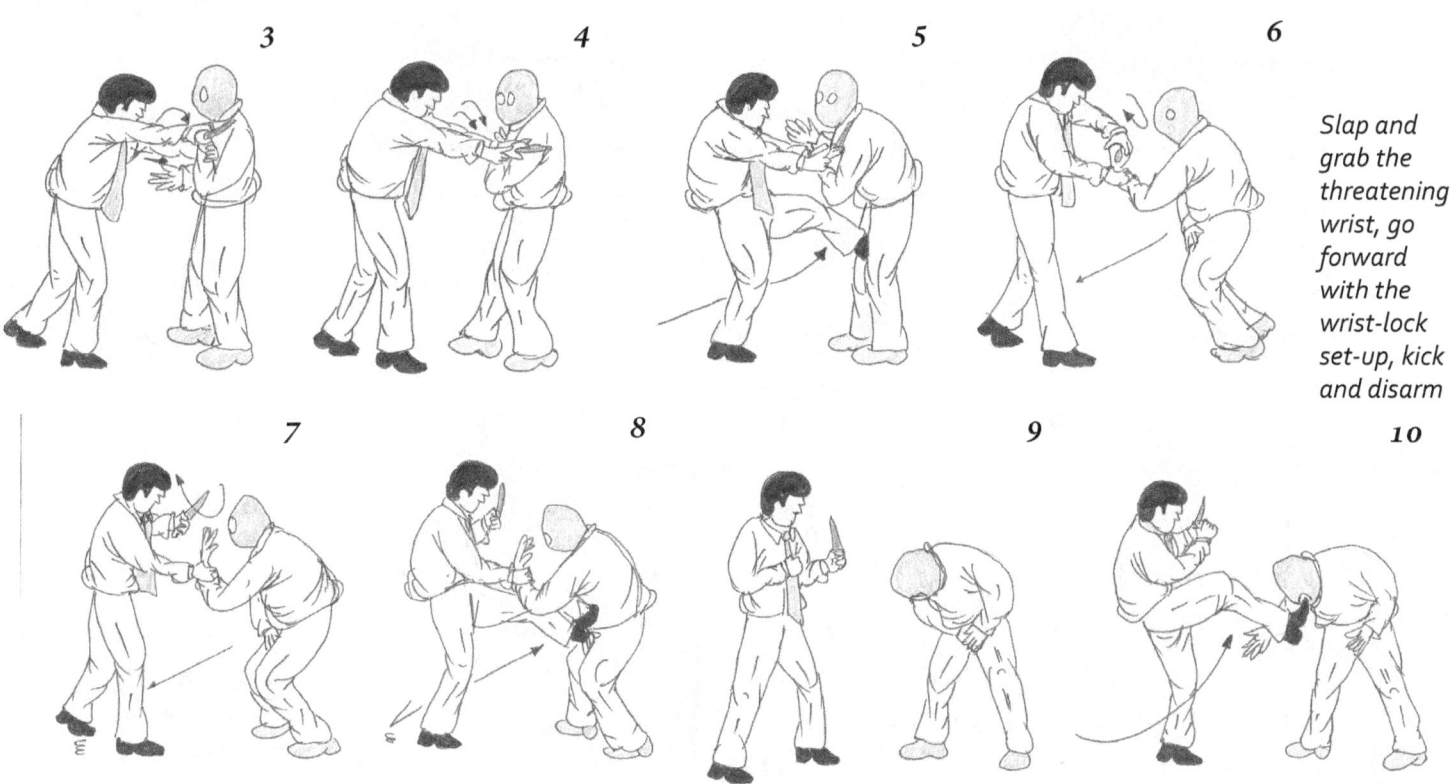

Slap and grab the threatening wrist, go forward with the wrist-lock set-up, kick and disarm

The next example is a more advanced technique with a **sophisticated Disarm**. Do not start drilling it before you have mastered the basic techniques. The reaction to a *straight carotid threat* is based on a simultaneous <u>triple</u> move: you move the upper body away from the knife, you strike his eyes and you grab and twist his armed hand (into wrist lock position)...

...It is more difficult than it looks. The moves must be nearly simultaneous, and the ability to twist his armed wrist with one hand is highly dependent on the success of the eye poke. With serious drilling it becomes a very fast and effective maneuver. Your eye strike becomes an Elbow Strike as you come closer forward, and the hand comes to disarm by grabbing the blade itself out of the opponent's wrist-locked fingers (See Illustrations below). Again, a maneuver that requires training. You can use the return of the arm to elbow his head again and start your *Retzev*.

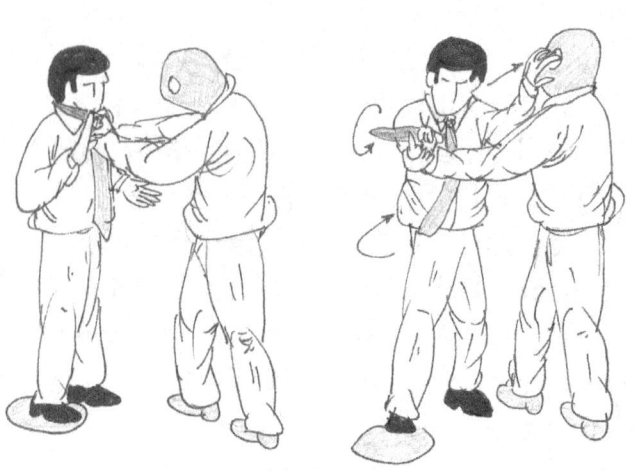

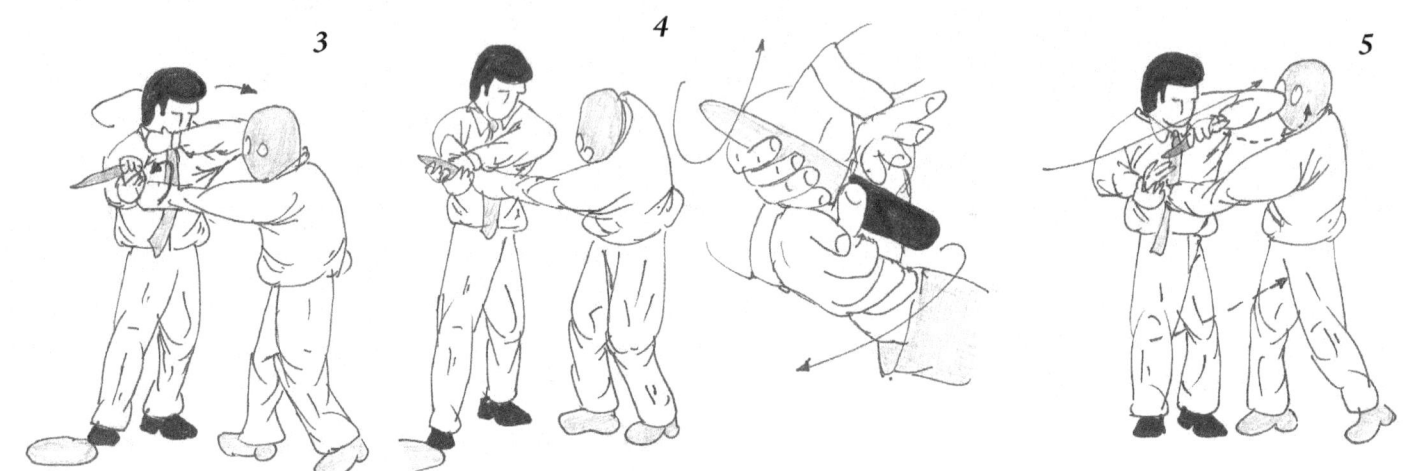

A difficult and sophisticated Disarm defense, but that is worth drilling

We shall conclude this section with another sophisticated defense including **Armlocks and 'use his own knife against him'.** The knife threat is straight but across the throat. Lean forward while trying to talk your way out of it and lift your hands in clear surrender. You will then strike his forearm down with *all your power* while pulling your neck back. You should use your body weight and aim at striking close to the wrist and close to the elbow in order to bend his arm as well. Press his arm to your body with both hands and use your hips and trunk to keep him under control. Twist violently for a full 360 pivot that will place his armed arm in Armlock under your armpit. Remember that the purpose is to inflict joint damage: you should act *brusquely*. As soon as you have damaged his elbow, change your hold into a classic Figure-Four Lock. Do another violent half-circle pivot to place him off-balance, and then suddenly change the direction of the circular move. By doing so, you release his arm from under your armpit so you can push his knife into his face with the force of both your arms and of his own reaction to the circular pull.

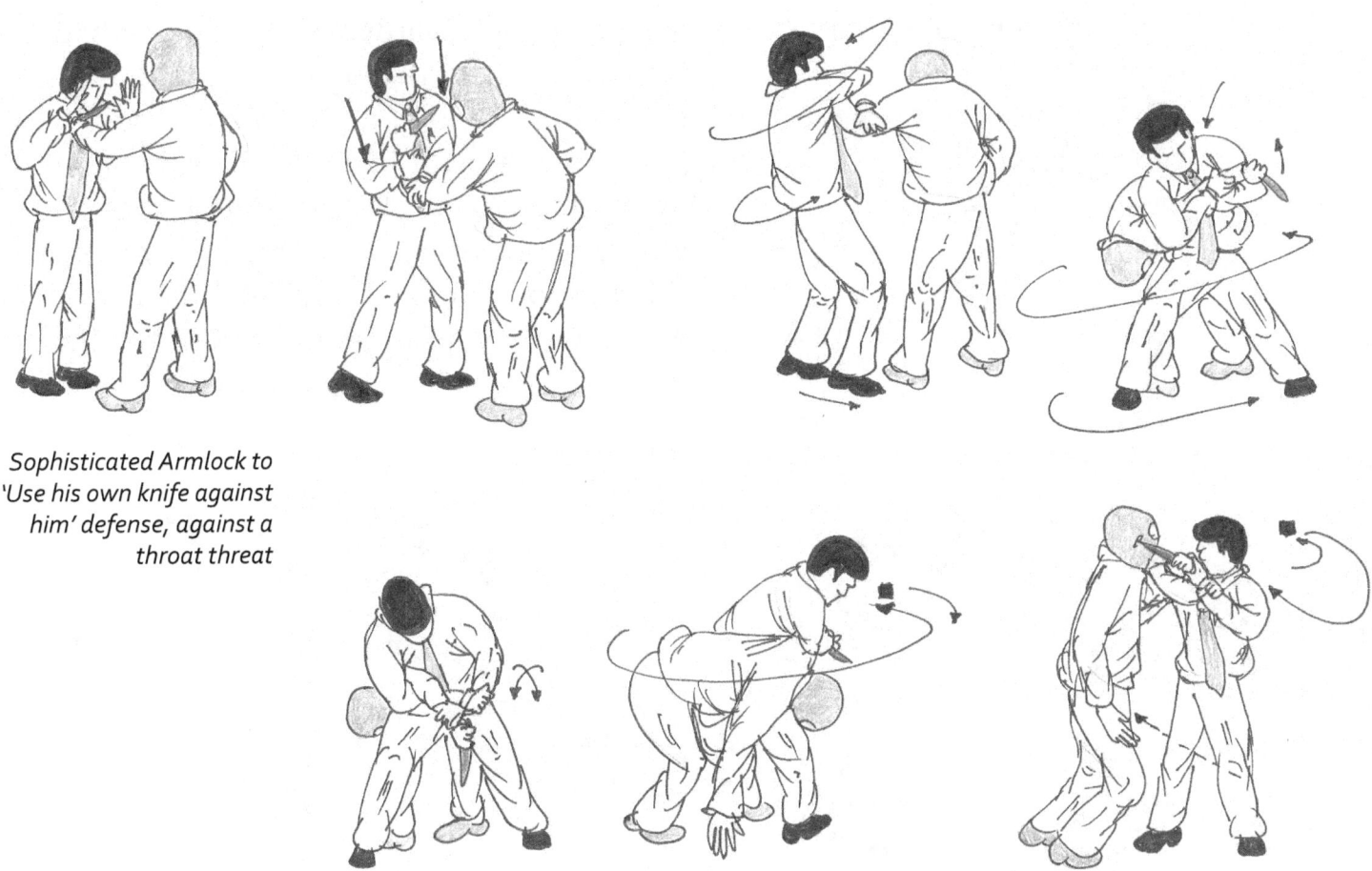

Sophisticated Armlock to 'Use his own knife against him' defense, against a throat threat

7.7.3 <u>Back threats with blade contact</u>

Being threatened in your back puts you, on top of everything, at a psychological and tactical disadvantage. If relevant, make sure you lower your opponent's guard by agreeing to all his demands and appear totally cowered … before exploding into action. The most common back threat, and the easiest to deal with, is the Hollywood-like stab contact to your lower back. If you drill the defense below, you will fast realize that getting out of the threat is pretty easy, because fast and natural [*It is, by the way, the same for a gun threat with back contact*]. To convince yourself, you can try with a partner who is to push the (fake) knife in as soon as you start your defense: you'll see.

Do not lift your hands but pivot in place with the shoulders. This is the key move that will remove your back from contact while allowing for your arm do deviate the knife wrist. You should start with the pivot, but nearly simultaneously, also move slightly sideways…

...As soon as your back is out of danger, you should lunge towards the aggressor while extending your arm below his. Headbutt him with your momentum and use the energy of the pivot to elbow the side of his head. Get control of his armed wrist while you pull his shoulder towards you and kick his groin. Grab his wrist in Wrist Lock position with your other hand, disarm him and keep kicking

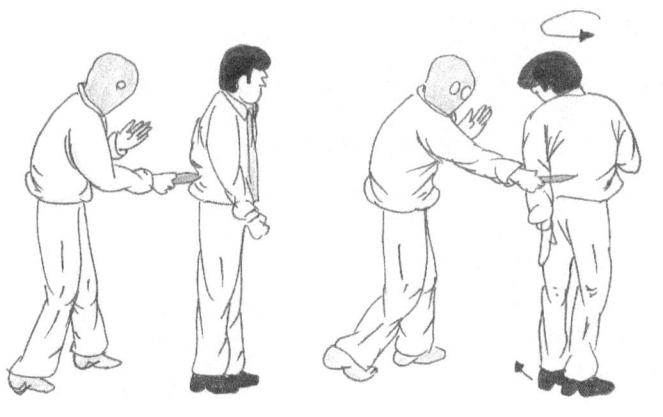

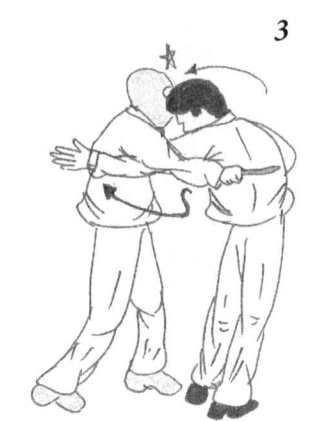

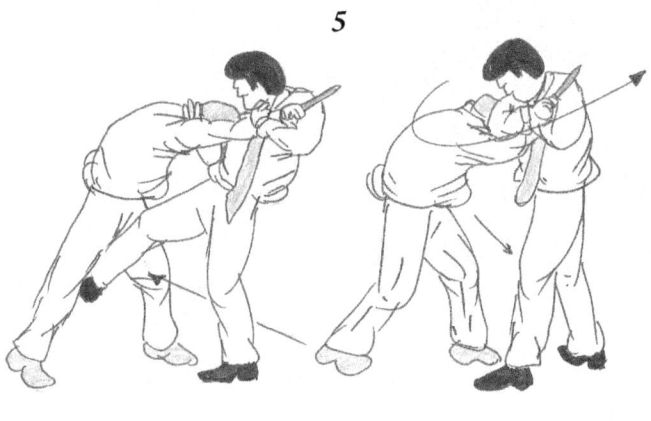

A fast pivot and block will get you out of a lower back knife threat; then lunge at the assailant with a headbutt and more

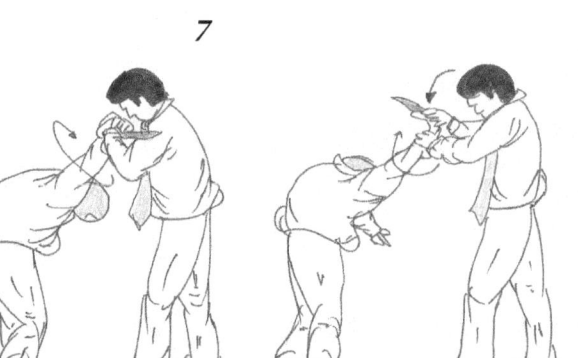

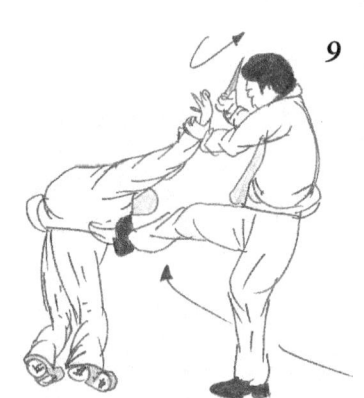

The next set of Drawings shows another way to go after the same simple and effective pivot: strike his extended elbow and go into violent simple Arm Lock. Start hammering from there.

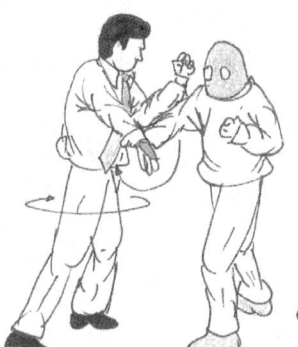

Simple Armlock maneuver after the simple pivot defense

ADVANCED KRAV MAGA

A much more difficult situation to get out from is the **throat threat from behind**. Remember that a sharp knife can easily cut through the throat cartilage or the muscles around the arteries. The idea will *always* be to first grab and lower the armed wrist to get the neck out of danger.

The **first** example illustrated below shows how to grab and lower the threatening knife. Hit his groin with your bottom as you bend to pass under the armed arm. Get a double hold on his arm to place him in Armlock position. Kick his face, lift his arm and get behind him while wrist-locking him into releasing the knife. Stomp the back of his knee and catch his chin for a violent head twist.

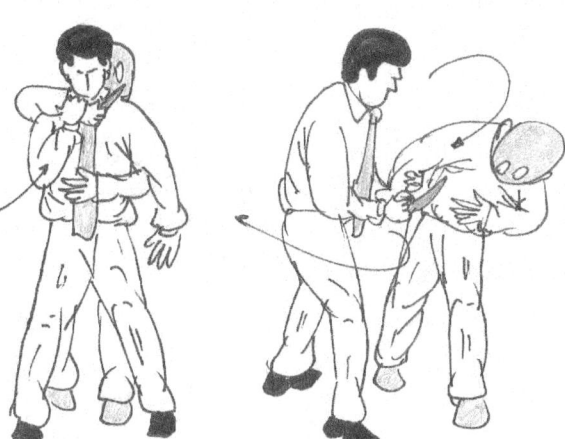

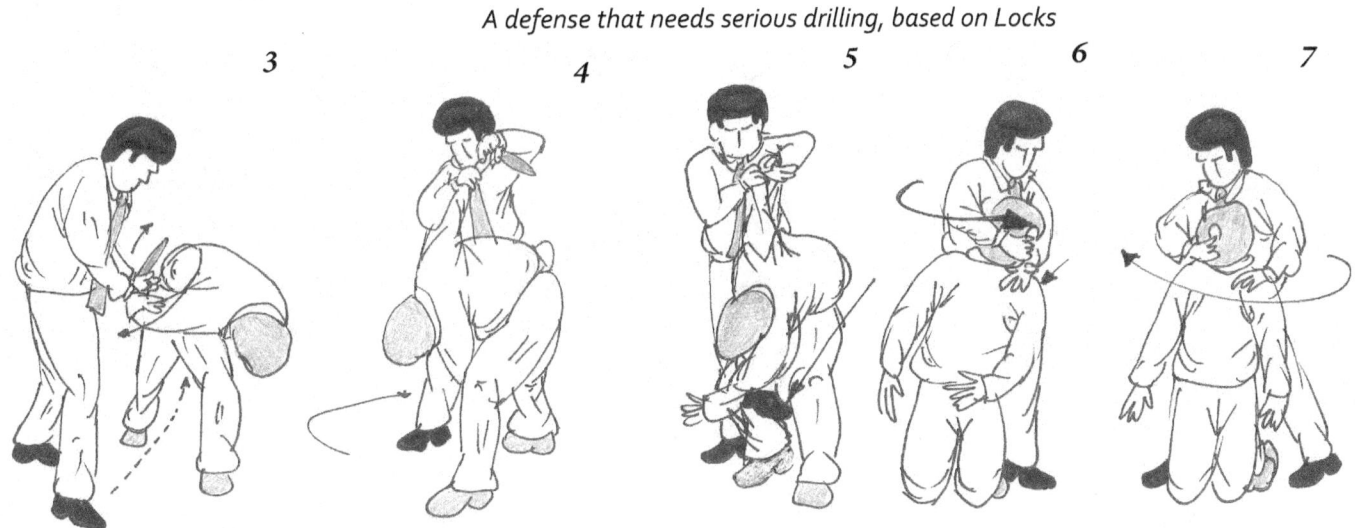

A defense that needs serious drilling, based on Locks

The next series of Figures, at the top of next page, illustrates how you grab the threatening arm **with both hands and use all your body weight and power to pass under the arm**. Keep using all your body to thrust the knife towards and into the aggressor's side. Get behind him and stomp the back of his knee into the ground. Keep control of his shoulder and eye area. Keep at it if necessary...

KNIFE ATTACKS 175

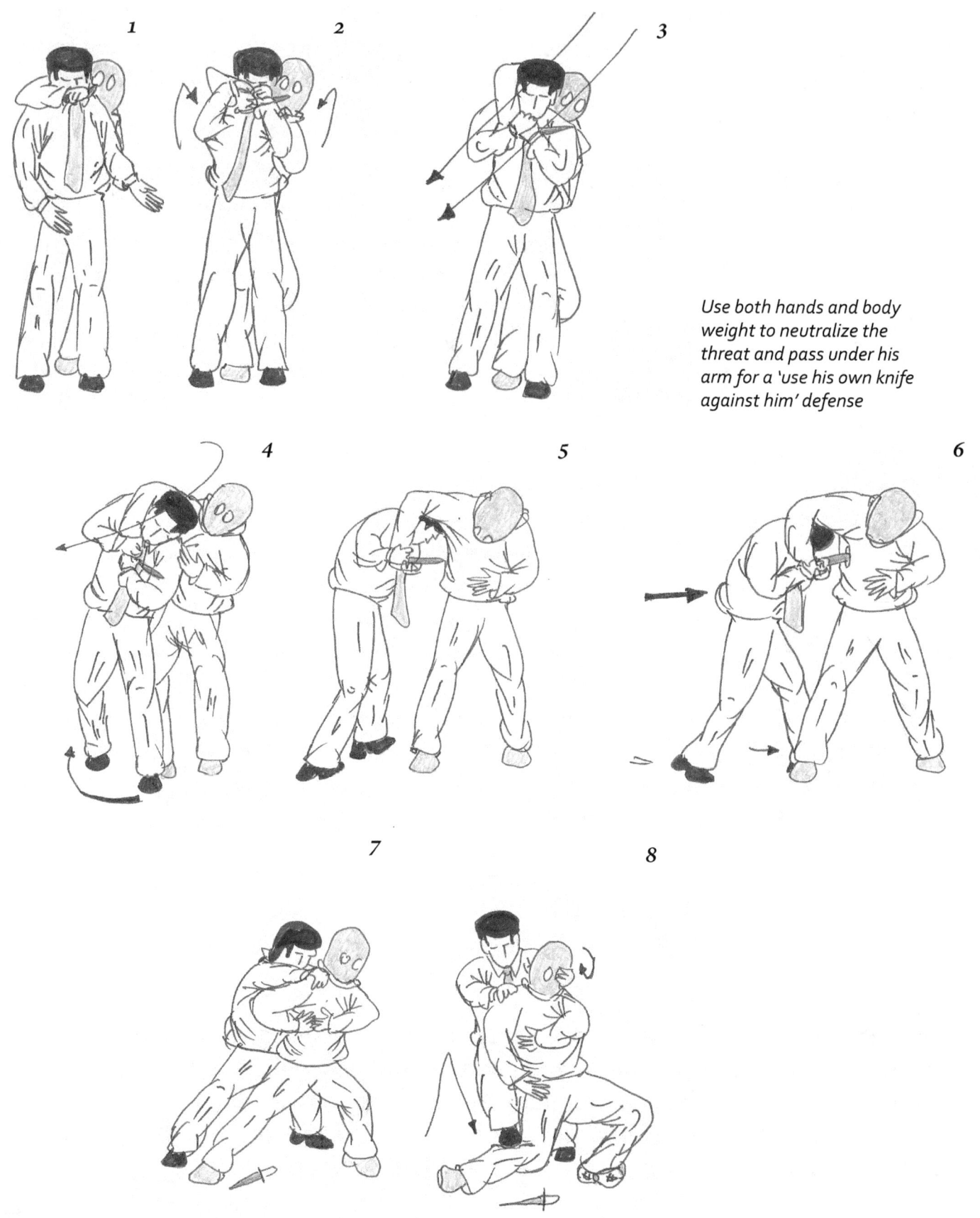

Use both hands and body weight to neutralize the threat and pass under his arm for a 'use his own knife against him' defense

ADVANCED KRAV MAGA

7.8 Downward 'Icepick' Knife Attacks

The **Downward Icepick Knife Strike** is probably the most common 'true' attack. It is not a threat, but a life-threatening move with no other purpose than kill or seriously wound. It will be the attack of an assailant in crazed state or of a terrorist, not of anyone trying to scare you into giving up your wallet. It is extremely dangerous because of the power it entails and the fact that nearly anything pierced from that angle is potentially lethal. The good news is that the attack requires a very clear chambering that makes it easy to identify early and to intercept on its way down. The *Krav Maga* handling will always to go diagonally forward to neutralize the strike by being closer than expected, earlier than expected and more sideways than expected. The Strike being powerful and needing a clear chambering, it will therefore be difficult for the aggressor to change his trajectory in mid-course. Once you are close and in control, many possibilities arise.

Our **first example**, and probably the most important, is illustrated below. It is clear how to go forward and out with a rear-hand deviating Block, and then use the momentum to simply push the aggressor away by the armed shoulder. You can then **run away** if possible, or, if you have no choice, to pursue him with a *Retzev* of Kicks.

Evade diagonally forward and push the assailant violently away

KNIFE ATTACKS

A much more sophisticated way to make use of a good evading forward step is presented in the next Drawings: you grab his armed wrist without blocking it and redirect it on its own momentum towards the opponent's trunk. Use both your hands for the redirect and your whole body for the push of the knife towards him. This specific **'Use his own knife against him'** technique is easier than it may seem, because of the use of the very powerful downward momentum. It still requires lots of drilling though, mainly for building the necessary self-confidence and ingrained automatisms.

After the evasion forward and out, simply redirect the knife towards the assailant's belly

It is important to first master the simpler **Striking Techniques** to come after the forward evasion and control. We explained that in the introductory training section. Once you become trained and confident, the strikes will flow by themselves and you can proceed to the more sophisticated lock and disarm techniques. So here come a few striking options to drill, and to complete by your own preferred *Retzev* routines. Knife-hand Strikes, Palm Strikes, Knee Strikes,... Of course, never forget the eyes as a target!

Evade forward and in with a Knifehand Strike to the neck

178   **ADVANCED KRAV MAGA**

Another way to go: Palm Strike to the face or chin, and grab to pull the head into Knee Strike

The next sets of Photos will illustrate the evading move combined with a **Knife-hand Strike to the armed forearm**. The Strike's purpose is to hurt the arm and accelerate the downward trajectory of the knife; *it is not to disarm*, although disarming can be a side benefit that sometimes happens. This kind of attack on the armed forearm is kind of a Block and MUST be immediately followed by a strike to vital points as the start of a serious *Retzev*. We shall also illustrate an option in which only one hand is used, as if your second hand is encumbered or wounded.

Evade and strike the armed forearm coming down; follow immediately with a Palm Strike to the chin

KNIFE ATTACKS

A one-arm defense: evade in and strike the armed forearm down; follow up with the same strike becoming a Knife-hand attack of the throat; keep striking

Of course, evading out follows the same principles.

Evade out and strike the back of the neck; you could follow with a stomping kick into the back of the knee as the start of your Retzev

Once you have mastered the instinctive 'evade and strike' pattern, you can start to work on the **locking and disarming maneuvers**. Remember that they will only work after mollifying strikes to the opponent's vital points.

The **first** example, illustrated below, with evading out and redirecting with the rear hand. You can then grab the armed wrist with the other hand while poking the eyes of the attacker. Start the basic disarming technique on the wounded assailant and attack his eyes again as soon as you have grabbed the weapon. Keep your fingers around his eyes to pull his head back. You can now use the handle of the knife for another strike to the side of his face.

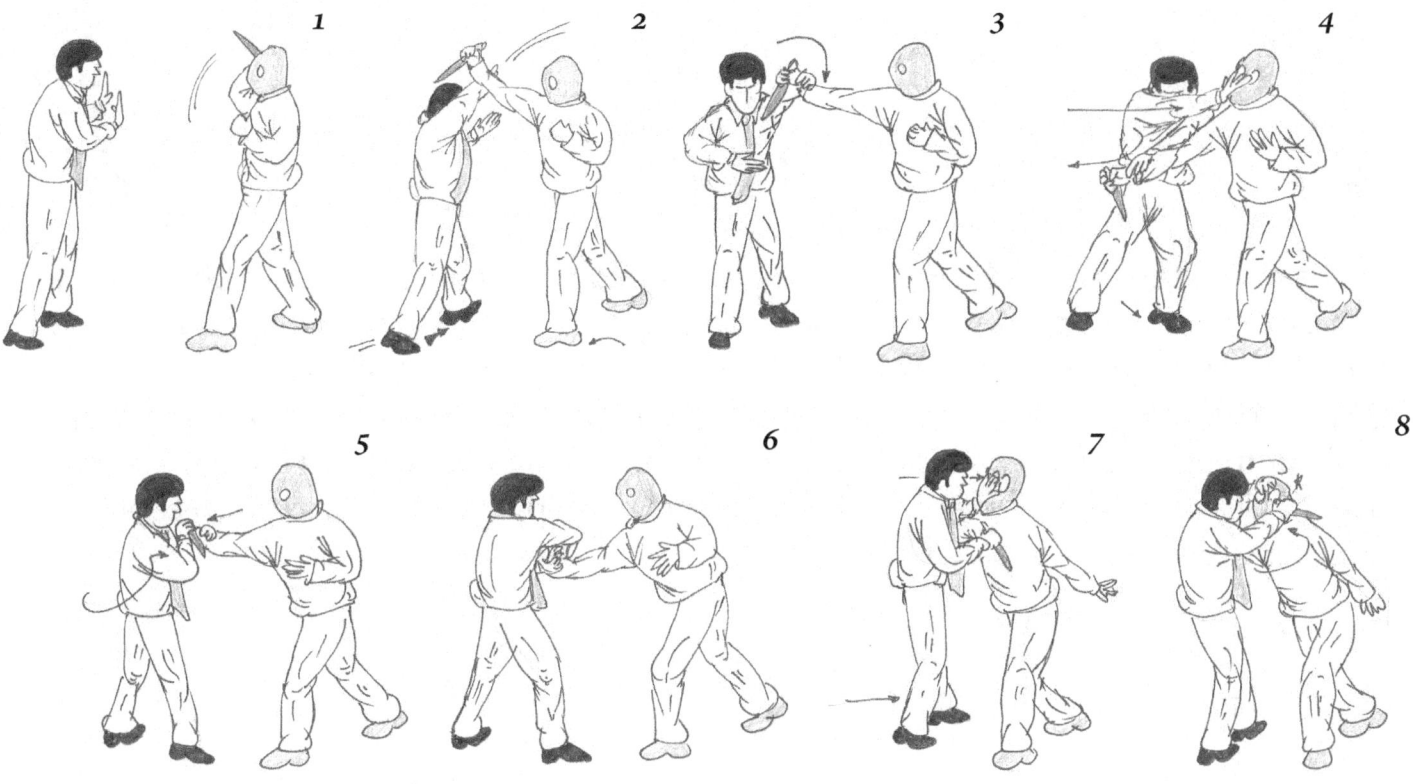

Evade out and attack the eyes to allow for an easy disarm

Our next example will start with an **inside evasion**. The Drawings at the top of next page illustrate how to go *forward and in* while attacking the aggressor's eyes and while blocking. Your block becomes a grab and you kick the opponent's groin while controlling his shoulder. Your Groin Kick rebounds back on the floor for a knee strike and your shoulder hand goes to grab his ear. Lower your leg deep rearwards while pulling his ear towards you and twisting his armed wrist. He should be sufficiently mollified for a Disarm that you can cap with another Groin Kick.

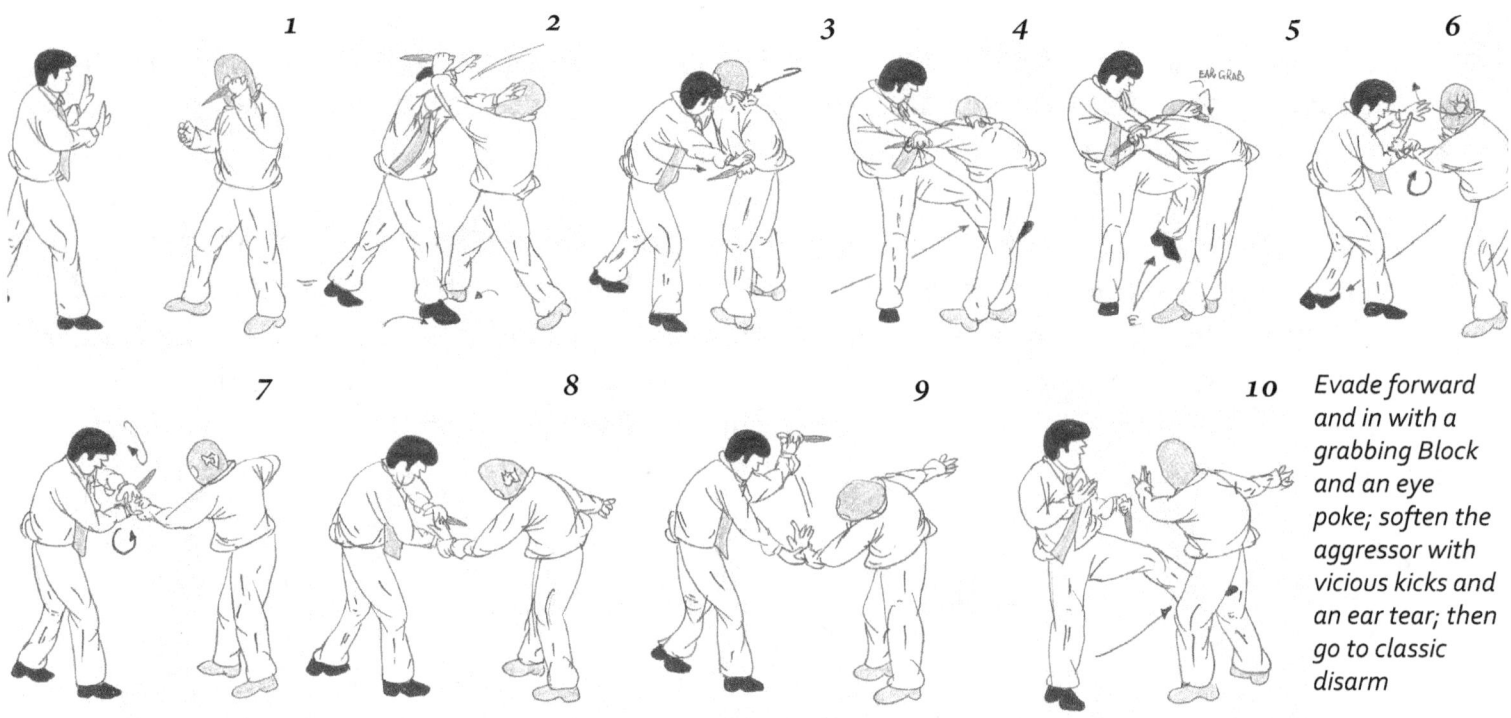

Evade forward and in with a grabbing Block and an eye poke; soften the aggressor with vicious kicks and an ear tear; then go to classic disarm

Our last set starts with a **forward-inside evasion** and a simultaneous Grabbing Block and Eye Poke. Use the forward momentum to strike his throat with your forearm and twist his caught armed wrist. Your forward momentum drives the Groin Knee and neck pull, and you can let your foot rebound on the floor for a second Knee Strike to the groin or midsection. Go back and pull his grabbed arm while twisting it further and use the distance for a Groin Kick. He should now be ripe for a classic Disarm capped by another Groin Kick. Keep at it.

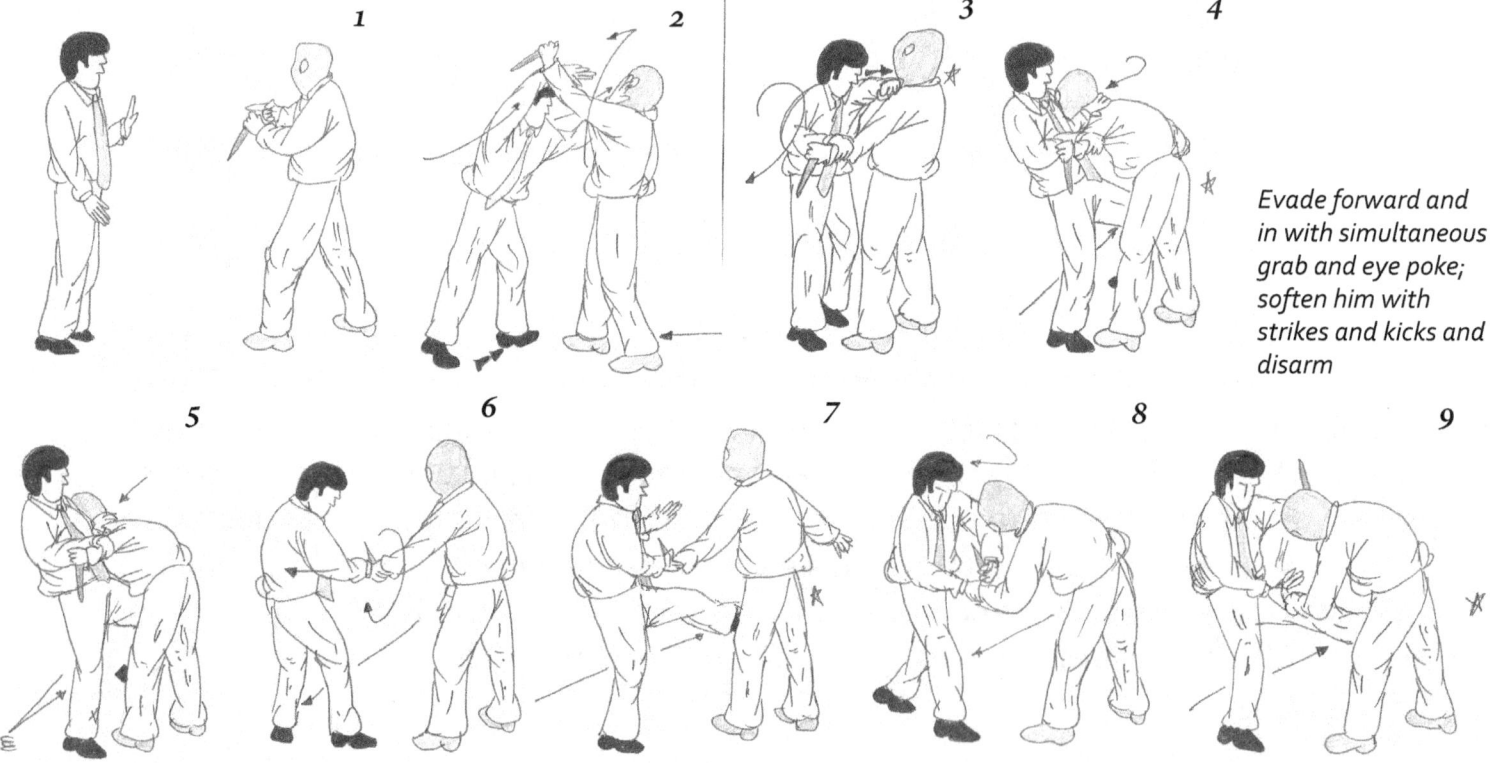

Evade forward and in with simultaneous grab and eye poke; soften him with strikes and kicks and disarm

7.9 Straight Pokes and Stabs

Pokes and Stabs are attacks that are more difficult to deal with: they are fast and do not require chambering. They also are less impulsive and more planned, and they lend themselves to feints and misdirection. Again, it is best not to be there on grounds of having fled; but if you have no choice…

These attacks are simple extension of the arm, just like punches. They can be directed high, towards the face and neck; at middle level towards the stomach and heart; or low, in a generally upward trajectory towards the lower belly.

Dealing with **Pokes and Stabs** will usually be with forward evasions and vital points strikes; and for more advanced fighters, with additional locks and disarms. Sometimes, you can be surprised with an attack and will have to rely on blocks instead of forward evasions.

Pokes and Stabs are often used after lots of playing around, fake stabs and threatening moves to intimidate the victim. Remember that in such a case of a threatening assailant moving his blade around in front of you with overconfidence, you should launch a preemptive attack as described in the previous sections; do not wait for a possible real and dangerous stab.

The first stage in learning to deal with **Pokes and Stab** will be the drilling of evasions followed by strikes.

The first Photos show a simple **block and evade** move that places you in control of his back for a follow-up.

Evade out and Block

The coming Illustrations, at the top of next page, show in turn how to **evade and kick**. You evade *forward and out* against a full Stab and keep general control of the armed hand while kicking the assailant's groin with a fast Body-bent Roundhouse. Follow up with a Stomping Side Kick to the back of his knee and keep at it.

Evade and groin-kick

One of the possibilities after an evading and blocking a Knife Stab, is to reserve the **first subsequent Strike for the attacking forearm**. One can hope to help release the knife, although it will not happen every time. But the Strike will hurt, numb the arm, further deviate the knife strike and give you the time to start your *Retzev*. In our example, you evade a low (*and slightly upward*) belly stab *forward and in*. You block and deviate the strike out and upwards in order to bring the elbow up for a Downward Knife-hand Strike. Stat a *Retzev*, preferably with an Eye attack.

Evade forward and in and strike the offending elbow before starting your vital points strikes

184   **ADVANCED KRAV MAGA**

Of course, you can also forget the strike to the attacking elbow and go directly for the start of your Strikes series. In the Photos below, with a **Knife-hand Strike to the neck** and a Knee Strike for starters.

Evade, block and start striking

The point of the coming Photos is first to show the **numbing Arm Strike** from another angle. It is also to illustrate the fact that, in dealing with an attack from close up, you will not always have the time to evade forward but will have to rely on blocking only.

From close up, just block and strike the armed elbow first

KNIFE ATTACKS

Of course, even from close up, your reaction can also be to block and **follow up without hitting the attacking arm**. In the examples below, you can see a Knife-hand attack to the neck **or** a Palm Strike to the chin *as starting points*.

Pull your belly back as you block; knife-hand the neck for starters

Block a close Stab and palm-strike the chin with all you have

Of course, blocking a low stab from close-up can also be done **outside-in**, with a following Palm Strike as a start of the *Retzev*.

Outside Downward Block on a close low stab followed by a Palm Strike

186   **ADVANCED KRAV MAGA**

We will conclude this 'drilling strikes' part with a **one-arm evade/block/strike** sequence that is good to practice for a deep intuitive understanding of evading, of blocking and of striking an armed forearm. It also could be relevant to dealing with an assailant in spite of being wounded in one arm. Evade a committed low stab forward and in. Block the stab with a powerful Downward Knife-hand Strike on the forearm. Keep the momentum of the Strike to come back with an Outward Knife-hand Strike to the throat.

One-armed defense: evade, strike the attacking arm and go for the throat

When you are *surprised* by a stab, evasion will sometimes have to be **rearwards**; and it is sometimes the instinctive thing that will happen and on which you will have to build your defense. The coming drill is therefore important. Against a committed low stab, you retreat and grab the armed wrist from above in something very close to an instinctive reaction. Drill it and it will become fully instinctive. Keep retreating while pulling the armed wrist forward *violently*. In doing so, you make use of the momentum of the assailant's attack and slightly deviate it. Once the attacker loses his balance forward, you come back in a classic and very effective 'Clothesline Maneuver'. It will get him on the ground with a bruised face. From there you either run away or stomp-kick his limbs.

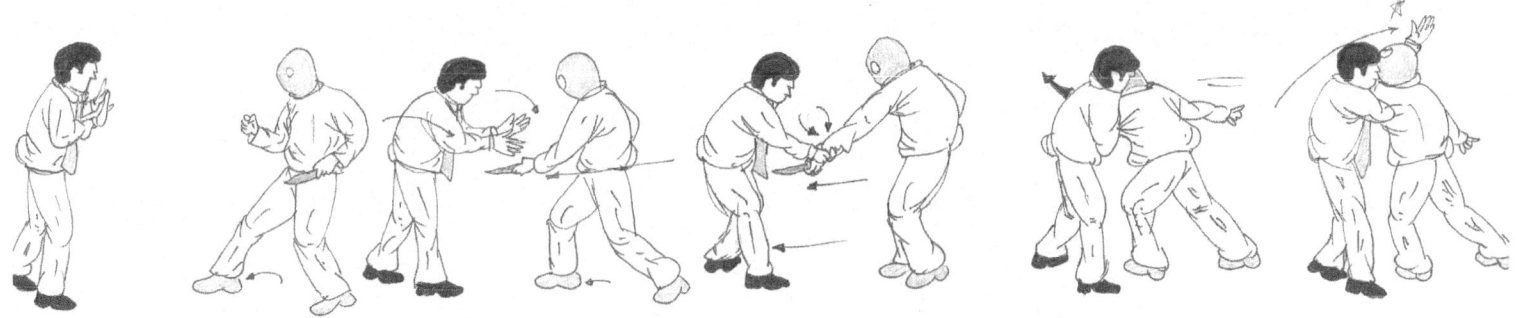

Evade back while grabbing armed wrist; pull violently and "clothesline"!

KNIFE ATTACKS

But the preferred evasion, like always in *Krav Maga*, will be forward if possible. In the coming Drawings, a mid-level stab is **evaded forward and out**. The rear hand will then immediately grab the armed wrist while the other goes for the eyes. Keep your forward momentum and keep your fingers in the attacker's eyes. Knee his groin. You have now softened him enough for a pivot and an elbow-break (=violent Lock) on you shoulder.

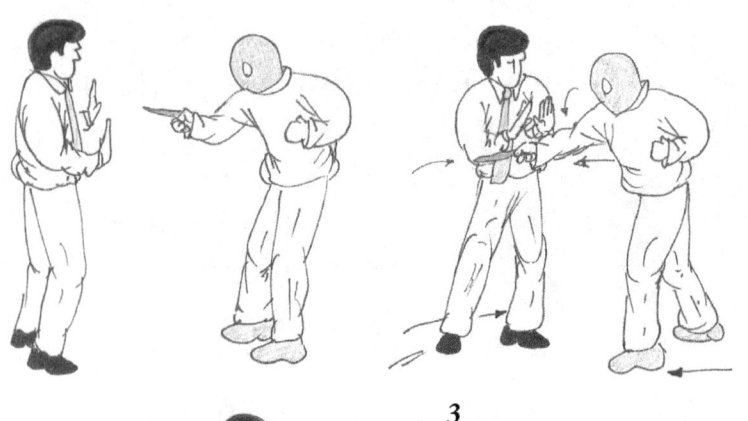

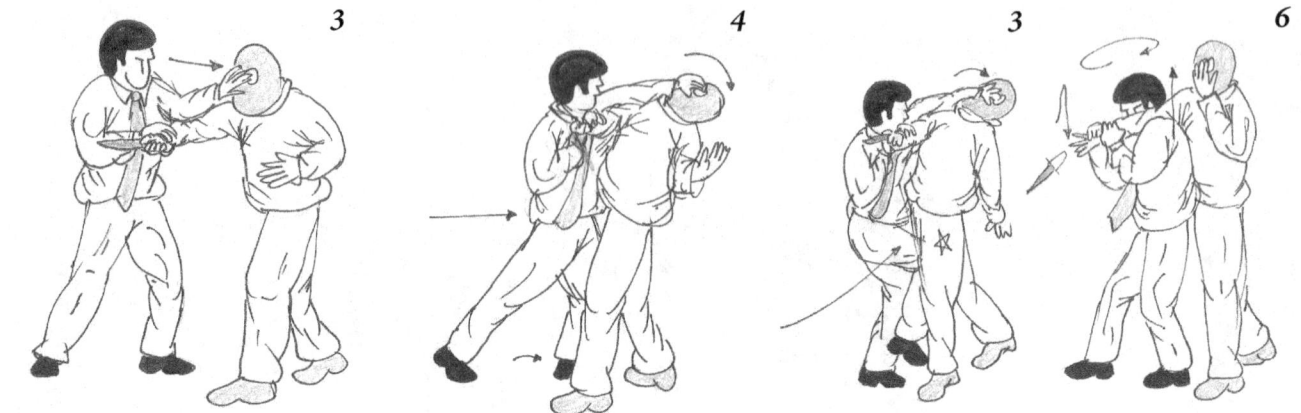

Evade forward and out, grab, poke the eyes and knee the groin, pivot for armlock

The following Illustrations will show an **Inside Evasion and the more classic Disarm**. You diagonally evade a mid-level stab *inside and forward*. Grab the armed arm while going for the eyes, and let the poke evolve into a Hammer-fist Strike to the nose. A groin Kick will soften him even more to allow pulling back and setting up the hold for the classic Wrist Lock. Twist his wrist and peel the knife out if possible. A groin kick and rebounding knee to the face should put you firmly in charge.

Evade forward and in, grab, strike repeatedly to prepare the Disarm

ADVANCED KRAV MAGA

Of course, the same kind of series is applicable to an **outward evasion**: strike, disarm and keep striking. The Drawings illustrate how to evade a mid-level stab *forward and out,* and grab the wrist while attacking the eyes. Kick the groin while setting up the Disarming Lock. Keep kicking after the Disarm.

Evade forward and out, go for the eyes, kick and disarm and keep kicking

If the attack **surprises you from too close,** you should learn to *go for the Block forward without evasion*. The series illustrated at the top of next page illustrates how to block and poke the eyes *simultaneously*. Envelop the stabbing arm from inside out and kick the groin while the eye-poking hand pulls his shoulder forward. The kick rebounds into a knee strike and you can use your hips to come over his arm with your own in order to get a two-handed grip for the classic Wrist Lock. This move is *violent* in order to cause also some elbow damage; use all you body. Once you have the grip, kick his groin again and pivot back into the full Wrist Lock. Kick his face as he bends in pain and peel the knife out. Keep at it.

Self-defense is the only honourable course where there is unreadiness for self-immolation.
~Mahatma Gandhi

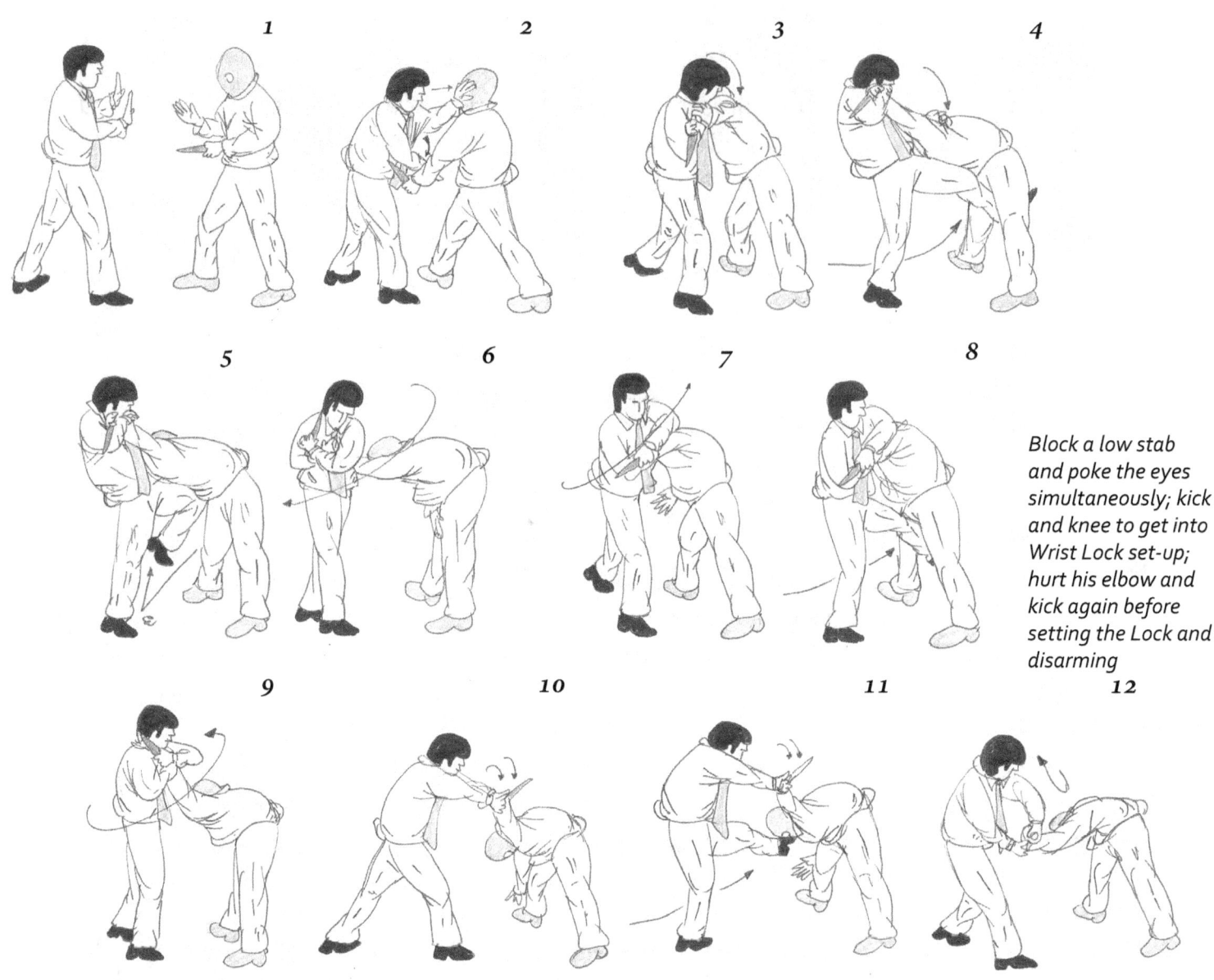

Block a low stab and poke the eyes simultaneously; kick and knee to get into Wrist Lock set-up; hurt his elbow and kick again before setting the Lock and disarming

There are several ways to **block and then get into a Wrist Lock set up**. It will have to be your body on autopilot and therefore it is good to drill several possible ways. In the Drawings at the top of next page, you evade a low stab *forward and out* while blocking down with your *rear* hand. You should then switch hands to get in set-up position with your front hand, while the rear one goes for the eyes. You can now go for the Disarm on the locked hand. Use your elbow to strike his face as you peel off the knife and stomp the back of his knee before starting a *Retzev*. Drill this for a fast hand switch and a one-handed Lock for Disarm.

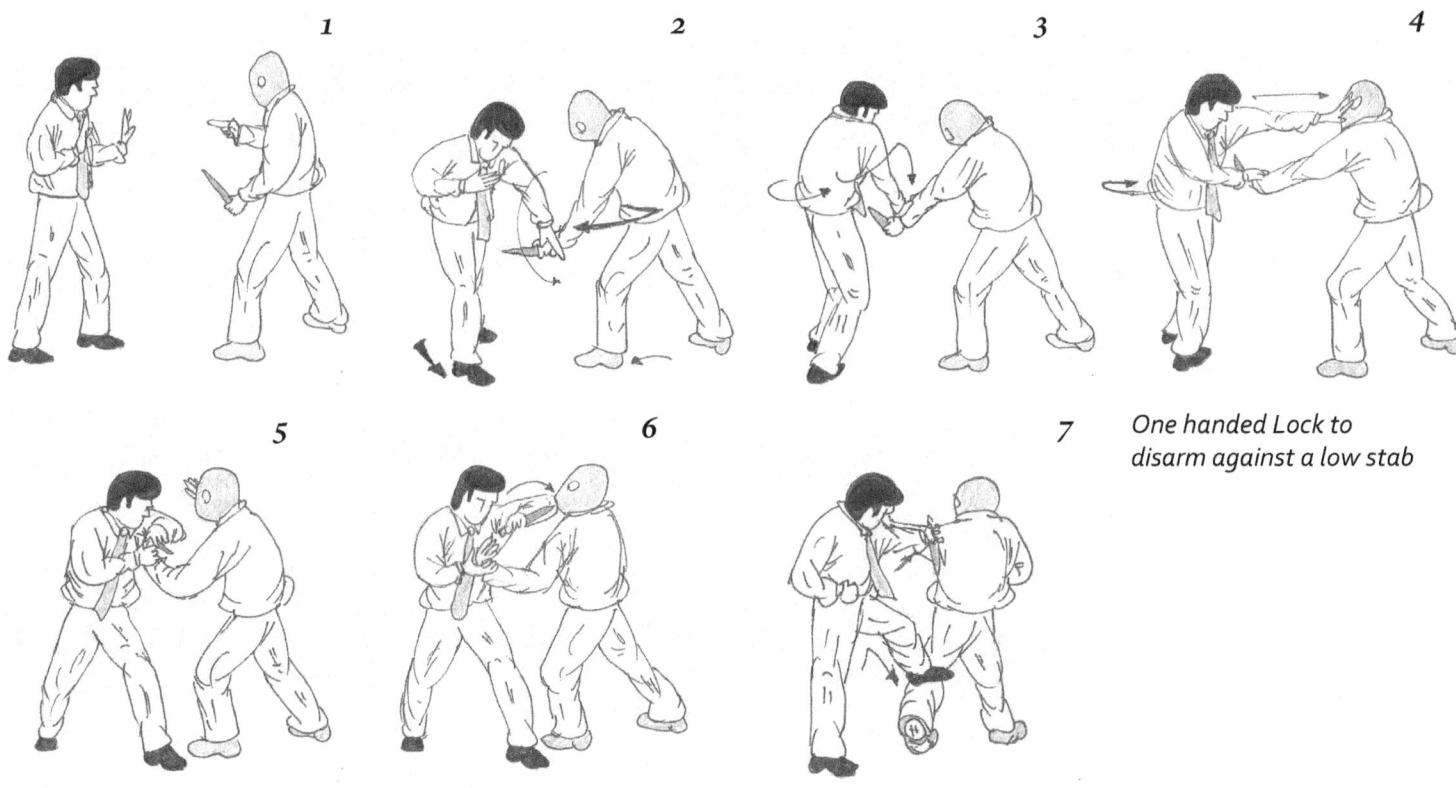

One handed Lock to disarm against a low stab

The next Illustrations show another type of **Arm Lock** in a defense against a <u>close</u> upward stab to the lower belly. As you are surprised, you pull back your belly while blocking down and striking his eyes. Your block becomes an enveloping of his arm while you knee his groin. The groin strike should allow you to set the classic elbow and shoulder lock. Remember to set it up *brusquely* for maximum damage. Knee his face and then twist violently down to force him to the ground. Place your knee on his *neck* to maintain him in place as you twist *violently* to dislocate his shoulder and elbow. You can leave him and run away or stand up to stomp his ankles.

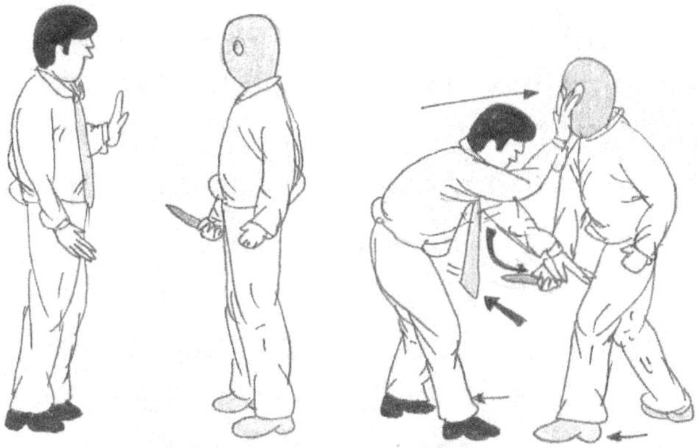

Pull back to evade a sudden low stab and block while striking his eyes; strike to allow the set up of a classic Shoulder Lock

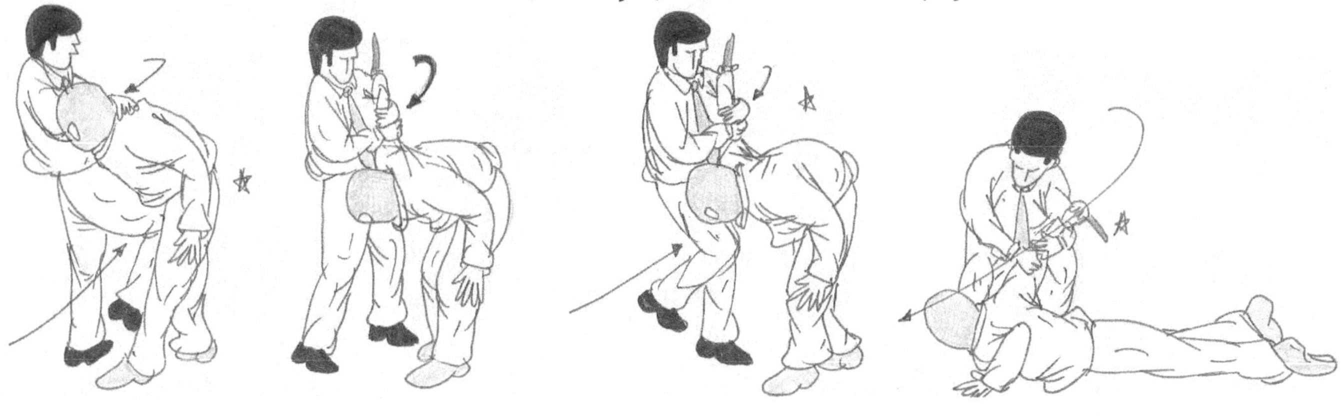

KNIFE ATTACKS

You should also drill the **'switching hands'** on a sudden low stab. In the Illustrations below, you can see how to do a Downward Block with the 'rear' hand and then *switch hands for a grip that leads to the Wrist Lock set up*. Strike the eyes and twist his grabbed wrist to get into full Lock position. Kick his groin to facilitate the subsequent peeling off of the knife. A circular Elbow to the head will then stun him further. You can catch his head violently, *using the handle of his own knife*, and knee his groin.

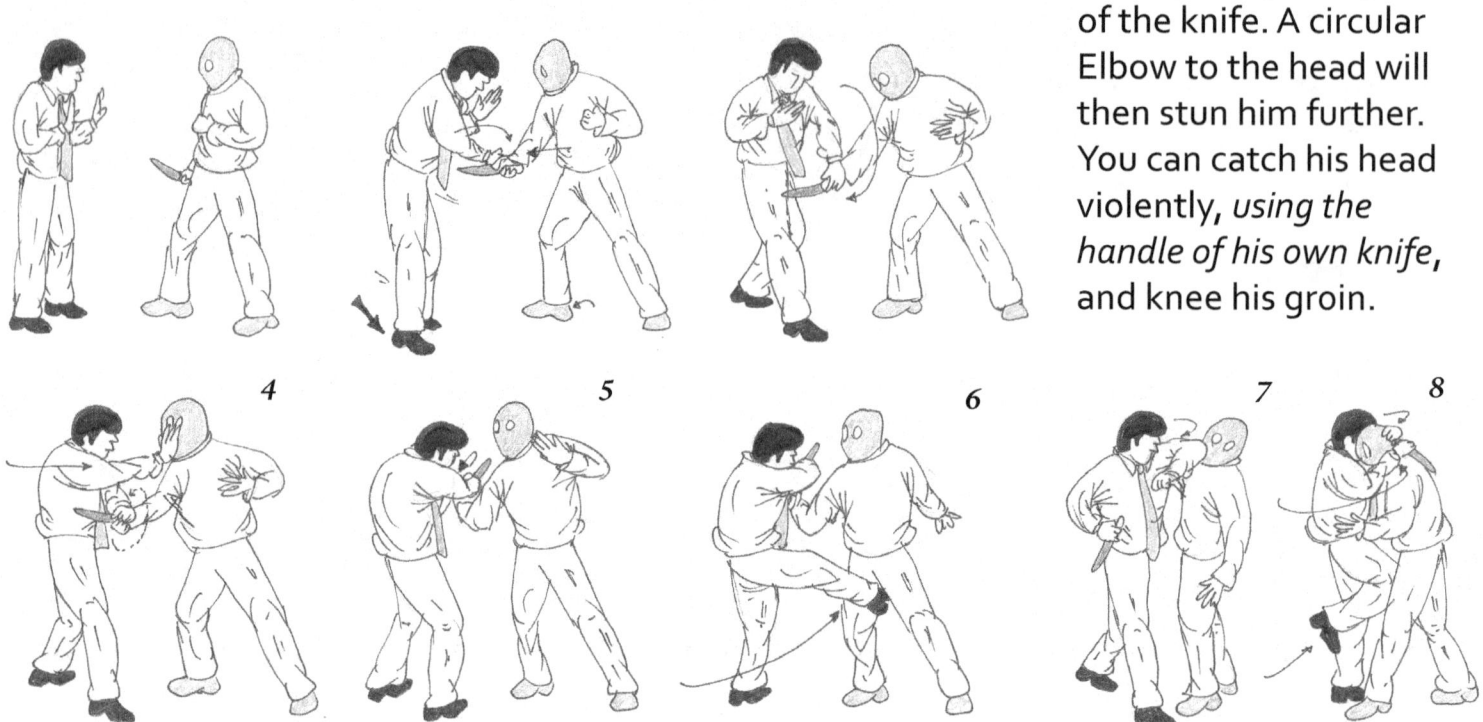

Block a low stab with one hand and grab the wrist with the other; strike and disarm; and keep striking

The instinctive pulling back of the belly and grabbing of the attacking wrist from above can be used to build a very efficient **'use his own knife against him'** defense series. Evade back and grab his attacking wrist with both hands. Twist his wrist violently with *both* your hands and kick his groin. Use *both* hands to bend his arm and stab him with his own knife, wherever you'll be able to push. Use *both hands and the whole body* to lunge at him and stab him. To help explode towards him, you should think of also headbutting his face. Use the momentum to push him away and 'low-kick' his knee as he stumbles back.

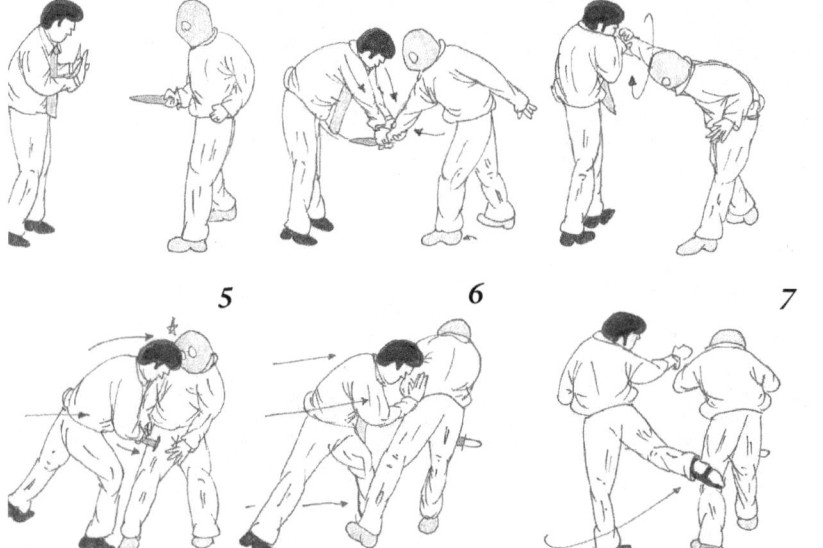

Learn to use the instinctive pull-back-and-grab reaction for an all-out 'use his own knife against him' explosion

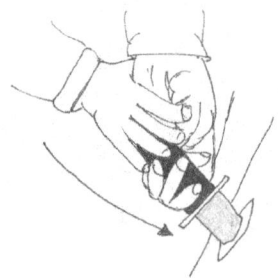

The **high stab towards the head and throat** should be dealt with like a punch: evade diagonally forward and block. Then strike. The Illustrations below show how to go *forward* with a deviating front-hand block and then palm-strike his groin violently. You use the forward momentum for the groin strike and in order to pass behind him and 'own' his back. Grab his shoulders (or eyes from behind) and pull him down brusquely. Stomp him as he lands.

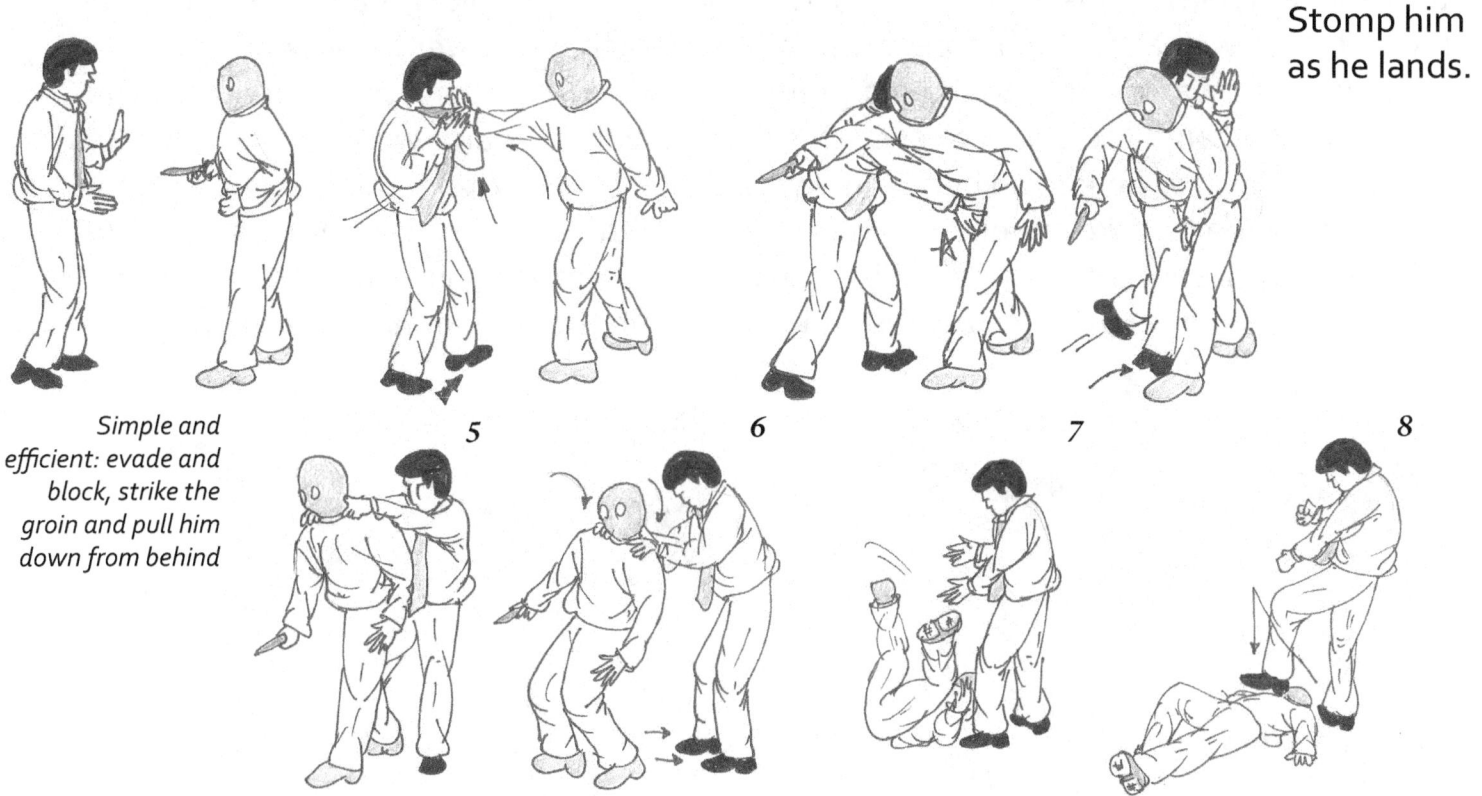

Simple and efficient: evade and block, strike the groin and pull him down from behind

The advanced '**use his own knife**' defense against a **high stab** is as follow: Evade and block, and then use your other arm to come in around his elbow to hyperextend it. You can then bend it and *use all your body* to push it towards him and stab him wherever you'll get. Simple, efficient but requires training. Do not attempt before you have mastered the strikes version and the lock versions.

Block, hyperextend, bend and push the knife towards the attacker

KNIFE ATTACKS

We shall conclude with a **low stabbing attack from behind**, in which the assailant grabs you by the shoulder to turn you around and try to eviscerate you. Of course, a defense from an attack from behind will only work if you are in a state of readiness. You know that trouble is to be expected and your sixth sense is hard at work; or you are trying to turn and leave when this happens. In fact, you block this just like for any other surprise low stabbing we have seen before: block while keeping you lower belly away. But as he pulls you towards him, use the momentum to crowd him with your upper body and strike his head with the elbow or even the head. Envelop his arm while you keep striking him on the neck or head, and bend him in classic Armlock. But do not proceed with the armlock. Instead, strike his inner elbow to bend his arm and explode towards him *with all your body.* Headbutt the side of his head and stab him with his own knife. Use *both hands and the power of your hips.* You can then stomp the back of his knee to bring him down.

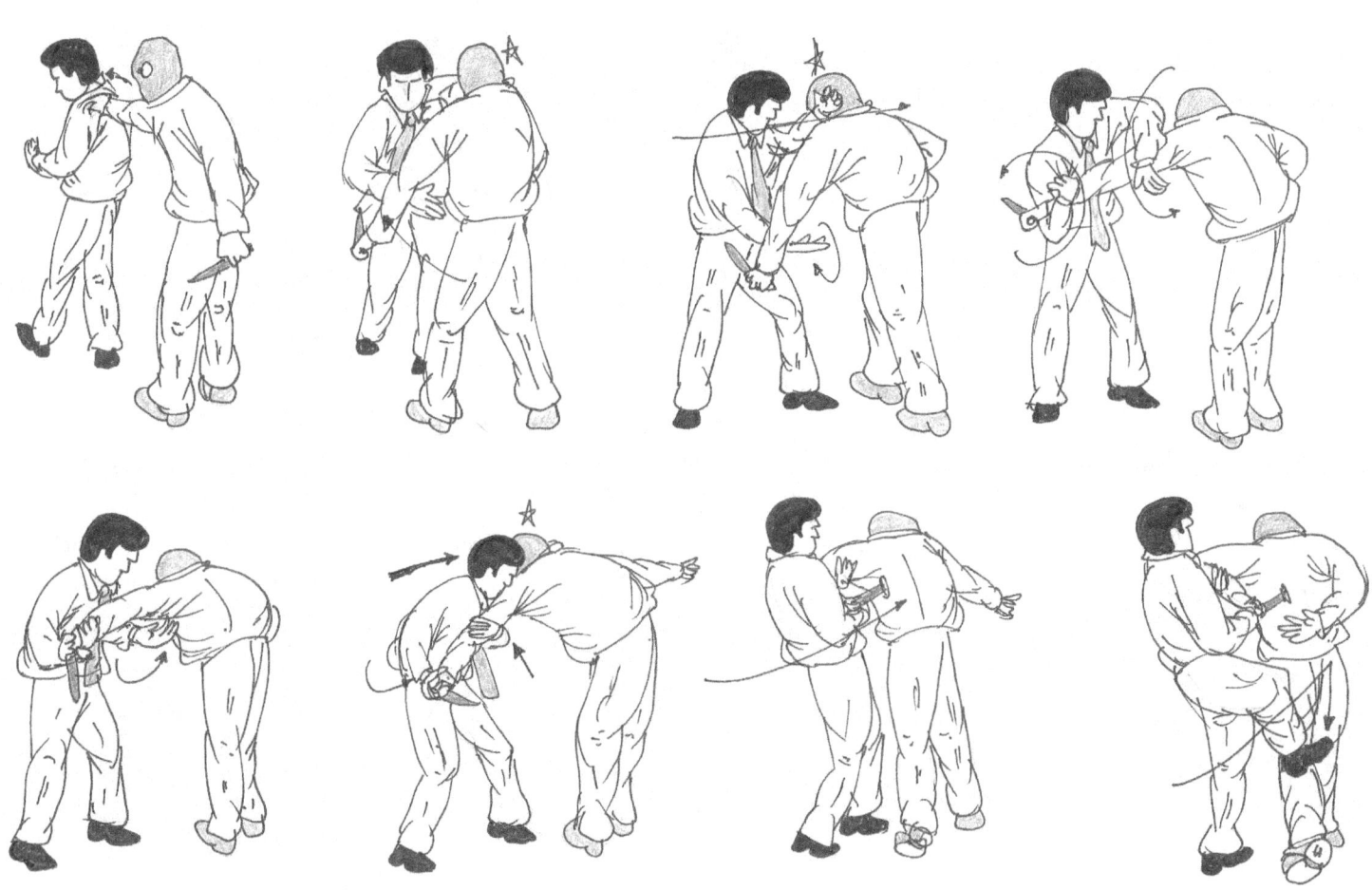

Use his own knife against him in this advanced defense against a low stab from behind

7.10 Slashes

Inward and Outward Slashes are also dangerous attacks. They are fast and difficult to block, and they lend themselves to easy feinting. Just like stabs, they are also much used as threatening moves or as misdirecting moves before a real full-out attack. **Slashes** are also ideal small moves to cause bloodletting without being lethal. Attrition by small cuts contributes to the demoralizing psychological effect of having the victim see his own blood.

There are only <u>**two**</u> ways to deal with **slashes**, irrelevant to them being regular inward slashes or backhand outward slashes:

- *Jump into the attack* before the knife can reach the centerline, or
- *Evade rearwards* and then jump back forwards as soon as the knife has passed.

<u>*The first option*</u> will always be preferred in *Krav Maga*, but it is not always practical. In order to be able to *explode forward*, you must identify the slash early. It is most suitable when the attack is energetic and passes through a large and clear chambering.

<u>*The second option*</u> of *back evasion* is very instinctive and suitable when the attack is too fast or too sudden. It is imperative to seriously drill the *rebounding in a forward explosion* in order to counter safely. If you do not jump back forwards as soon as the knife has passed in front of you, you place yourself in a very dangerous defensive situation. The opponent will be able to keep attacking, and you will be on the defensive with no option to regain control of the fight! Remember that your attacker will always be able to run faster forward than you'll be able to flee backwards!

<u>Before drilling defenses against slashing attacks, it is imperative to drill those two options with a partner.</u> Drill the preemptive jump-in, and especially drill the aggressive rebound forward after a back evasion.
Once you have mastered these moves, and only then, you can start drilling the techniques presented below that use either of those openings.

And first comes the Photo series at the top of next page that illustrates the "**let the knife pass and jump back in to control said knife**".

KNIFE ATTACKS

Evade the slash back and jump in with a block and Palm Strike

The second option is illustrated by the following Drawings. You 'helmet' your head for protection and *explode forward before the knife can get to its median axis*. The attacker does not expect this and will hit you with the forearm as you keep going with your forward momentum to crash into his face with your protective elbows. Keep the forward push with a Forearm Strike to the side of his neck that will turn into a hard catch as you headbutt him. Put your hips into the subsequent Circular Elbow Strike and stomp the back of his knee.

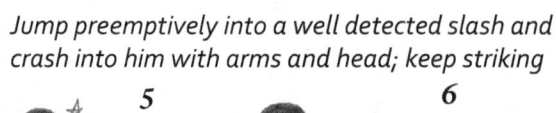

Jump preemptively into a well detected slash and crash into him with arms and head; keep striking

196   **ADVANCED KRAV MAGA**

Of course, instead of a forward crash with your head protected by your elbows, you could also simply **lunge forward with a classic block** of the incoming arm. The preferred option should then be a grabbing block with simultaneous Eye Strike. You should then twist the grabbed wrist while kicking his groin, and conclude with a hip-propelled Circular Elbow Strike to the side of the head. The attacker should now be sufficiently softened for a Lock to Disarm maneuver. Start the subsequent *Retzev* with a Small Groin Roundhouse Kick.

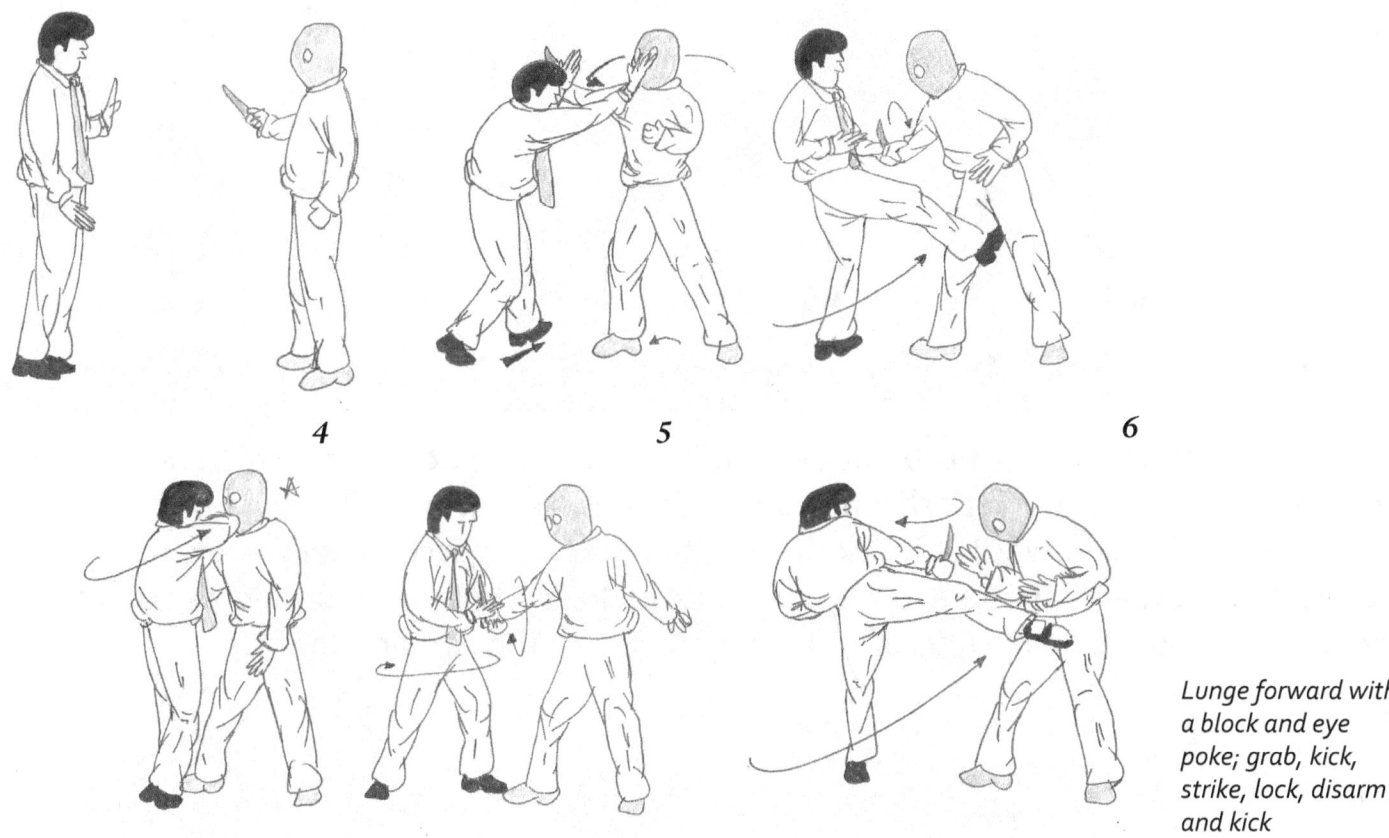

Lunge forward with a block and eye poke; grab, kick, strike, lock, disarm and kick

If you have to evade rearwards because you have been surprised, it is imperative to jump back forward immediately. This has been underlined before. A regular Inward Slash will usually be followed by a Backhand Outward one: it is a completely natural combination that happens even without being planned by the attacker. To avoid being put on the defensive and lose the control of the fight, you must interrupt this 'double' slash by lunging with a block in between. The Illustrations at the top of next page show how to do that with a lunge that stops the backhand return at its very beginning. Block and grab the armed wrist while striking the eyes. Switch grabbing hands and punch the attacker's nose. Kick his groin while setting up the Lock position. Disarm and kick the groin again as the start of your finishing moves.

KNIFE ATTACKS 197

After an instinctive rear evasion, it is imperative to jump back forward immediately to prevent a 'return' slashing move; block, grab, poke, kick, strike lock and disarm

There is a **little variation of the back evasion** that can also be instinctive: bending down under the trajectory of the slash while going back as well. What follows stays the same though: jump back forward to block the arm that has just passed you. The example illustrated below also shows a more sophisticated lock and disarm; remember that these techniques must be drilled only after having mastered the simpler defenses.

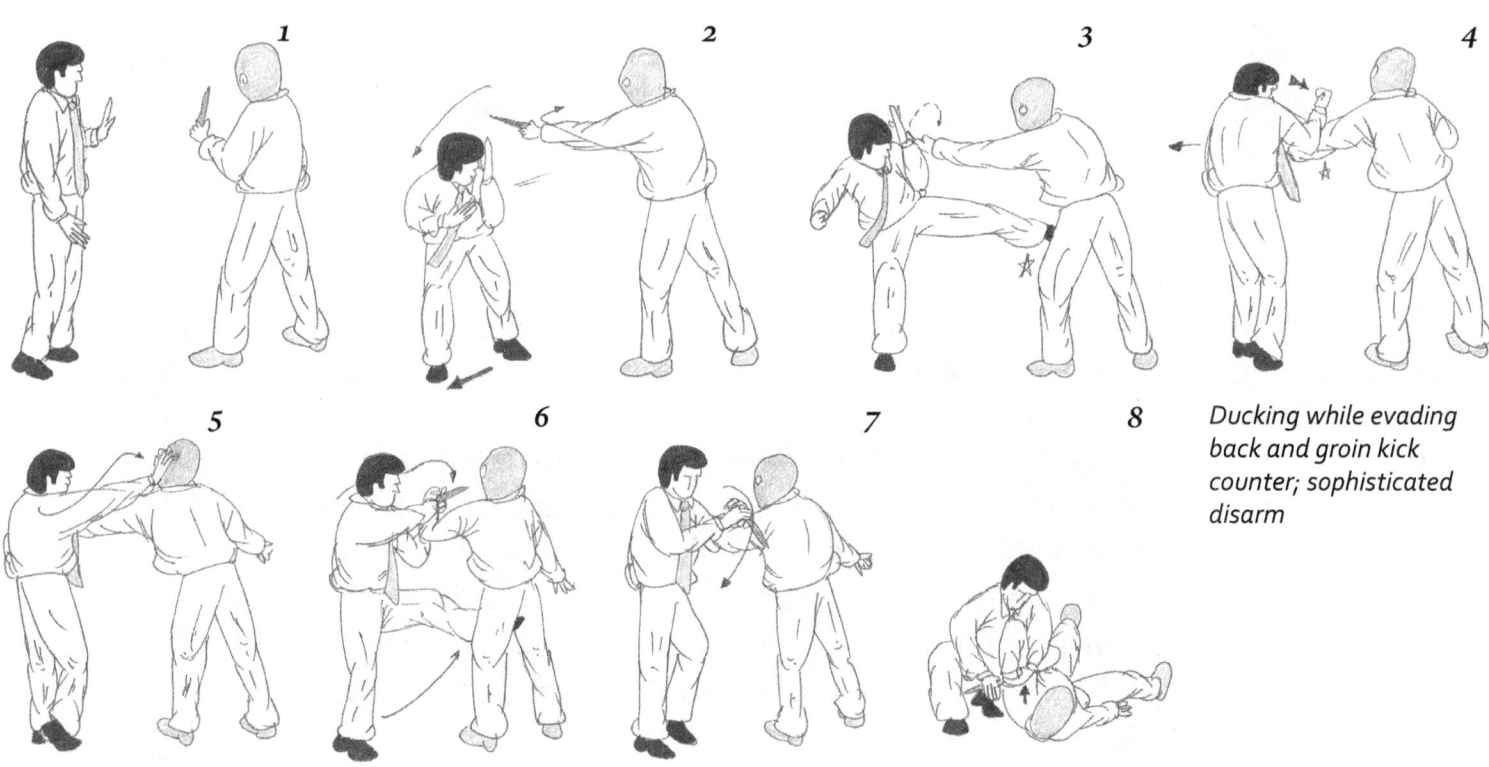

Ducking while evading back and groin kick counter; sophisticated disarm

ADVANCED KRAV MAGA

The Drawings at the bottom of the previous page show how to bend low and away under a slash and then rebound forward with a groin Roundhouse. The hand is ready to block a return of the slash and then grabs the armed wrist. *Use the hips and the whole body* for an elbow break of the caught armed arm. Strike the eyes to allow for the set-up of a locking grip and further soften him with a groin kick. Get him to the groin with a violent Armlock (Based on Aikido's *Shiho Nage*) and disarm him by locking his wrist (his elbow is stuck under your arm). The Illustrations make all this clearer.

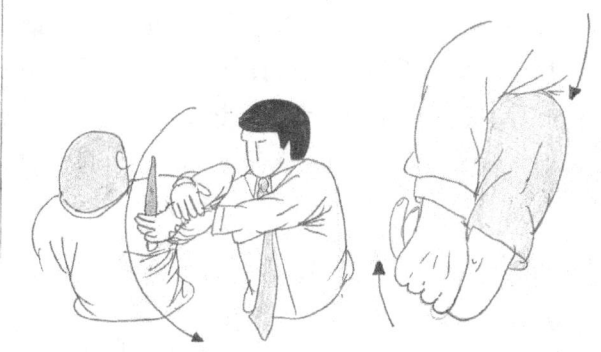

Details of the lock - figures 7 and 8 of previous page

The classic Disarm is therefore illustrated again in the next set of Photos, in a move starting with the *preemptive forward lunge and block*. You explode forward before the slash can develop and block while striking his eyes. Grab the armed wrist and the shoulder to pull him in into a Groin Kick or Groin Shin Kick. Let the kicking foot rebound for a Knee Strike to the ribs or head. You can now twist the grabbed arm to go for the Lock and Disarm; he should be stunned enough. Start the finishing moves with a Groin Roundhouse.

Go forward with a Block and an Eye Poke and strike to prepare a classic Lock & Disarm

KNIFE ATTACKS   199

A more sophisticated Lock that needs drilling is now presented in the same reaction to the classic slash. You lunge diagonally forward while blocking and striking the eyes. Grab the armed wrist while keeping the forward momentum for a Double Elbow Strike to the head: Circular Inwards and then natural return in Lateral Outwards. For both strikes, you pull him in by the grabbed arm and that will place you in perfect position to envelop his arm from above and set up a Figure Four Wrist Lock. Using *the strength of your whole body and both arms against his one arm*, it will be easy to twist around him and place him in a Back Shoulder Lock. Keep twisting and get him on the floor by *violent* pressure of the lock. Easy to disarm him there.

Forward Block and eye Poke and Elbow Strikes to allow the set up of a Figure-4 Armlock

And now for a "**Use his own knife against him**" defense. Start drilling this only after you have totally mastered the more classical techniques. As illustrated, you go forward to block the incoming slash and deviate the Strike down and around. Switch grabbing hands while striking the eyes. Twist his wrist and lift it up; come with the other hand on the back of his hand to reinforce the coming push. Use *all your body and both hands to push the knife towards his face* or neck. It will now be easy to disarm him and start a *Retzev*, for example with a Groin Kick and Elbow Strike. ➡

200   **ADVANCED KRAV MAGA**

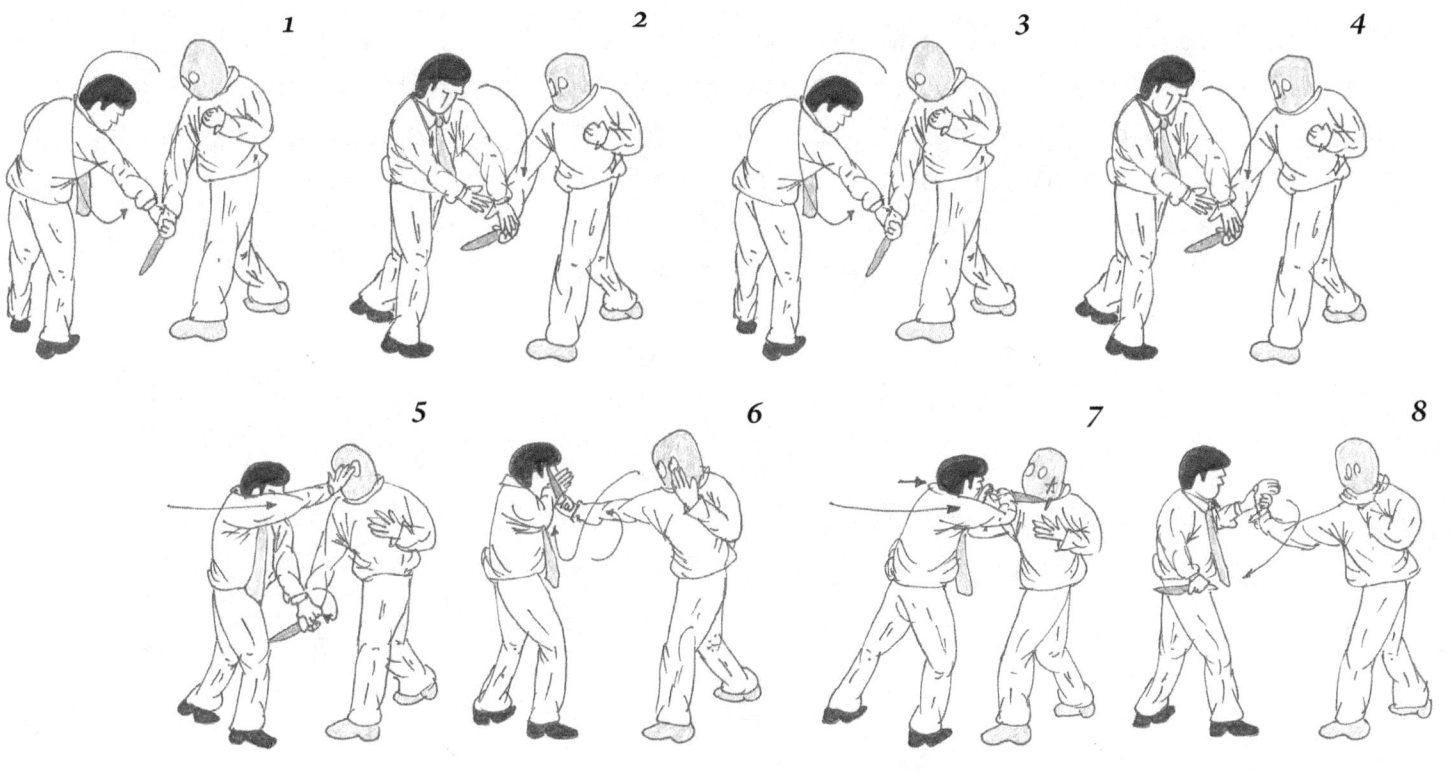

Go forward, block, lead the strike down and grab; strike the eyes and use both hands to push the knife towards him

If the slashing **attack starts with a Backhand Strike,** the jumping forward defense allows naturally for an easy arm break. The Drawings show how you can explode *diagonally forward* with the arms protecting your head and then grab the armed wrist to strike the extended elbow 'with all you have'.

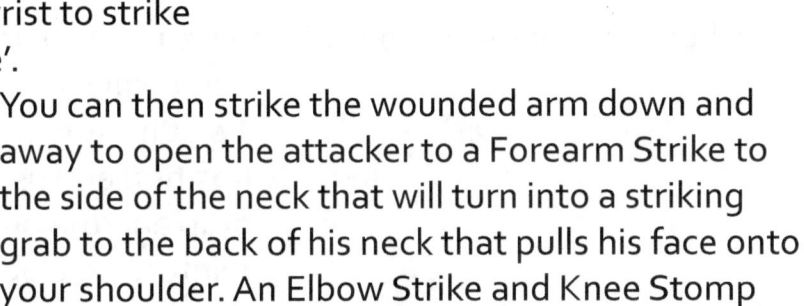

You can then strike the wounded arm down and away to open the attacker to a Forearm Strike to the side of the neck that will turn into a striking grab to the back of his neck that pulls his face onto your shoulder. An Elbow Strike and Knee Stomp should complete the series.

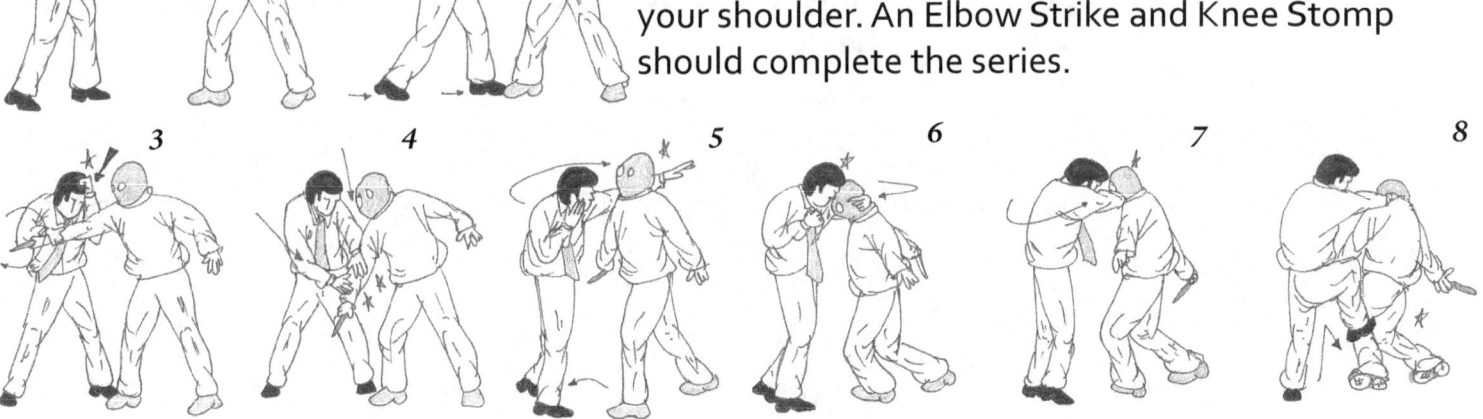

Against a backhand slash, jump diagonally forward and break the attacking elbow before starting a vicious Retzev

KNIFE ATTACKS 201

And now a "**Use his own Knife against him**" defense against a Backhand Slash. You lunge diagonally forward and block while poking the eyes. Immediately twist his armed wrist and grab it with both hands to push the knife *with all your body* towards his ribs. Pull the wrist back and twist it more to allow for a Disarm. Use his knife to poke his chest and pull it back across and under his arm in a (light) slash of your own. Palm-strike his chin and stomp kick his knee joint. Keep at it if necessary.

'Use his own knife against him' series against a Backhand Slash

Another less bloody version is presented in the Drawings below. You will again go diagonally forward for a Grabbing Block and Eye Attack. Twist his arm into single handed classic Wrist Lock position and use your other arm to reinforce the wrist grab and the push towards his ribs. The position of the reinforcing elbow allows for a more powerful push into the ribs.

Another 'Use his Knife against him' defense against a Backhand Strike

The next set of Drawings illustrates an **'Arm-break Disarm'** after having poked the slashing assailant with his own knife. Drill all possibilities seriously, and then let your body choose intuitively in free-fighting which is most suitable. In our example, you lunge *forward diagonally* while blocking the backhand slash and while poking the attacker's eyes. Pull the arm to extend it and palm-strike his elbow to weaken it. Pull it further and place your other hand on the back of his hand as illustrated. You can now use *both hands and all your body* for a sudden and *violent* push of the knife towards his ribs. Pull the knife back after contact and extend it for another hard Palm Strike to the elbow for disarming him; after being poked by his own knife, he'll probably be much keener on letting go.

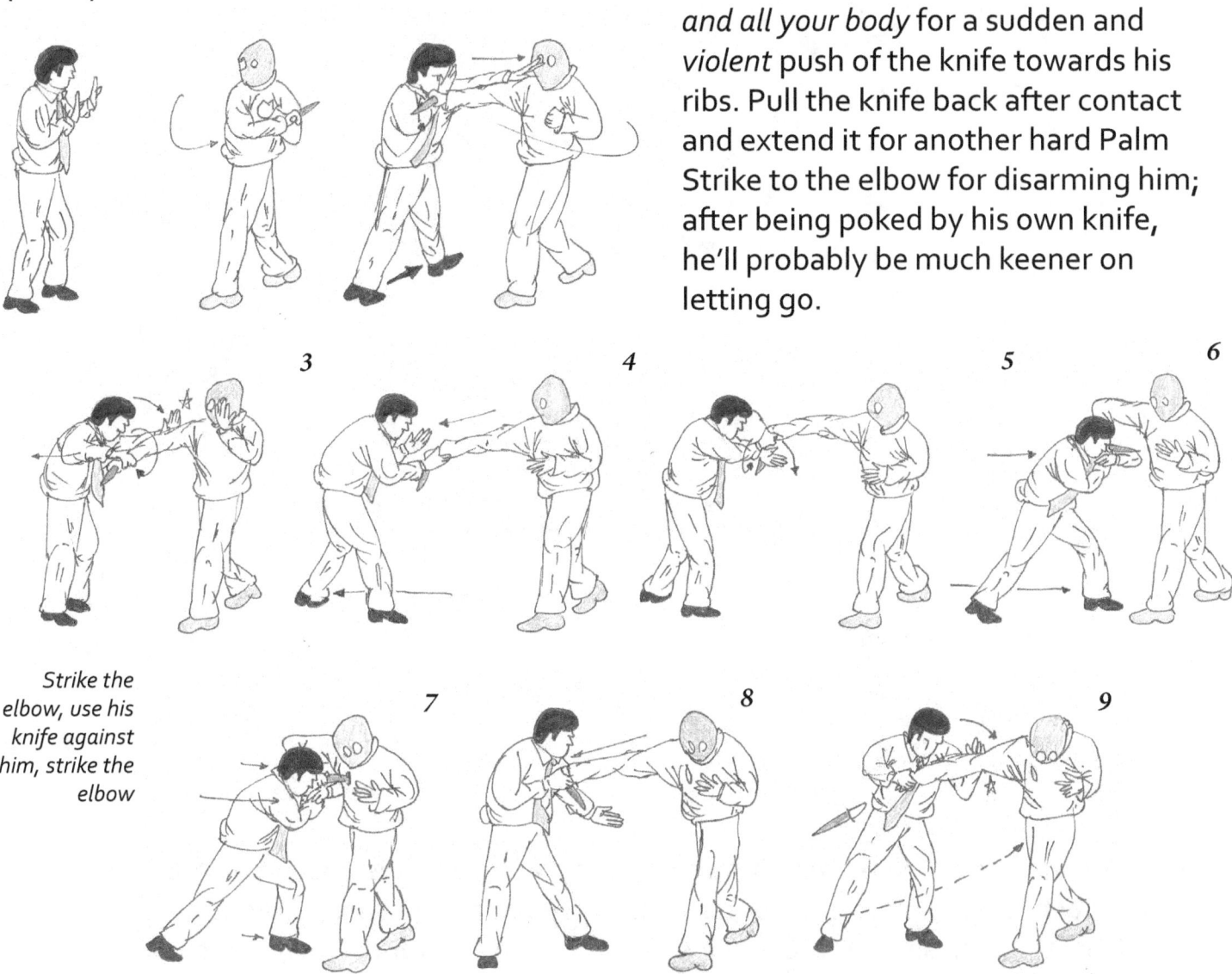

Strike the elbow, use his knife against him, strike the elbow

But *not always will you be able to jump forward before the slash*. We now present a **back-evasion Disarm** series against a clear and full Double slash, in and out. This is, of course, valid against a single simple Reverse (backhand) Slash as well. Evade <u>back</u> instinctively a regular slash that has come too fast for a forward move. *But you will lunge back forward as soon as the knife has passed in front of you*. Block the return backhand strike with both arms. Immediately lower the armed arm and push it towards the attacker's body with all the power of your forward momentum. Simultaneously you will poke his eyes as he concentrates on his armed wrist. Kick his groin to allow for an easier grabbing of his armed hand in Lock grip. Peel his knife off and kick him again in the groin.

KNIFE ATTACKS

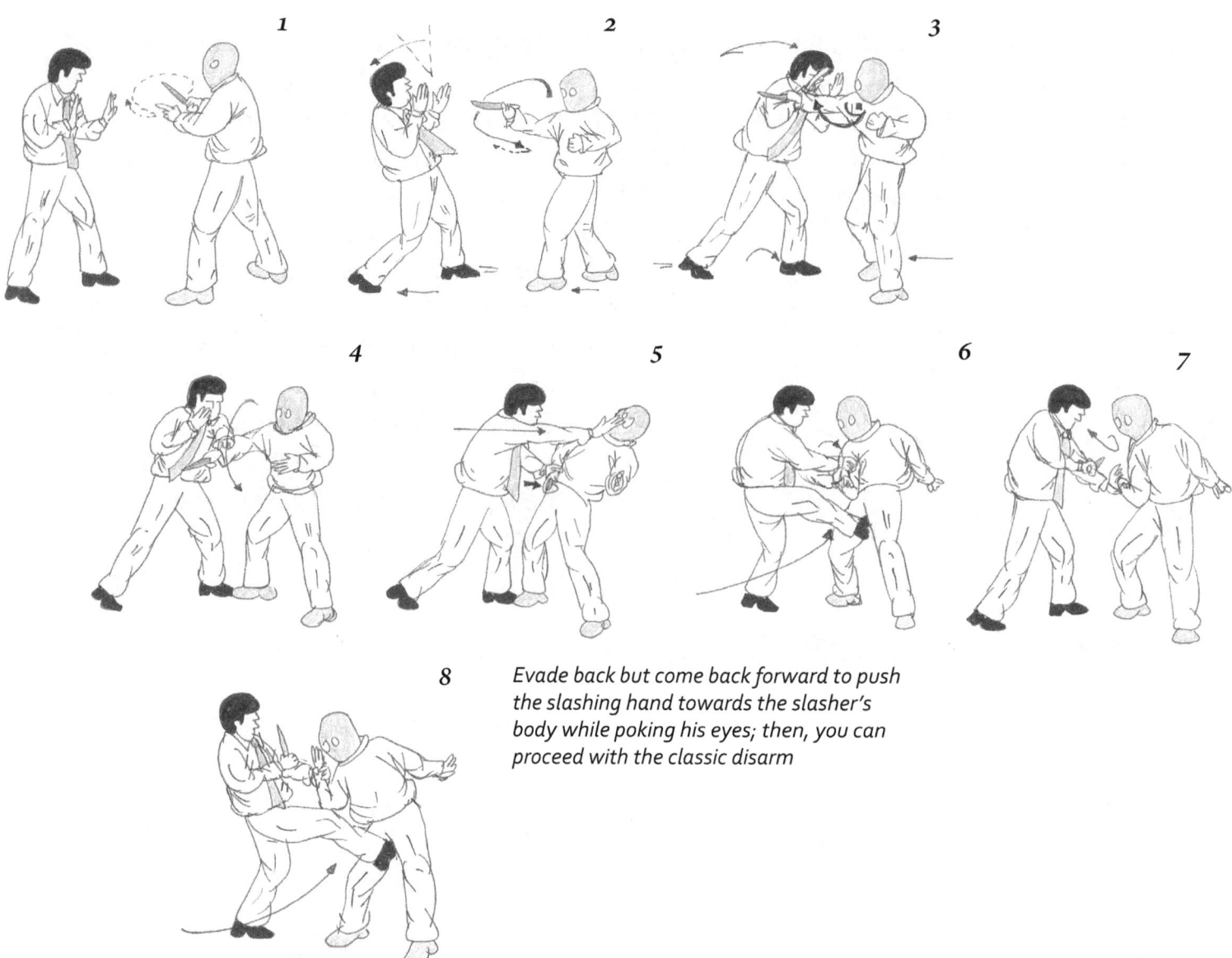

Evade back but come back forward to push the slashing hand towards the slasher's body while poking his eyes; then, you can proceed with the classic disarm

We shall conclude this Chapter with a **sophisticated** technique against an **early low regular slash**. Do not start drilling this before you are an advanced practitioner able to defend himself with simpler techniques. Mastery comes gradually! In our example, the attacker starts low with a regular slash. You lunge forward preemptively and block him low (classic Downward Block). You keep your forward momentum to come close and lift his arm. Strike a painful armlock with the blocking forearm on his elbow as his hand is stuck on your upper arm. *Strike* the elbow *violently* and join hands over his arm for the subsequent Lock. This will keep him in place for a groin Kick or Knee. As he bends in pain, strike his back neck and then push it down and under his shoulder. Pull his arm in the same circular motion to bring him to the floor. *Bang his head on the floor* and put your fingers in his eyes.

ADVANCED KRAV MAGA

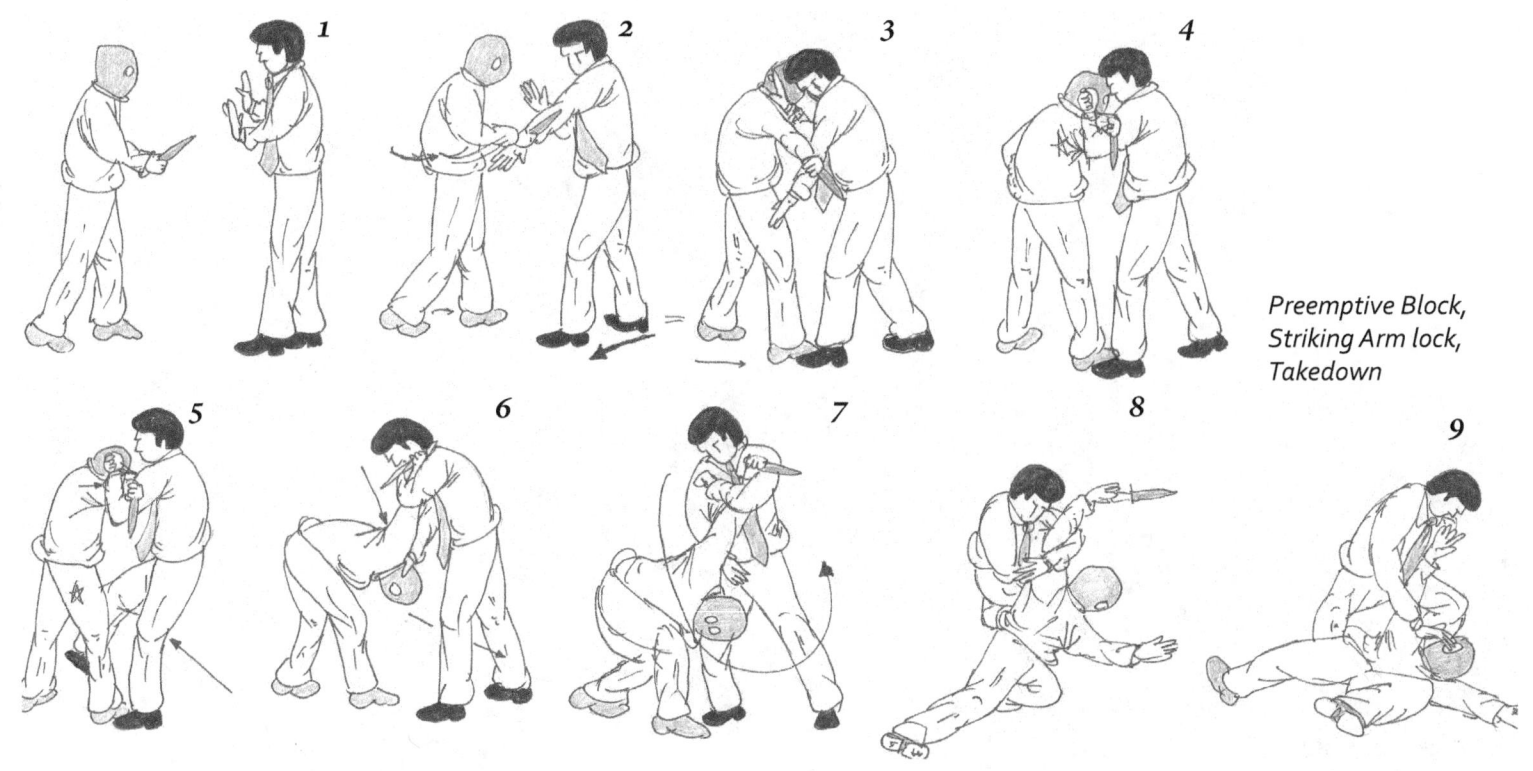

Preemptive Block, Striking Arm lock, Takedown

The world is a dangerous place, not because of those who do evil, but because of those who look on and do nothing.
~Albert Einstein

PART EIGHT

Defenses against Gun Threats

הגנה מפני איומי אקדח

Everything we have ever said about 'choosing not to fight' is even truer in an altercation involving firearms. Even the densest of persons will understand that using a finger to squeeze a trigger is easier and faster than any self defense technique imaginable. Relinquish your wallet or anything of value, if it is what the threat is about. **No material wealth is worth putting your life on the line**.

Of course, if it is also clear that, if nothing will save you or a loved one from execution, kidnapping, serious bodily harm or sexual attack, you should consider resisting. The problem is that no Hollywood stunt will help you **if you are not close** to the assailant. A gun is a weapon to be used from a distance and an experimented thug will not let you get close enough to do anything. Forget James Bond from the Seventies movies that could kick a gun out of the villain's fingers. From some distance, it would be imperative to weasel your way closer in a subdued and totally non-threatening manner.

The good news is that a gun threat is a *threat* and not an attack; if the attacker wanted, he would have shot you already and easily. He wants something from you and he could be cocky or stupid enough to come close to you or let you approach. You could get close by offering your wallet, or he could be inclined to touch you with the gun barrel to intimidate you (also an Hollywood favorite).

If you find yourself in a situation where you are threatened by contact with a gun, then there certainly is hope. Many readers will be surprised to learn that taking the initiative in this situation is pretty safe and easy. The only caveat is the danger of collateral damage posed to eventual onlookers; and it is to be taken into account.

The reader should first convince himself that, with a little training, one can easily shift a gun touching him before the assailant can pull the trigger. It may seem surprising or counter-intuitive. Just try with a toy gun; have a partner hold you at gun point with your hands up. Simply twist and deviate the gun with one hand; your partner is supposed to shoot as soon as he discerns your exploding into the move. Believe it and check by yourself: you'll win each time because you are the one taking the initiative. This is what all gun threat techniques are about. The problem is that it works only if you are very very close and it will not be possible against a professional attacker.

The other little piece of good news is that once you have started your defense, the disarming of the assailant is pretty easy too. Think about the fulcrum you have when holding the attacker's wrist and the barrel of the gun: it is long and around the axis of one finger into the trigger guard. Twisting the gun will be easy and will also break the trigger finger. Pulling the gun away after that will be child's play.

In a nutshell: dealing with a gun is exceedingly dangerous to you and to your surroundings; it should be avoided at any cost. But if you have no choice and are "lucky" enough to be threatened from close up, taking the initiative *Krav Maga*-style will probably give you more than a fighting chance.

8.1 Body evasion and Disarming

Unlike dealing with sticks and knives, **gun threats** can only be dealt with by disarming the assailant. The effort needed to squeeze a trigger is so minimal, that anything else will keep you in danger. All the self defense techniques presented will be about *taking the gun away* from the attacker. Eventual strikes are only complementary moves to help or to conclude the disarming technique.

As mentioned, taking a gun out of the opponent's hand is basically very easy: you make use of the fulcrum between the end of the barrel and the opponent's wrist or even grip. And you make use of the searing pain of the trigger finger joints being violently damaged. All disarming techniques will therefore be based on the following simple scenario: (1) you move the armed wrist so as to get out of the line of fire, (2) you catch the barrel of the gun with one hand and the armed wrist with the other, (3) you twist the gun violently around the axis of the trigger (in a way that does not place you in the line of fire at any time), (4) you pull the gun away.

And then comes the following: you are now in possession of the attacker's firearm; *what is to be done?*

Here are the golden rules when holding a gun:
1. **Do not make the attacker's mistake of staying close**: immediately retreat (or push him away) to keep about 10 feet (or 3 meters) between you and him. A handgun advantage is at mid-distance, not for close or for very far.
2. **Do not threaten anyone with a gun if you are not ready to use it**; for example, shooting at his lower limbs in case he gets closer or tries to attack you again. Having a gun can give you *a sense of false security* and slow your reactions if you are not ready to use it. Remember that it could be taken away from you too and then place you in jeopardy.
3. **Do not threaten anyone with a gun if you do not know how to use it**. Unless the gun is a revolver that just requires to pull the trigger, you may need knowledge to be able to get a discharge. Automatic guns come with various safety features and require arming before you can shoot (getting a bullet into the chamber). Moreover, unlike in Hollywood, guns often jam and clearing a jammed gun in real time is a skill you only can get by good instruction and practice. If you are not familiar with a gun or not willing to use it, it is best to get rid of it (throwing it far away), to run away with it or to place in your pants or pockets before using *Krav Maga* to completely subdue the attacker (**crushing his fingers and wrists** would help ensure his inability to further threaten you).

Before we consider the Disarming Techniques, we should also present a very important exercise <u>to be drilled seriously</u>. Getting out of the line of fire will always be based on **two** components: move the armed hand <u>AND</u> removing yourself simultaneously. This can be ingrained by the following drill.

Have a partner poke you with a gun (Poking someone with a gun is also Hollywood-derived; it is totally stupid and unprofessional). He can poke you anywhere: in the gut, in the chest, on any side, on left or right shoulder. Your job is to 'give in' fast and remove the intended target from the poke *and the line of fire* by twisting your body. Do not grab the gun hand; this drill is there to ingrain the need to pivot with the body. All full defenses to be drilled later will have a natural component of twisting evasion together with the gun grab to deviate it. It is common sense but it requires getting used to.

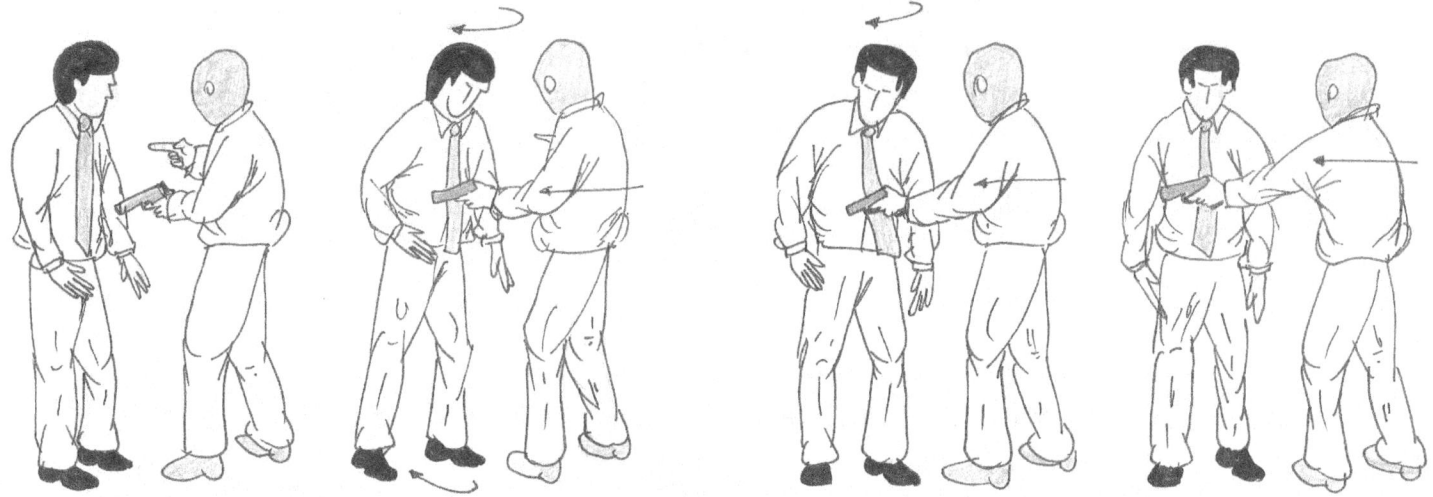

Drill the necessary body twist evasion that complements all defense techniques

We shall now present the **basic Disarming Techniques** that you should drill first to get familiar with the principles of disarming a gun-holder. Drill those slowly and smoothly with a partner who *keeps his finger out of the trigger*. Increase speed gradually but drill carefully so as not to hurt your partner's joints. Later in the text, some defenses will be presented where the more advanced disarming is different. The principles stay the same and must be first mastered by the techniques we are presenting now!

Maybe needless to add, but we shall say it anyway: <u>**Never practice with a loaded gun!**</u> It is best to use a fake gun, but if unavailable use only an unloaded gun that has been checked at least twice for its absence of bullet in chamber and in magazine; all munitions should, at that time, be under lock and key, far away, to avoid any possible miscommunication. This cannot be underlined enough!!

The first Disarm we shall present is **the Vertical Disarm**. We present it first because it should be used whenever possible, on account of lifting the line of fire towards the sky during the technique. This has the advantage of minimizing possible collateral damage during the Disarm. Remember to also remove yourself from the line of fire during the grab. **The Vertical Disarm** is based on grabbing the barrel from below and grabbing the wrist. You can then lift the barrel to make it pivot around the trigger area, while keeping the wrist in place. Do this *violently* and you will break the opponent's trigger finger while disarming him. You should then strike the attacker in the face with the gun in line with the natural continuation of the Disarm movement. *Remember to immediately retreat* to keep him in check with his own gun from 3 meters at least.

The Figures illustrate the Disarm and present an applied example.

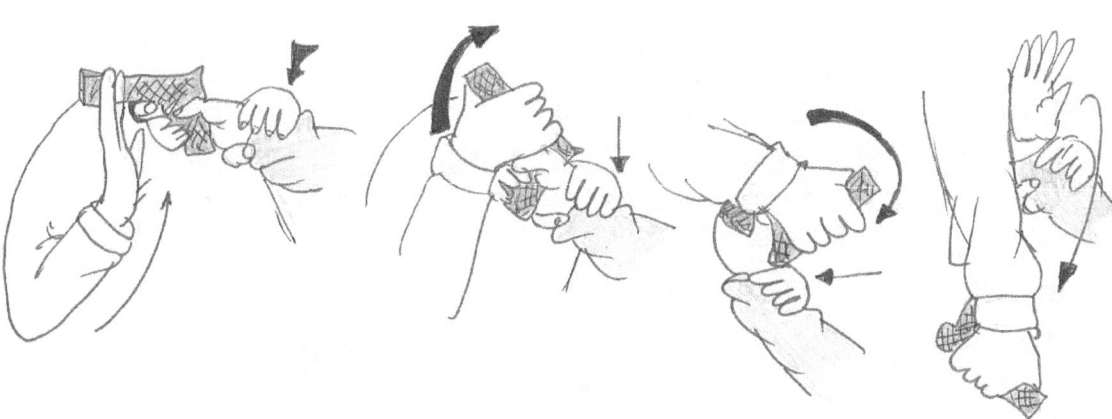

The Vertical Disarm: safest for standers-by

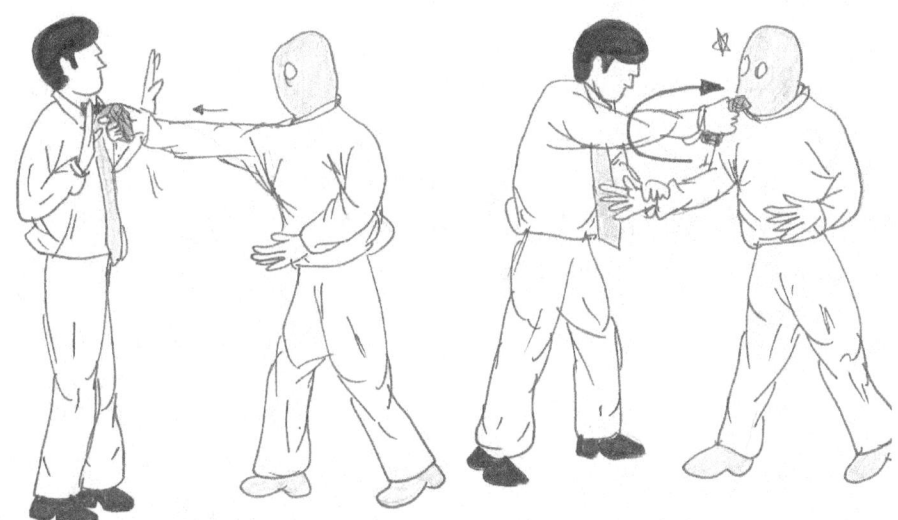

Vertical Disarm against close high front gun threat

We shall also present a **variation of the Vertical Disarm** that illustrate that it is the principles that matter and that there is no dogmatic way to follow. The Application illustrated at the top of next page is especially useful in a situation where the gun is '*in your face*' and you are also grabbed by the assailant. Lift your hands near your face in a non-threatening way: you are clearly surrendering in fear. From close-up, you can now explosively grab the barrel of the gun *with both hands* and *violently* lift it in place around the trigger area! Make sure you pivot around the trigger that should be stuck in place by your move.

➔

GUN THREATS

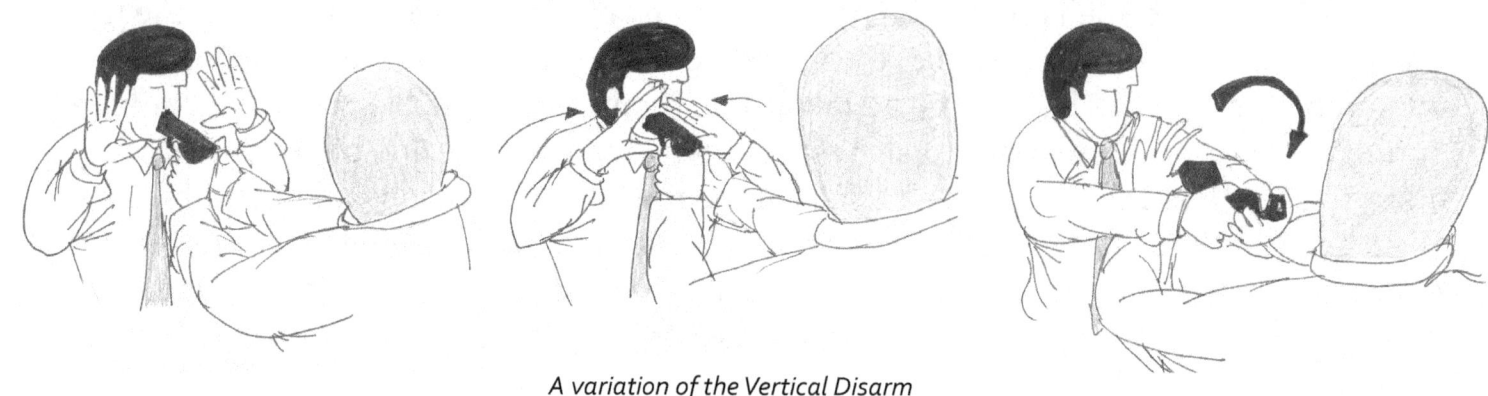

A variation of the Vertical Disarm

The Second Disarm is **the Lateral Disarm**, based on the same principles. You grab the barrel and the wrist and then push the barrel *horizontally* back towards the opponent. This move also pushes the palm of his hand towards his forearm, which has the advantage of causing his fingers to open naturally. But, of course, you execute the push *violently* in order to break his trigger finger, while pulling his wrist towards you. As soon as he lets go of the gun you push it forward with the momentum to hit him in the face with it. You should then immediately take your distance, eventually after a groin Kick or groin Knee if you are in control.

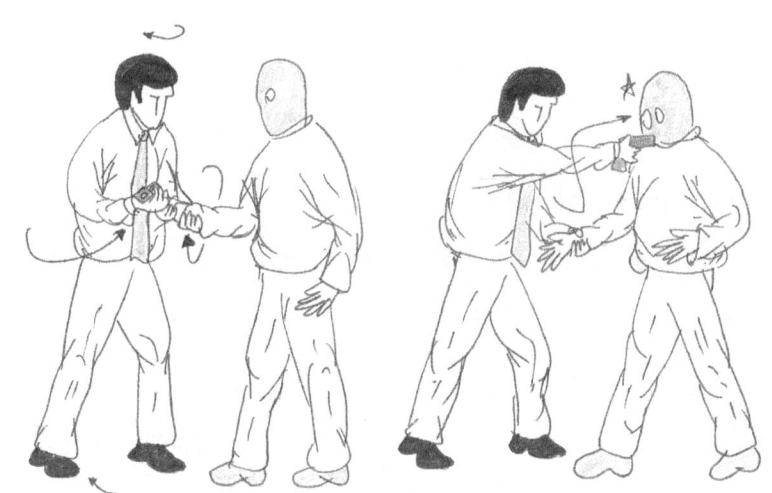

Applied Lateral Disarm against gut-level close front gun threat

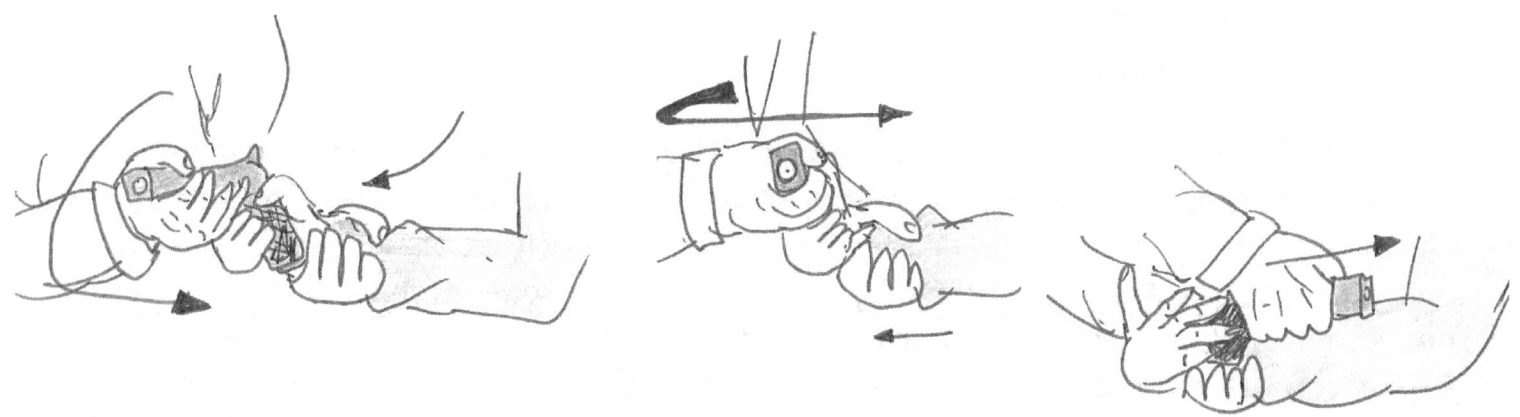

The very common Lateral Disarm, horizontal version of the previous technique

ADVANCED KRAV MAGA

The Third Disarm, **the Corkscrew Disarm**, is very efficient but it requires a special control of the opponent's arm. It is very useful when you find yourself in a wrestling tug-of-war for the gun with the opponent. Again, you grab the barrel and the wrist, but this time you *twist the gun on itself around the trigger*. The violent twist will both damage the trigger finger and make him release the gun. Regarding the necessary set-up to execute the Disarm, the following example will make things clear.

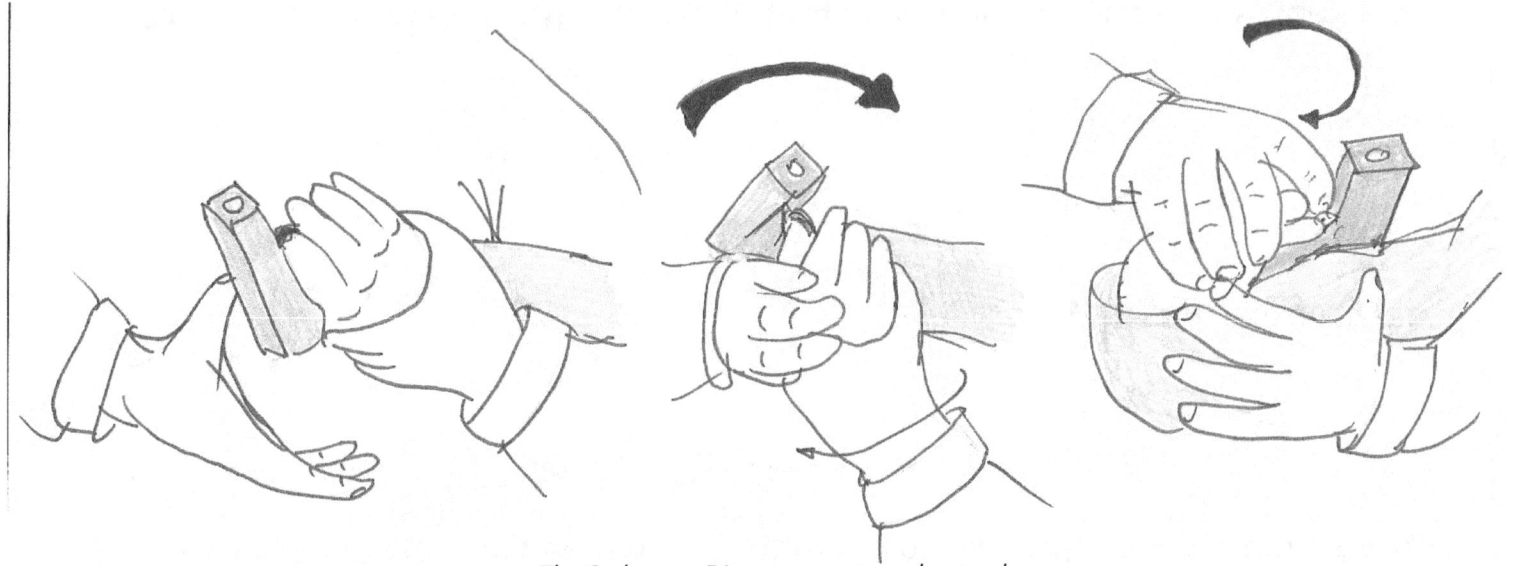

The Corkscrew Disarm, easy to understand

Our application for a **Corkscrew Disarm** is illustrated by the Drawings below. Your attacker threatens you with a gun touching your chest. Lift your hands in a clear and well-understood sign of surrender. Once you have broken inertia and are in movement,

grab his wrist and push it away and towards him while twisting out of the line of fire. Keep pivoting in order to place him in classic armlock *under your armpit*. <u>Use all your body to get in position and strike his arm violently with the armpit</u>. Immediately grab the gun barrel and execute the **Corkscrew Disarm** while pushing even more on his arm joints. Take the gun and take your distance.

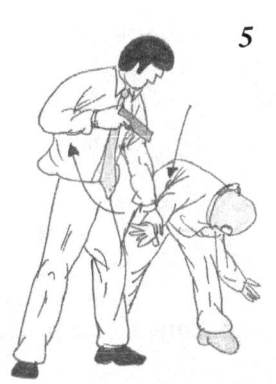

Applied Corkscrew Disarm in classic Armlock position

GUN THREATS

All other *Disarm Techniques* are variations of those just presented and are based on the same guiding principles. A few more advanced techniques will be presented later on with a different approach, but they should be reserved for advanced trainees with a full mastery of the basic techniques. Drill the basics first and proceed in due course.

Before we go to the Techniques themselves, it is important to remember: **the purpose of Gun defenses is to take the gun away from the assailant!** Certainly *not* to tumble and rumble.

8.2 Threats from the Front

Threats from the Front are the most common, as a threatening attacker usually wants something from you. Here are a few ways to deal with it. Try and drill all defenses presented; some are very similar. After lots of drilling, you'll see what best fits you and you should then concentrate your drilling on those.

The first example is an **applied Lateral Disarm** as it should be drilled by beginners: *using the whole body in the technique* to make sure to have enough power. Against a gun placed on or poking at your gut, you pivot out of the line of fire while grabbing both wrist and barrel from below. Twist back *with all the power of both your arms and your hips* to break his fingers and disarm him. Move away.

Full-powered Lateral Disarm against gut-poking with gun

Our first set of Photos illustrates same simple **applied Lateral Disarm**, but in a more advanced version. In this example, it is the opponent's *hand* that is controlled, but the principles stay the same. You pivot while grabbing and moving the armed hand. Twist the hand and weapon violently and move away with the gun.

Lateral 'wristlock' Disarm

Next comes a **hybrid between Lateral and Vertical Disarm**. As illustrated below, you lift your hands in surrender against a gun pointed towards your upper chest from very close. As soon as they are level with the gun, you grab the barrel and deviate it out while pivoting simultaneously out of the line of fire. You then grab the armed wrist with your other hand and start pushing the barrel both up and laterally out. Of course, the pushing pivot is centered around the trigger and you hold the armed wrist firmly in place. The pivot is *violent* and should break the trigger finger. You can then kick the opponent's groin before pulling the gun away forcefully *with both hands*. Take your safe distance.

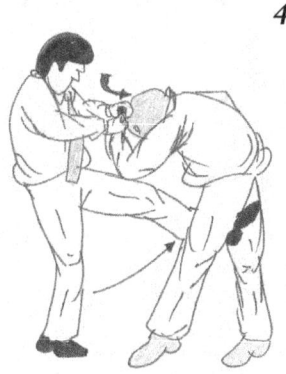
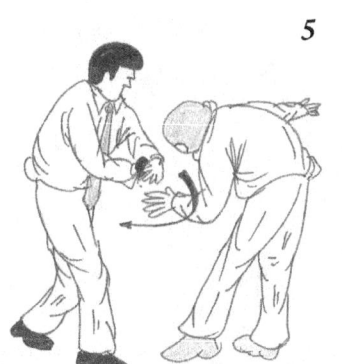

Applied 'Diagonal' Disarm with groin Kick

GUN THREATS   215

The next set of Photos shows the **more advanced version of the Lateral Disarm,** in which *you grab the armed hand with both hands* rather than barrel and wrist. It is a Wrist-lock type of grab that is faster but requires more training and strength. The principles are exactly the same though.

The advanced 'wrist-lock' version of the Lateral Disarm

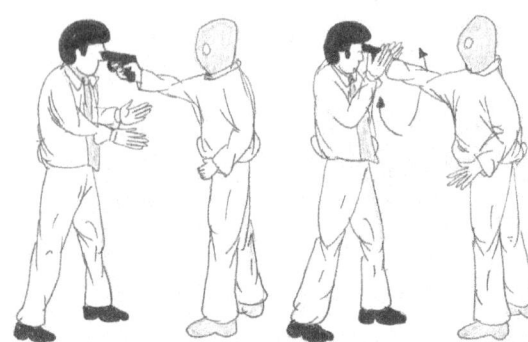

The coming Illustrations show a simple classic **Vertical Disarm against a gun hold to your face.** You grab the gun hand with both hands simultaneously while getting out of the way (Of course, you have broken the inertia by lifting your hands in clear surrender). Immediately start to lift the barrel of the gun around the trigger axis while pulling his wrist down and forward. Use your whole body for the violent pulling (down and forward) of his gun out of his grip. Push him away with your shoulder and take your distance.

Vertical Disarm clean and simple

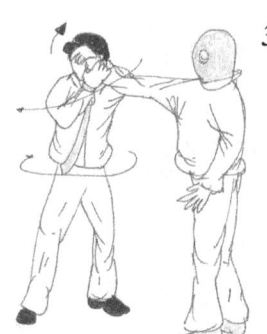
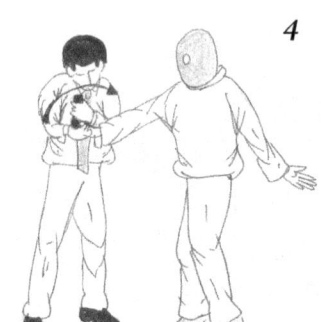
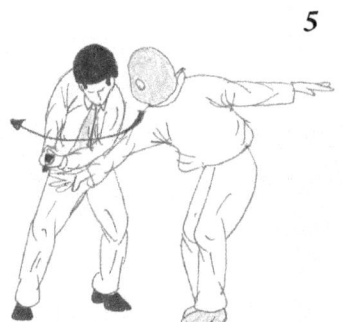

ADVANCED KRAV MAGA

And now for a full application of the **Corkscrew Disarm**. You are threatened by gun contact to your chest. Lift your hands and grab the armed wrist or hand with one hand. Deviate the gun by pushing it *out, down and towards the assailant*, while getting out of the line of fire. Keep the momentum to place the opponent in typical 'under-the-armpit' Armlock. This must be of course done *violently, explosively and with the use of your whole body*. In this position, you can grab the gun barrel and execute the **Corkscrew Disarm**. All the while, you let yourself fall down *with all your weight and energy onto his elbow*. Grab the gun, push his arm to the ground and place your knees on his wrist and elbow in order to safely stand up. Stomp his elbow or/and wrist and/or fingers to neutralize them, and take your distance.

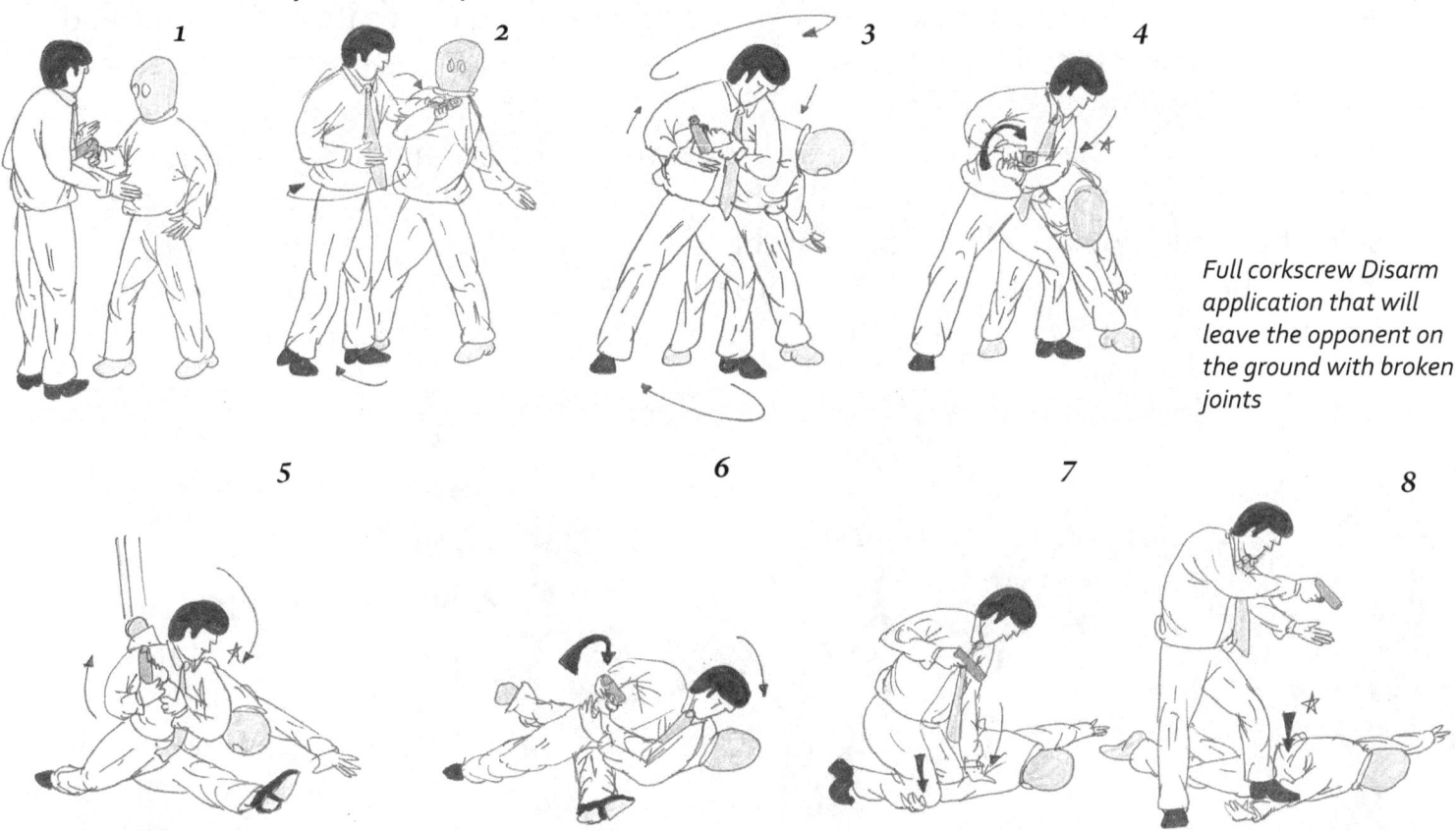

Full corkscrew Disarm application that will leave the opponent on the ground with broken joints

When you become familiar with the Disarming Moves, you should be able to execute them with narrower and shorter movements. It comes from practice and power management, but it requires drilling and explosiveness. The Figures at the top of ext page illustrate such an **economical Lateral Disarm**. Against a gun pointed touching your gut, you push the gun wrist straight into the opponent's belly *with all your body power forward*. The move itself deviates the line of fire. The push becomes a wrist grab, and your forceful forward momentum allows for a simultaneous headbutt aiming for his nose. Grab the barrel with your other hand and execute a *violent* Lateral Disarm. As soon as he lets go of the gun, keep your forward momentum and push forward while twisting and lifting his wrist. You can eventually kick his groin before taking your distance.

GUN THREATS 217

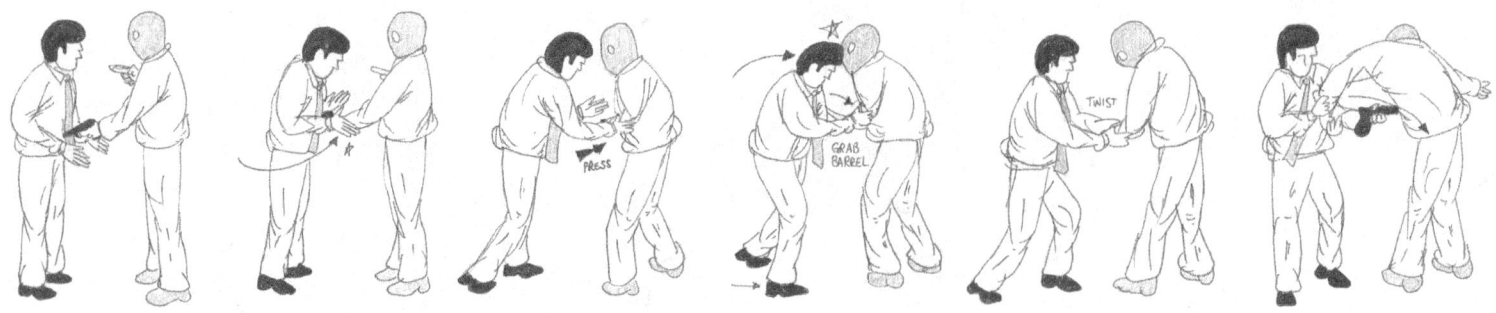

Explosive but economical Lateral Disarm with strong forward momentum

The coming Photos will show an **advanced technique** that should be enough if executed by an experienced *Kravist*. It looks simple but requires drilling for a safe execution. On the other hand, the whole series could also be the prelude to a classic Disarm as presented before. Drill this carefully at the beginning, and complete it with a Disarm if you feel it necessary. Against a high front gun threat, you slap out the offending hand (with same-side hand) and grab the armed wrist with the opposite hand. Attack the opponent's throat or side of the neck with the knife-edge of the 'slapping hand'. Simultaneously you pull on his grabbed wrist in order to pull him into the strike. Remember to strike *through the throat with everything you got*. You then use the same knife-edge to strike down through the armed forearm. You should twist the arm in order to target the upper forearm muscles near the elbow rich in nerve endings. If it has not been enough, you should follow up with a groin knee strike and a classical Disarm.

Advanced 'striking' gun defense that can also be the prelude to a classical Disarm

218   **ADVANCED KRAV MAGA**

Another advanced technique is presented below. The Photos show the use of the classic *Aiki-Jitsu* Takedown '*Shiho Nage*' to deal with a Front Gun Threat. The technique is easy to execute but it requires training to ensure success. The *Krav Maga* version is shorter than the *Aikido* version and is more about *dislocating the shoulder* than about throwing him down. The movement must be *short and violent* (but not in training obviously). It is important to go *forward* with the twist of the body and to push *through* the opponent's body. Do not try to execute this move from far away, and remember that it requires serious training for a complete mastery.

Advanced: Shoulder dislocation of a gun armed attacker

We shall conclude this Chapter with two applied Disarms against a **front gun threat from a longer range.**

The problem with a **longer range** is obvious: you have to be able to deviate the line of fire before the aggressor squeezes the trigger. It is still possible the gun is an arm length away from you. Of course, you have to be fast, explosive and well-trained.

The important point to remember for **longer range** defenses is that *your hand must start moving first*, before any body move. The hand is fast, and if you start with the body move at the same time, you will lose speed and have the opponent react earlier. So, *it is imperative to throw your hand fast to grab or slap the gun*, and then follow with the body move forward (and out of the fire line). Once you are closer to the attacker, the techniques will be identical to the regular Disarms we have seen before.

GUN THREATS

The first Drawings illustrate how you **slap and grab the gun wrist or hand with a fast hand move**. Only after contact do you lunge forward and push the grabbed wrist down and towards the opponent's belly. *Use all your body momentum* for that, and simultaneously, use your other hand to finger-poke his eyes without pity. Use the poking hand to grab the barrel from below and execute a Lateral Disarm while pushing him with your elbow and shoulder (for good hands alignment). Pull the gun out of his grip with *both hands and your whole body*. You can eventually kick his groin before retreating at a safe distance. The key to the technique is the starting hand-move and lunge, and it needs serious drilling.

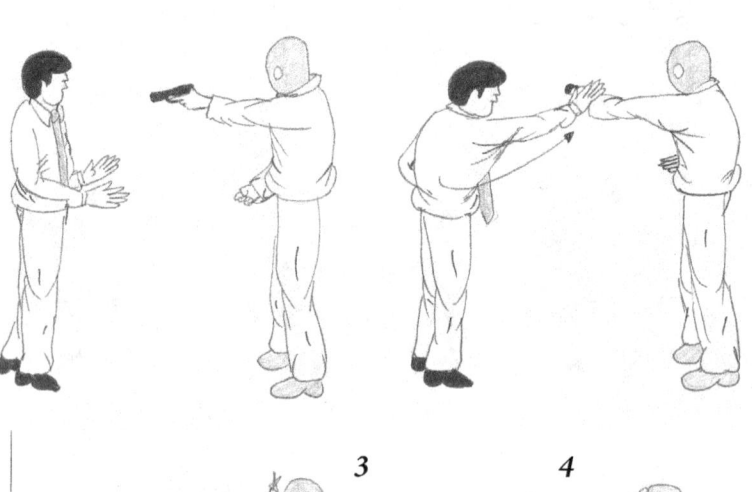

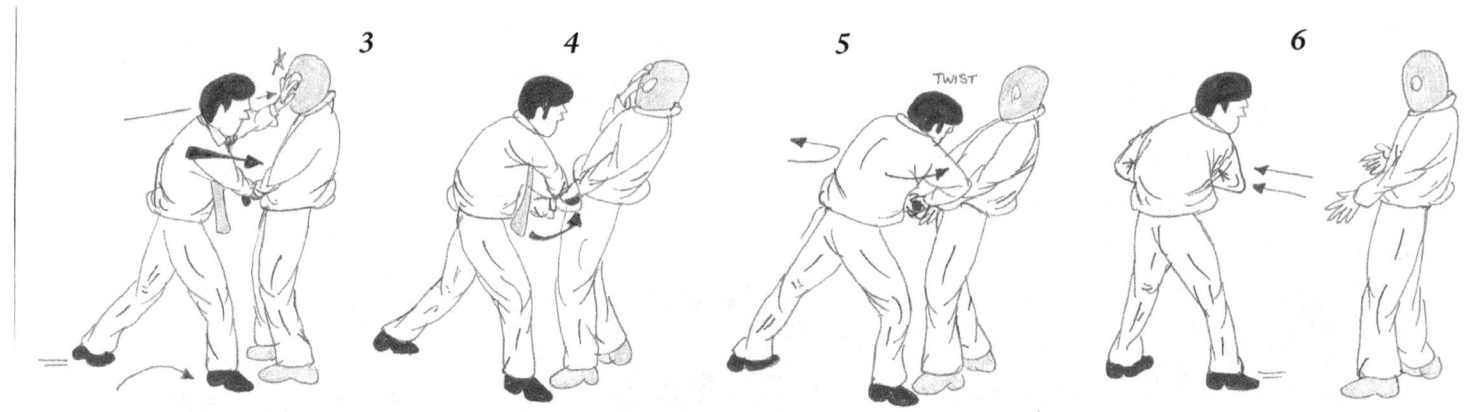

Mid-range gun threat: Slap and grab the gun before lunging for the disarm

The second example, illustrated at the top of next page, reinforces the same principle of **grabbing with the hand first before starting the explosive lunging move**. This is all there is to longer range gun threat handling. You grab and deviate the barrel of the gun (with same-side hand) before lunging forward. Use all your momentum to push his gun sideways and then grab his wrist from below with your other hand. Twist the gun around the trigger finger while keeping the wrist in place, and then pull it out *violently with all your body power*. Kick his groin and take your distance!

220   **ADVANCED KRAV MAGA**

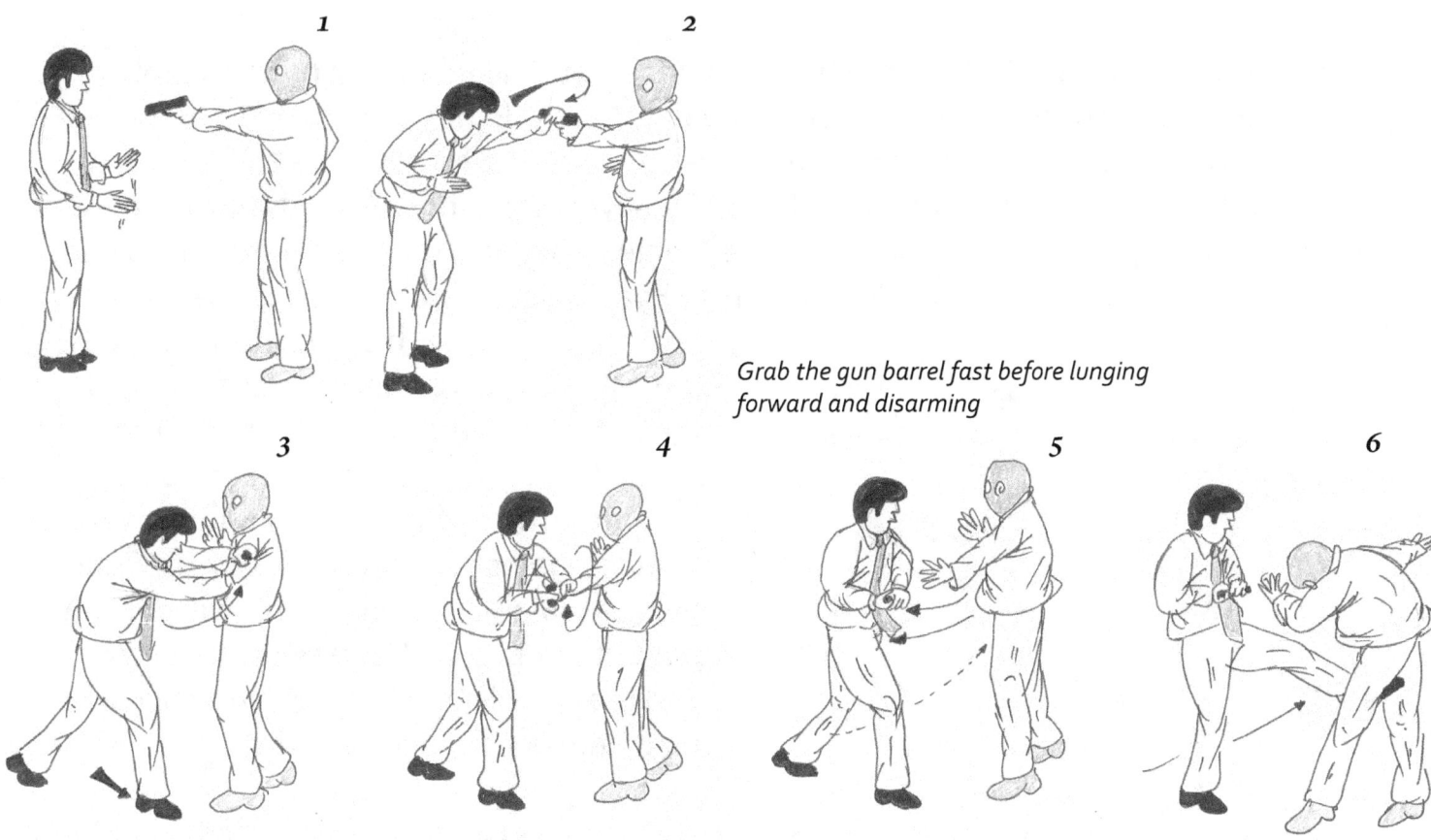

Grab the gun barrel fast before lunging forward and disarming

8.3 Threats from the Back

Being held at gun point **from the back** is even more problematic. It is imperative that you take a peek to assess the situation. Maybe the attacker is not alone, or he has a weapon in his other hand as well, or ... You need to lift your hands in a convincingly subdued way and turn your head to have a look, preferably a fearful look that will convince the attacker that you are cooperating. Do not turn with your body at this stage, only the head. If you then decide to fight, you'll have to explode into a body twist that will both *push the hand away and remove your body from the line of fire*.
The only good news is that the first move of all defenses is pretty easy, fast and effective. The rest follows the principles we already know from the front defenses.

The first example illustrated below shows how you explode in a **body twist** that also pushes the gun hand away. At this stage, you only twist; do not alert him by trying to also move towards him. Concentrate on the speed of the twist: this is the most important thing to get out of the line of fire. Then, you can lunge towards him with a Poke to the eyes, while your 'blocking arm encircles his gun arm from below. Press his gun hand onto your shoulder while going from Eye Poke to Elbow Strike, preferably to the throat. Press his neck down as you naturally kick his groin. Of course, you keep tight control of his gun hand. Now that he is seriously mollified, get hold of the barrel of the gun with the free hand. His wrist is hold in place against your shoulder by the other hand. A violent Lateral Disarm will pry the gun out of his grip. The natural trajectory of the Disarm will lead to a gun strike to the head before you take your distance.

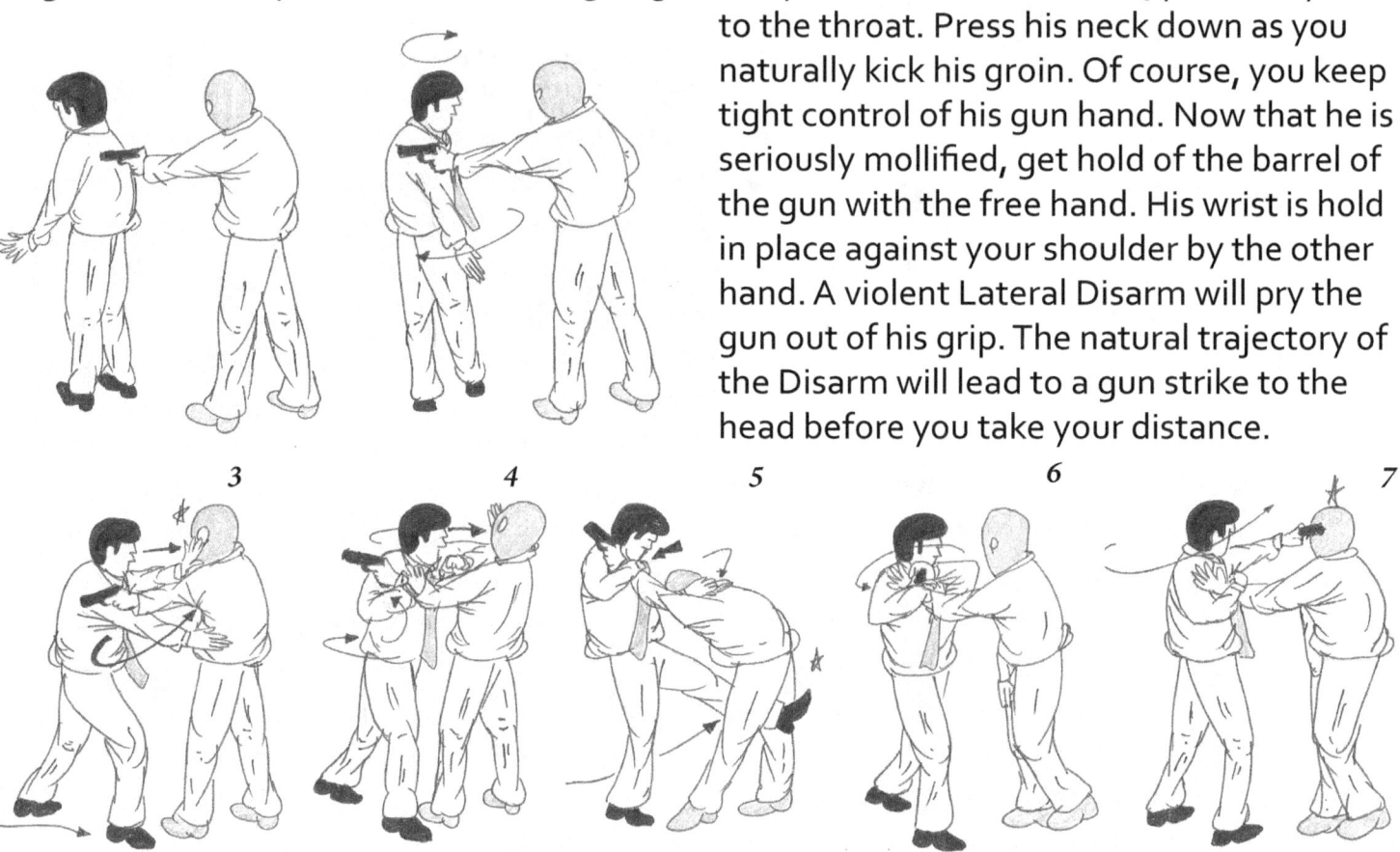

Basic defense and disarm against a gun threat from the back

As you can see from the second set of Drawings, at the top of next page, this basic technique stays nearly identical if you can **get closer to the attacker from the start**, which requires more training and proficiency. It is then easier to lift his head with the Eye Strike to better open his throat to the Elbow Strike. And the Groin Kick then becomes a Knee Strike.

Nothing is more harmful to the world than a martial art that is not effective in actual self-defense.
~Choki Motobu

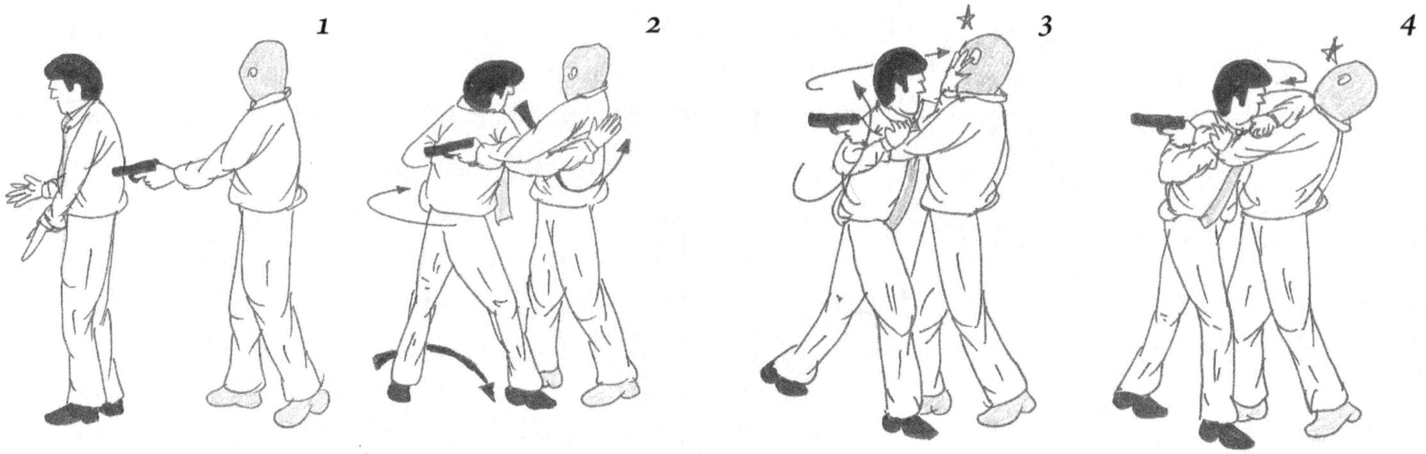

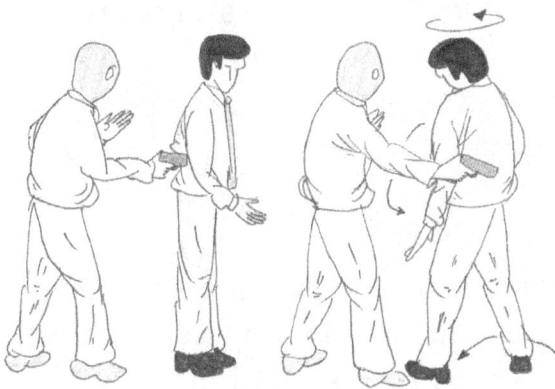

The more advanced 'closer' version of the basic technique

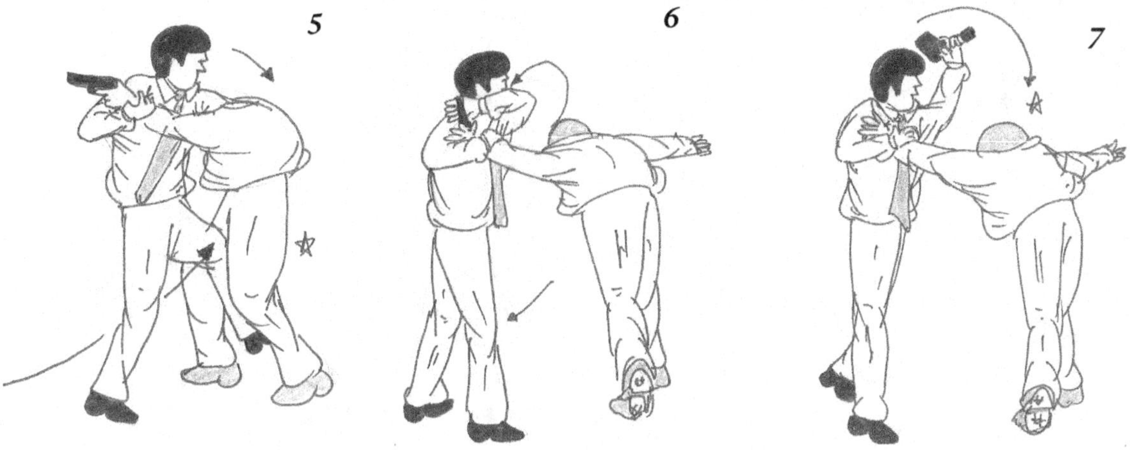

A more advanced way to deal with the threat is presented in the next Illustrations. It dispenses with all the 'mollifying' strikes and **goes right for the Disarm**. But it requires more training, proficiency and confidence. You should start drilling it *after you have fully <u>mastered</u> the previous versions*. After the pivot you immediately set a very strong vise on the armed wrist and go for the barrel with the other hand. The Lateral Disarm will relieve him of his weapon and then you can knee him (while striking him with the gun). Take your distance at once.

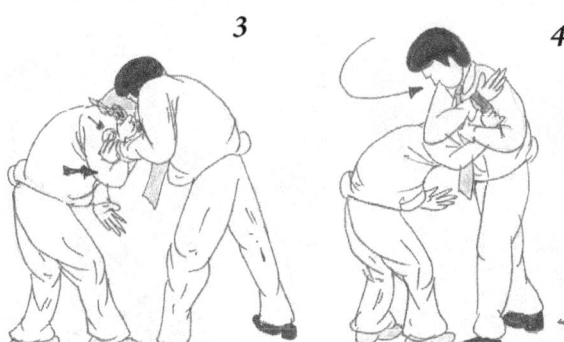

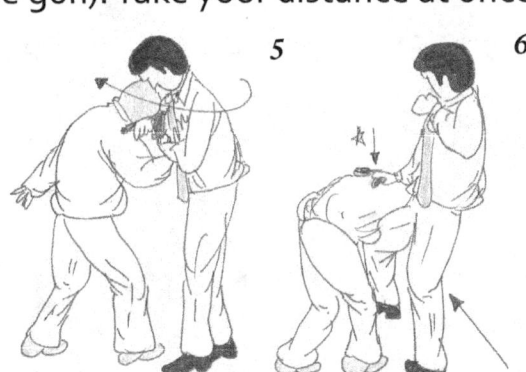

When proficient, go directly for the Disarm

GUN THREATS

Another advanced variation that goes directly for the Disarm is presented below. It also requires good drilling. In this example, you twist and deviate like always, but you keep pivoting to get hold of the opponent's armed wrist with the second (non-blocking) hand. You have quasi-simultaneously grabbed the barrel of the gun with the deviating hand, from below. The set-up allows for a *fast and violent* Lateral Disarm in which you *use the momentum of a strong lunge towards him*. You are pushing the armed wrist diagonally under his own shoulder for a better disarm. Push him away and take your distance.

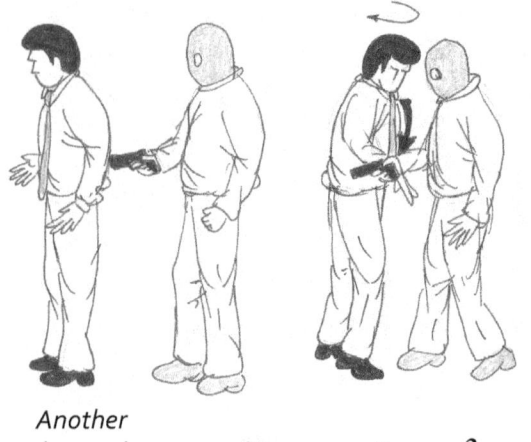

Another advanced simple and straight Disarm

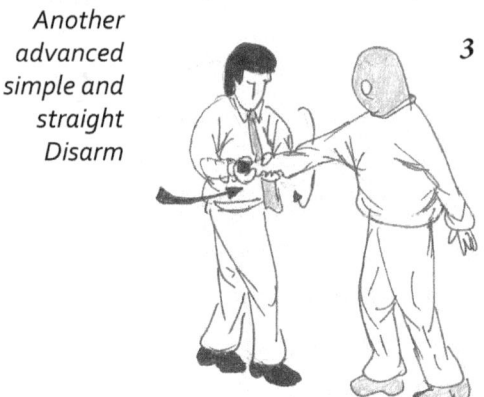
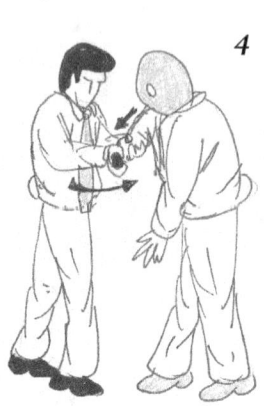

A different approach against a rear gun threat is presented in the Photos below. This is also an advanced technique that requires serious drilling. The Disarm is an optional addition at the end of the series. You pivot and deviate classically, but you then lunge and overtake him to his out-side while 'clothe-lining' him. Strike his neck *forcefully* and squeeze. Your shoulder pushes his own shoulder into his carotid, while your forearm does the same on the other side. Keep your strong momentum 'through' him to bend him backwards. At the same time, you reach for the gun with your other hand and bend his arm down. You can take him down and choke him, or you can twist the gun out of his grip.

Advanced 'clothesline and choke' defense; drill seriously

ADVANCED KRAV MAGA

And we shall conclude this section with an example of defense **when the gun threat from the rear is at some** (*reasonable*) **distance**. First you definitely need to peek to assess the situation: Really a gun? How far? Alone? Focused? Alert? For that you need to reassure the attacker by raising your hands and looking sufficiently subdued. If you decide to act, remember that the twist and necessary hip twist come <u>before</u> you start to move towards him. Speed and explosiveness are of the essence and any feet movement or body lunge will slow you down and alert him early. Just like for the Front defenses from some distance!

Here is the proposed technique, although, once you are safely closer, anything else already seen can work. Go with your gut!

The Drawings below illustrate how to *explosively twist and throw the arm to grab the gun barrel*. This is only after you have peeked to check the situation. You can start lunging towards the attacker only after the start of the twist and arm extension. Push the barrel to the side with his arm extended and go for an Eye Poke. Keep going diagonally towards his out-side while your poking hand comes to grab his armed wrist. Use your momentum to push him both physically and psychologically and execute a classic Lateral Disarm. You are superbly placed for a Groin Knee Strike, that can eventually be followed by a strike to the skull with his own gun. Take your distance.

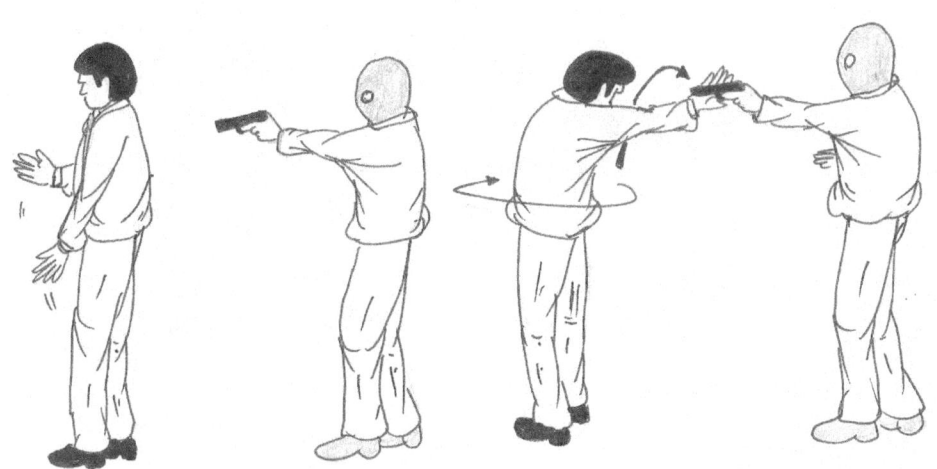

Applied Lateral Disarm against a mid-range Back Gun Threat; explode into the twist and reach to grab

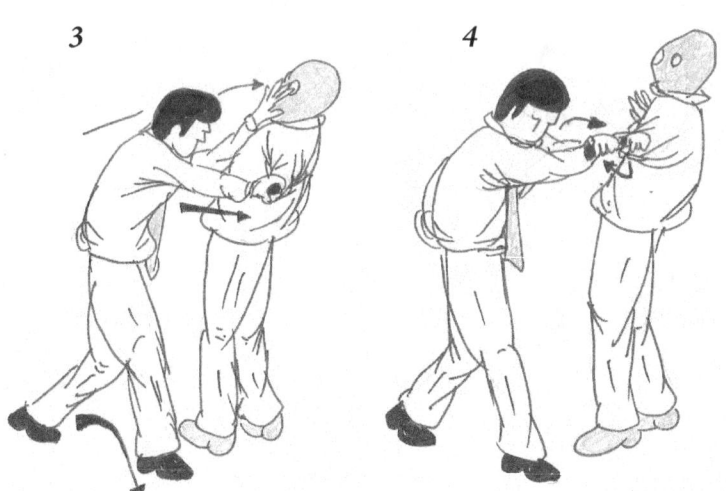
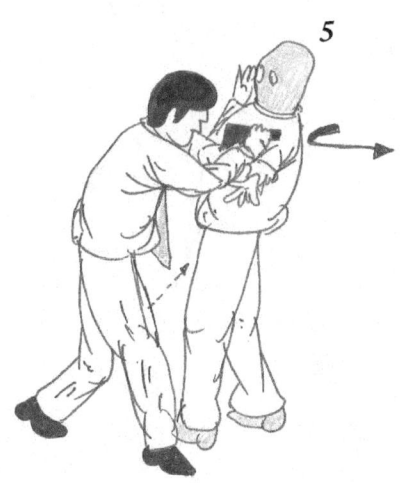

GUN THREATS

8.4 Threats from the Side

Threats from the side are not uncommon. They are usually linked to a mugger surprising you from a hiding place, although they can happen in a whole range of situations. The Disarms will be in line with what we have presented before for threats from the front and the back, but it is good to drill the specific situation.

The first set of Drawings illustrates how to **classically react to a gun being held close to the side of your head**: grab and deviate the barrel while removing yourself from the line of fire. You can then twist and lunge powerfully towards him. Push the gun hand towards his gut while attacking his eyes. Use the poking hand to come and grab the opponent's hand or wrist from below. Execute a classic violent Lateral Disarm while pulling back *with all your body* to pry the gun from his hands. Take your distance, eventually after a Groin Kick.

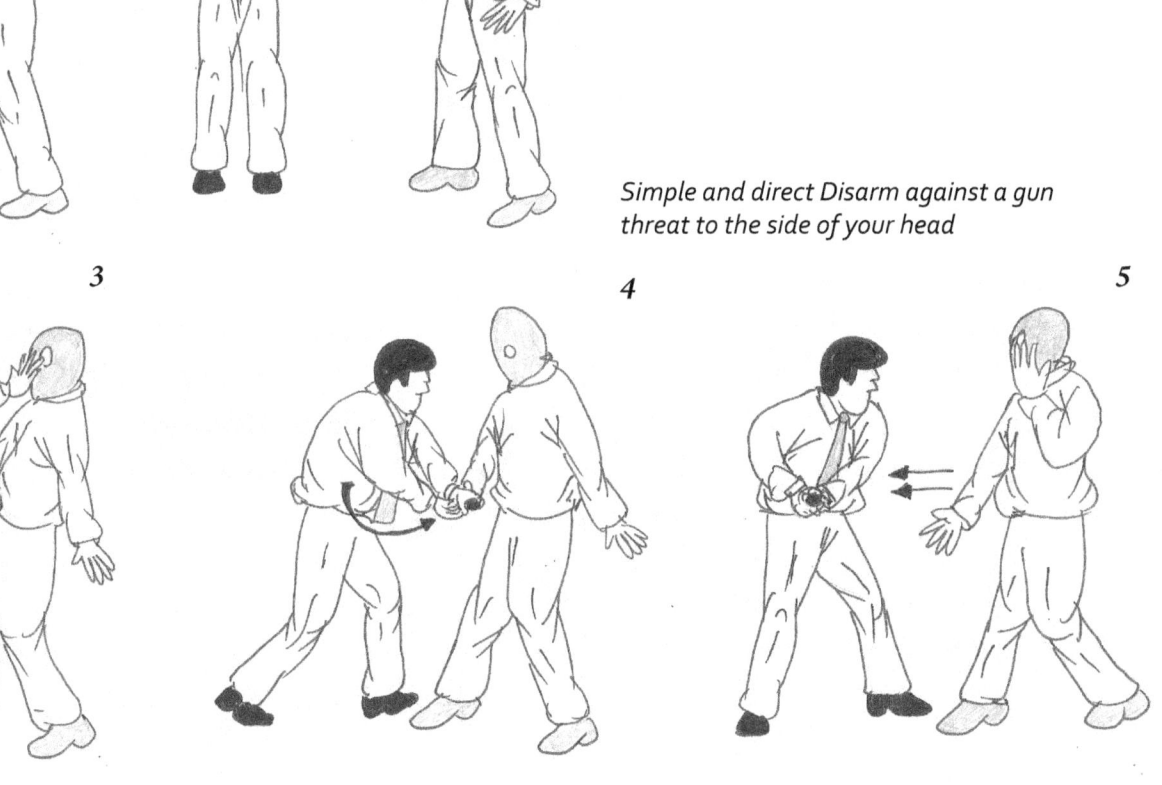

Simple and direct Disarm against a gun threat to the side of your head

Our second example, illustrated below, will have you **go to the out-side of the attacker**. You *explode* into the hip twist, the head evasion and the deviation of the gun line of fire. Using both your hands, you grab barrel and wrist simultaneously. Keep twisting and pull the armed arm forwards. Let go of the wrist grab to go over his extended arm and strike down on his arm with your armpit. Lock the armed wrist below your armpit and press it against your ribcage. Keep twisting: this is your way of using *all your body power* to control him. Stop the twist suddenly to change the direction of the hip twist. This will allow to use all your hip power while executing a classic Lateral Disarm. His wrist is blocked under your armpit and you violently twist the barrel of the gun towards him with all you have. Kick his groin and take your distance.

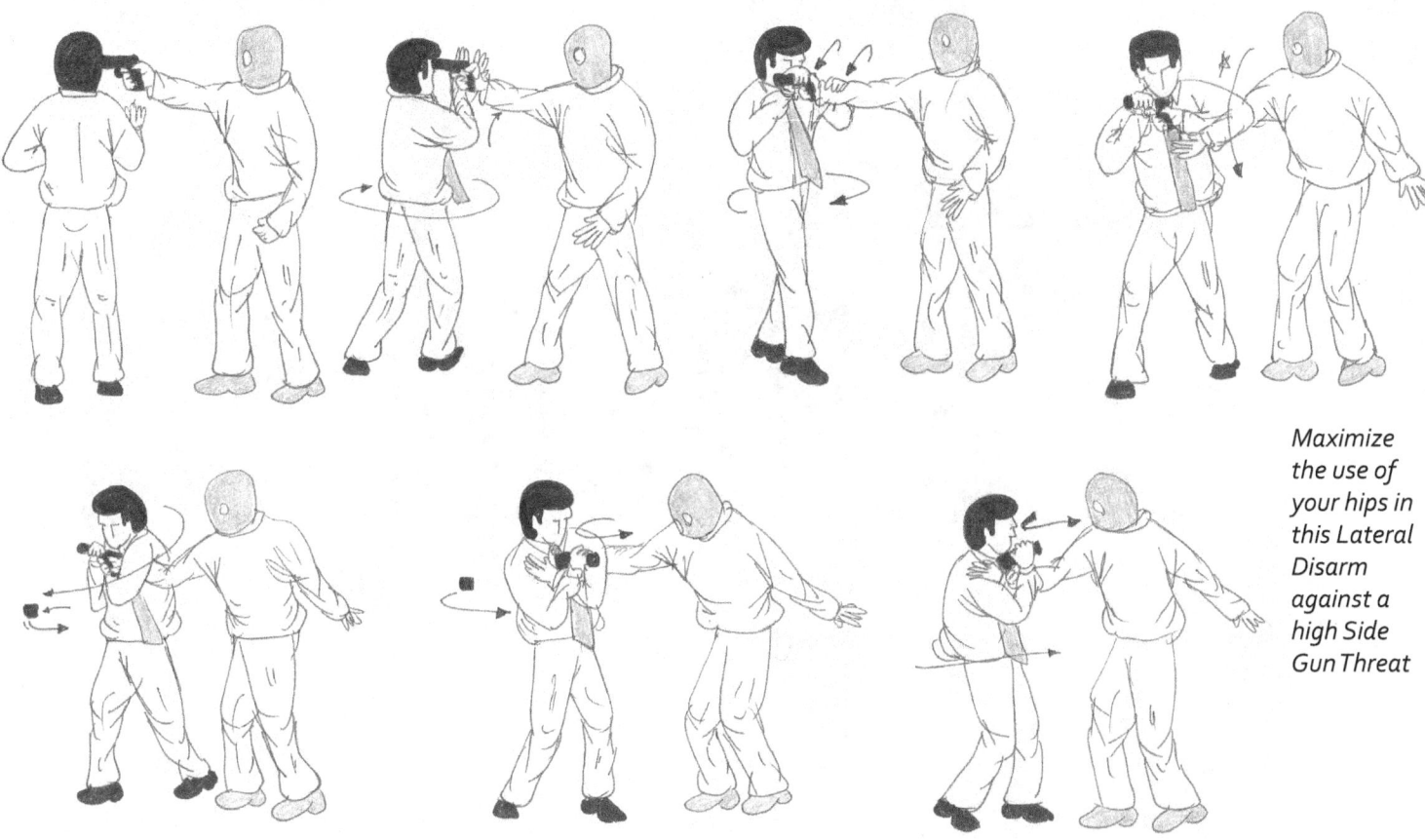

Maximize the use of your hips in this Lateral Disarm against a high Side Gun Threat

The coming set of Photos, at the top of next page, illustrates an **advanced version** of the preceding technique. You twist and remove the threat in the same way, but you proceed with the Disarm in place as soon as you have caught his arm under your armpit in what is a quasi-Armlock position. Twist the gun out of his fingers (and damage his trigger finger). You can then twist back to hit him with his gun, before you take your distance.

GUN THREATS

A more advanced version of the twist into 'under armpit armlock position' opening

8.5 Long Gun Threats

A long gun can be a carabine, a shotgun or an assault weapon. Unfortunately, senseless violence has become a feature of modern society and the availability of such weapons make this scenario a sad possibility.
Dealing with a **long gun** is a big problem. First, you'll have to pray that the assailant is stupid enough to get close to you. The advantage of a long gun is about mid- to long distance. Bringing the barrel at grabbing distance from you would be totally crazy. Then you'd have to pray that this is going to be just a threat to extract something from you. If it is just random violence or terrorism, your chances of getting close are minimal. But who knows? Maybe you can weasel or sweet-talk yourself into a close range.

If you are lucky enough to be close and "only" threatened by a long gun, you should remember the following: you'll have to get *as close to him as possible* in order to negate the possibility of being shot. Moreover, in order to control the gun, you will have to control <u>both</u> *the barrel and the area of the trigger*! You have to be in control of both areas where his hands are because controlling the barrel only allows him to move and place you back in the line of fire.

Techniques against a **Long Gun threat** are more difficult than against short guns. You are using the power of both your arms against the power of *both* his! Unlike for a short gun where both your hands are used in a fulcrum against only one of his wrists... This is why you'll have to drill hard and learn to use *all of your body* in these techniques.

I hope it has been made clear that this is very problematic. If it is about your wallet, I strongly suggest you choose the relinquishing option...

The first set of Drawings illustrates what is **one of the safest options** in the author's opinion. Grab the gun barrel and deviate it out while lunging in and head-butting him in the center of the face. Do not pull when grabbing, in order to avoid the reflexive pull-back that could place you back in the line of fire. Pull as soon as you are close to him, and slide your hand under his trigger hand armpit. Push your arm up and as far as possible under his trigger arm and come back with it under his trigger wrist. This is going to be the second point of your fulcrum. You will now twist his gun violently out of his grab by:

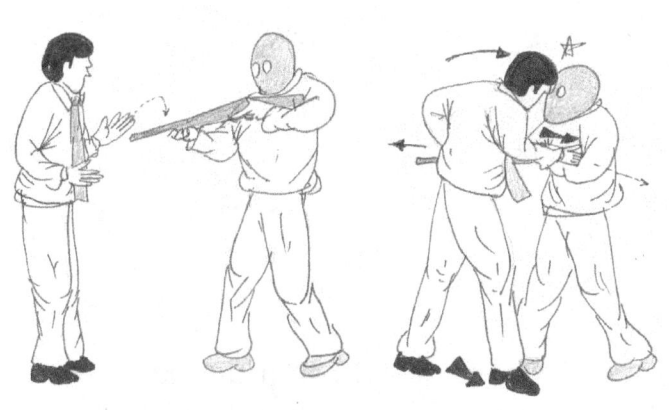

1. Using all your body (and your elbow) to pull his trigger grip forward,
2. Pushing and twisting the barrel of the gun in the opposite direction.

This is achieved by *pulling back your front leg and using a full pivot of your hips*. The twisting is also supposed to create pain at the trigger finger. Take your distance immediately.

Use your elbow over his trigger wrist as the fulcrum for twisting the barrel out of his grip

GUN THREATS

The second example will show a **deviation of the barrel to the in-side,** as you lunge and grab the barrel with the 'rear' hand. The front hand executes a quasi-simultaneous Eye Poke. Keep your forward momentum as your 'poking' hand extends violently in front of his face. Place your leg and hip behind and push his head back and down. This classic set-up will make him fall over your leg. Grab the gun around the trigger area while keeping the push-down to topple him. The other hand twists the gun *up and around* to pry it out of his grips. Use *all your body* for the pivot and takedown, and he will fall on his back without his gun. Strike him with the butt of the gun and take your distance. Remember: keep very close to him for as long as he holds the trigger area and keep tight control of the barrel, close to you and out of the fire line.

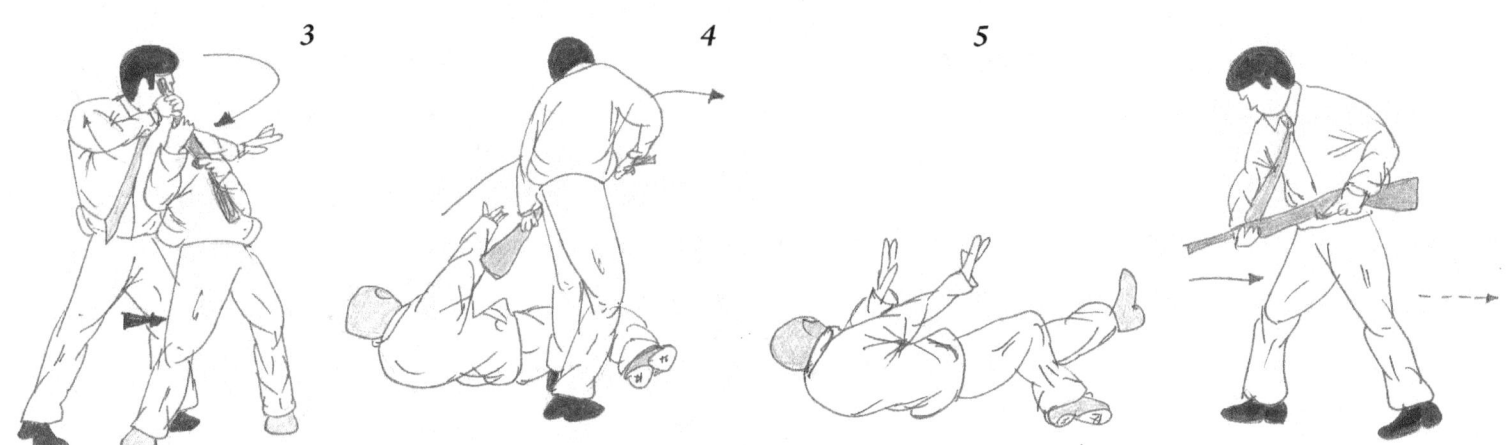

Eye Poke and Topple Takedown with twisting Disarm – effective but requiring more practice

The third series is a **classic maneuver** that is important to drill a lot: it reminds the trainee of the basic principles and uses **a variation of the 'elbow fulcrum' for the Disarm**. The basic principle of being close and of controlling both the barrel and the trigger area is underlined by the *double grab and forward lunge to his in-side*. Pull the gun forward and get 'sticky' close to him. Let suddenly go of the trigger area grab to lift your elbow and strike him in the head. Your elbow is, in fact, on its way down between his arms for an elbow fulcrum point. Strike down *hard and deep* between his arms, while pulling the gun forward; this will place the trigger area of the gun below your armpit. As he resists the pull, you now twist back violently with *all your hips and arms power* to pull the gun out of his hands. If he bends down from your pull, you will also be able to hit him on the head with the gun. Follow through with your twisting pivot and take your distance.

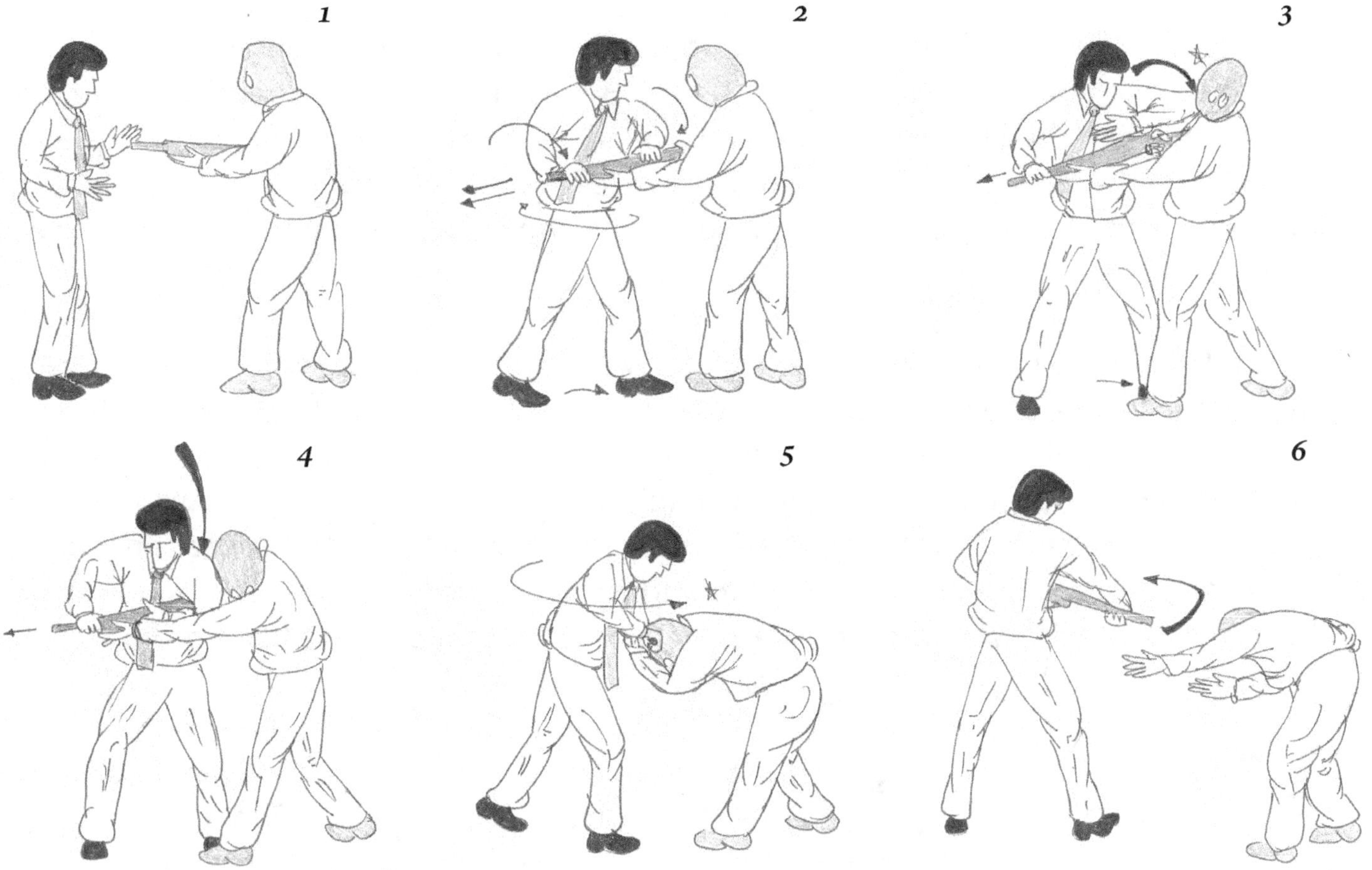

Classic elbow fulcrum twist defense; keep very close

After you drill the basic techniques and get intuitively familiar with the guiding principles, you can use **'simpler' advanced techniques**. It is all about deviating and then twisting the gun out of his grab after mollifying him with an eye or a groin strike. The next set of Illustrations show how to deal in such a fashion with a slightly longer-range threat. Grab and deviate the gun barrel out before lunging in to poke his eyes. Remember to start the lunge *only after having launched the arm for the grab*: the arm movement is faster alone while the start of a lunge is easily discernible. Launch the grab first, just like for the short handgun defenses. After poking his eyes, grab the trigger area and pull the gun forward (with both hands) while kicking or kneeing his groin. He should be mollified enough for you to twist the gun, in a full circle, out of his hands.

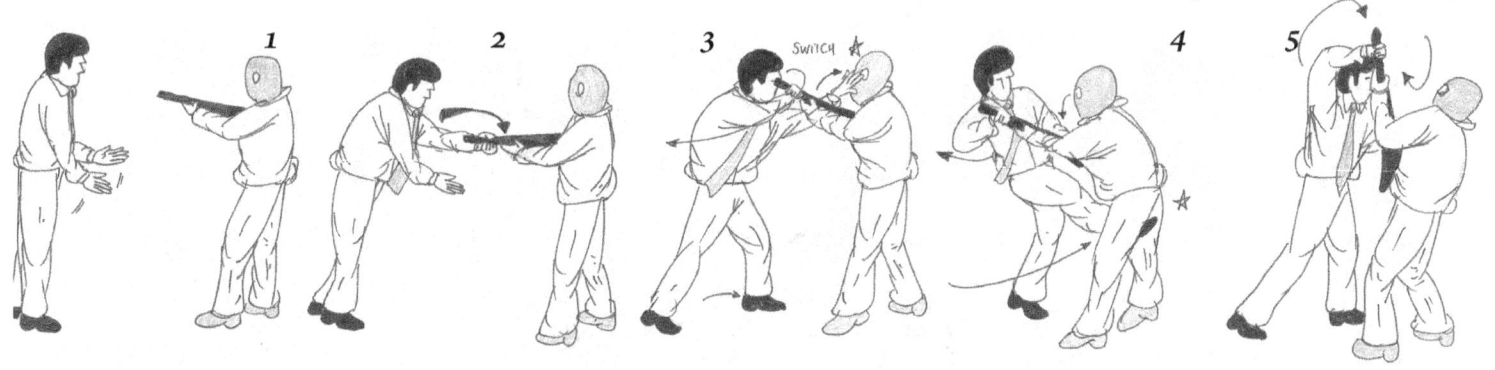

Mid-distance Long Gun Threat; grab, strike eyes and groin, twist gun. Simple technique but that requires drilling

GUN THREATS

Another approach in dealing with a long gun is to get close, throw down the assailant while going to the ground with him. By staying close, you neutralize the long gun and you can then bump the assailant's head on the floor to subdue him. These are advanced techniques that require a good level of *Krav Maga* proficiency, but they are, in essence, easy to execute. Drill them seriously, and only after having mastered the other defenses.

Our first example is a very effective classic. Deviate the barrel in while lunging forward with an eye attack of your 'rear' hand. Keep your lunging momentum to get behind him while your poking arm comes below the gun to push the gun against the weakened assailant's chest. The hand that used to hold the barrel can now come forward between his legs (from behind). This move is a *Strike* up in his groin for further 'softening' of his will to fight. You are, of course, crouching while keeping pressure on the gun to his chest. Your hand between his legs grabs "whatever possible" to his front groin area. Pull up while standing up straight in order to take him down. As soon as he is lifted with head down, push him down forcefully on his head and *go with him* to add your body weight on the floor crash. The gun is harmless under his body and you should immediately start striking his head and banging it on the floor until he is neutralized.

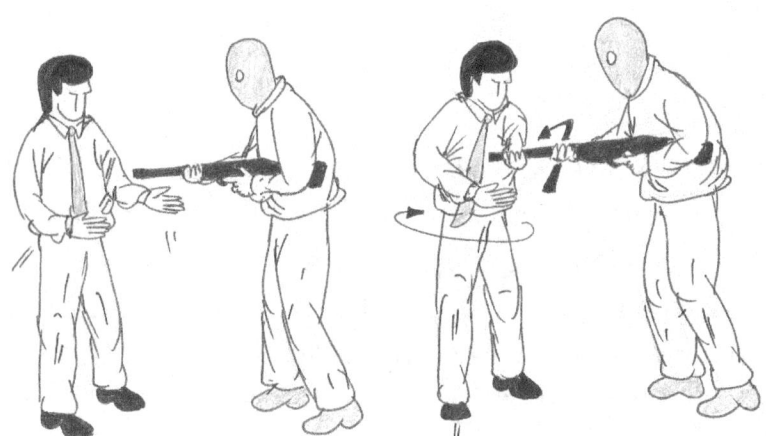

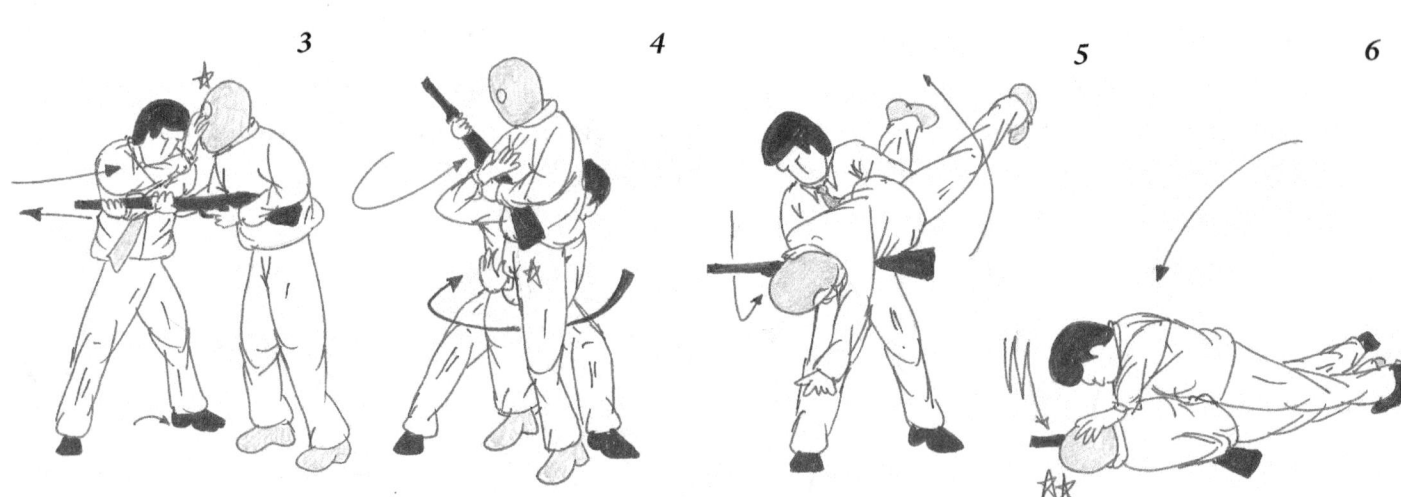

Eye poke and Groin Takedown Defense

The last Takedown Defense is illustrated below. The Drawings show how to deviate the gun barrel *out* while lunging forcefully straight into the attacker with a headbutt. Go over his barrel arm to control it and to keep the assailant close, and keep your forward momentum. Let your control hand glide into his lower back while attacking his eyes with the other hand. Take him down by pushing his head straight down with your fingers in his eyes and keeping his back in place. Push the head all the way down *into the ground*, while staying close. Keep control of his gun arms under your arm and keep banging his head hard into the floor until he is neutralized.

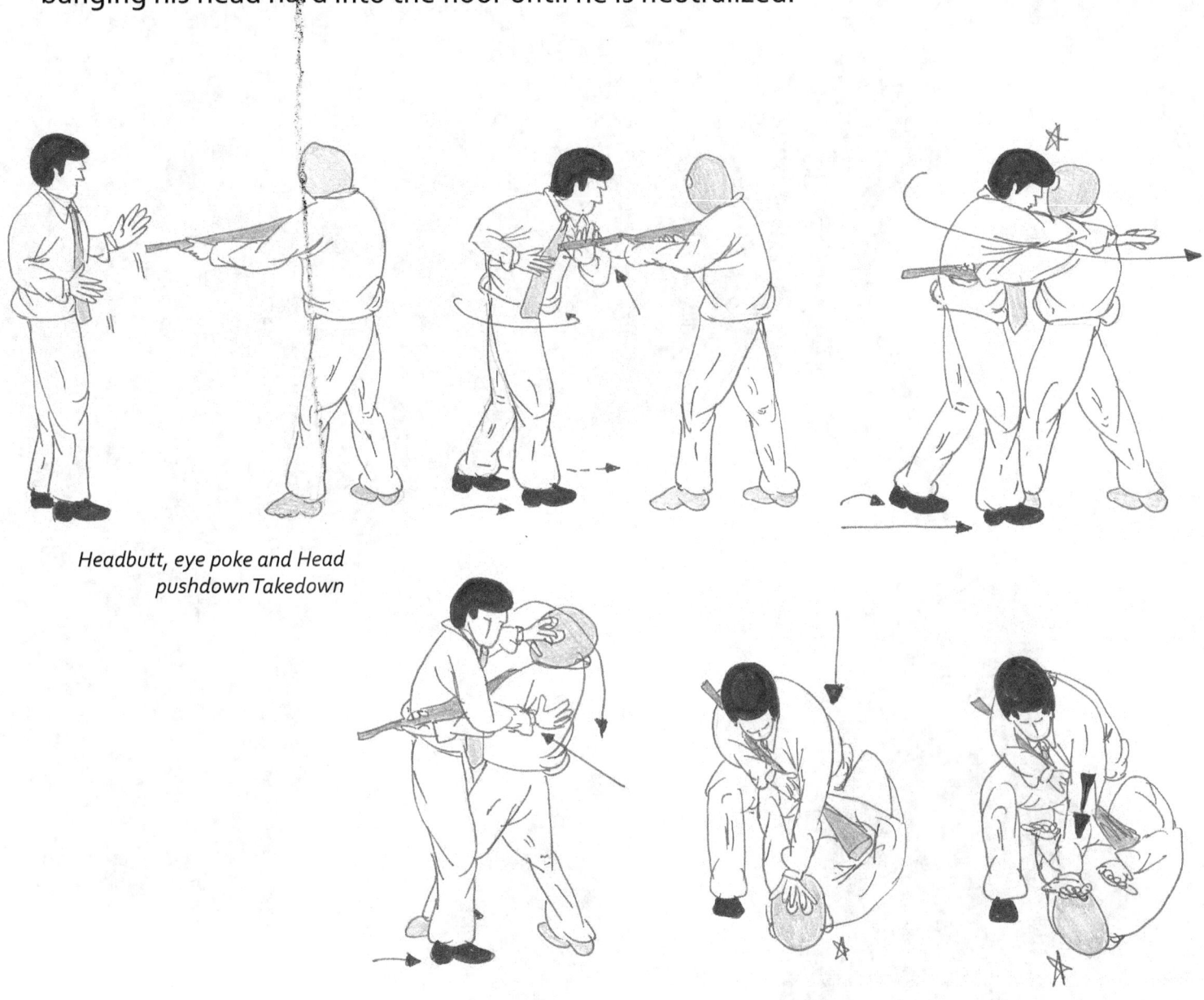

Headbutt, eye poke and Head pushdown Takedown

By failing to prepare, you are preparing to fail.
~Benjamin Franklin

PART NINE

Improvised Weapons

שימוש בחפצים יומיומיים

We are closing this work about *Advanced Krav Maga* with a short Chapter on **using everyday objects for self-defense**. One of the principles of *Krav Maga* is using everything around you to help you win the fight. That means getting the high ground on a stairwell as well as throwing hot coffee into the assailant's eyes. It means that banging the assailant's head against the nearby wall could be more effective than trying to punch him. The <u>use of your surroundings</u> should in fact be only limited by your imagination: it is more a state of mind than a collection of techniques.

We are not covering here obvious weapons, but **everyday objects** that seem innocuous but can very much improve your odds of winning a fight. A hammer, a screwdriver, a baseball bat, a cutter, a fire poker, a pepper spray, a telescopic baton or a kitchen knife are all true weapons to use if you happen to have them near you at the time. There is no need to talk about them. Let us talk about your backpack, your umbrella or your coffee to go…

We shall only present here a few illustrations, a few techniques and a few ideas. The reader will have to do his own thinking and consider what are the objects he is usually carrying and in which surroundings he is usually moving around. It is important to visualize all this and also to practice with everyday objects. The reason is not, this time, about intensive drilling but more of having thought about it before. *In times of stress, grabbing something useful will not necessarily be straightforward and you will not be in a situation you can think and concentrate.* Think about it, use it a few times with a partner and be ready.

<u>The first important move</u> to always remember is the *throwing of anything possible towards the assailant's eyes*. It should always be nearly automatic in any case it is possible. Even the best trained opponent will close his eyes and lift his hands if anything is coming directly for his eyes. Even if it is only for an infinitesimal part of a second, it will allow you to launch an attack to his unprotected body; preferably to go for the groin and follow up with an eye strike as soon as he lowers his hands. From there any *Retzev* series will do. Simple, easy, efficient. Just make sure the throwing is sudden, explosive and comes directly straight towards his eyes. You can basically throw anything you have in your hands: your keys, your wallet, your bag, hot coffee, any drink, a bottle, coins from your pocket, dirt or sand you have grabbed from the floor, groceries, your smartphone (as heartbreaking it may be to some), your watch,… The list is certainly not exhaustive, and, as you can see, anything goes

The set of Drawings below illustrates the concept. In this example, you are confronted as you hold your coffee to go. It will of course work best if it is still hot! And anything  else will work as well, as explained before; you just have to cause him to close his eyes and lift his hands instinctively. Our example shows that you make sure to be non-threatening while getting ready by unlocking the cup cover. If the confrontation is inevitable, explode into throwing the (hot) beverage towards his face. As he reacts atavistically, kick his groin and then attack his eyes as he lowers the hands. Start your *Retzev*, for example with a Low Kick to his front knee.

Throw anything towards the opponent's eyes and kick his groin as he lifts his hands

The second important object you should look for in an emergency is a **chair**. A **chair** is built with a seat that can be a shield against blades and strikes, and with legs that are formidable poking weapons. Of course they can be heavy and unwieldy, but you should use them for a short time, just to get the upper hand. **Chairs** and stools are everywhere, and should be used whenever possible, especially if the attacker is armed with a stick or with a knife. Grab it in any way you feel comfortable with and use the seat as a *shield* from punches, kicks or knife pokes. Use the pegs or legs as *poking weapons* against the most vulnerable spots of the assailant's body. Concentrate on one leg and aim with short poking moves towards the eyes, the throat, the nose or the solar plexus. The other legs will probably connect somewhere else as well, all for the best. DO NOT use the chair like in the movies, in wide moves aiming at crashing it on the opponent's head or back. These wide moves require momentum and are slow; they open you totally to the opponent. At most they could be used to conclude a fight that you have already won, when they can be executed with no danger of a stop strike or a counter strike. ➔

A Chair is obviously a fantastic shield

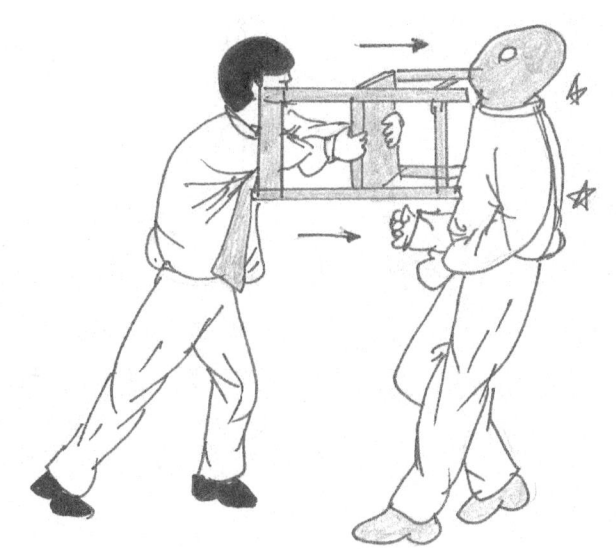

Use the chair exclusively as a poking weapon; concentrate on one peg and target the eyes, the throat or the nose

The principles are clear; you should now grab a chair from time to time and handle it just to get the feeling. You could even work a little with a partner for familiarization and hit a hanging bag with precision strikes by concentrating on one of the legs only. It will make you ready, just in case...

We shall now give an illustrating example of dealing with a knife. The drawings show how you are ready behind the shielding by the chair seat. Do not wait for the attack but preempt it by going forward into his approach and striking his knife directly with the seat. Keep going towards him with a series of poking moves and concentrate on one of the upper pegs for targeting the eyes. As he is hit, lift the chair (and his hand as well) just enough to kick him in the groin for good measure. You can now use the chair legs to hit his armed arm repeatedly up and down to hurt the elbow. From there on you should repeat your forward poking attacks towards sensitive points of his body. You can also eventually relinquish the chair at some stage to go for more traditional *Krav Maga* techniques.

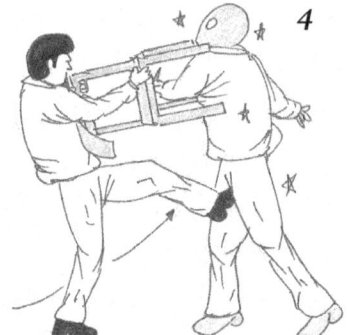

Using a chair to deal with an approaching knife-wielding assailant

ADVANCED KRAV MAGA

We shall conclude by mentioning that a chair can also be used *as an obstructing diversion* in a very easy move. This trick is incredibly effective and very easy to succeed with; *the key is to conceal your intentions* by being non-threatening and unobvious in your preparations. As illustrated below, you stand near one of those ubiquitous chairs, or maybe beside the chair you were just sitting on before being confronted. As your assailant gets close, you suddenly push the chair down into his legs. No need to use force or big moves, just push it down unobtrusively, but suddenly. As soon as he is struck and stuck, lunge for his eyes. Go around the chair to keep striking in your own *Retzev*.

Tilt a chair into the legs of an approaching assailant and attack his eyes as he concentrates down

Another very useful everyday object for self-defense is a pen or anything hard that looks like it. Pens and pencils are everywhere, and you maybe even have one on you right now. But hardly a weapon shall you say? Just think about the effect of a pen strike into the eye, and you'll be on board...

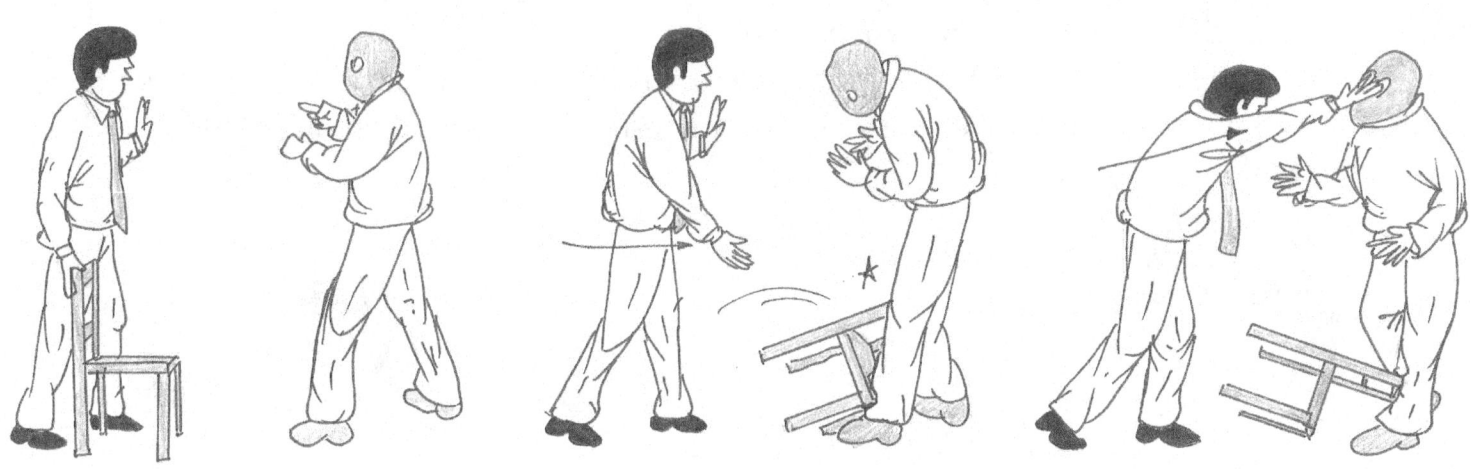

Of course, it may seem an overreaction and an even something unthinkable for a normative citizen. But one must remember that *Krav Maga* is about survival in extreme circumstances. Poking someone's eye is both gross and extreme. Of course, you will not attack the eyes of your drunken friend because he pushed you. *These techniques are about situations in which your life or physical integrity are at risk from criminals or terrorists*. This is not even about dealing with a purse grabber or a drunk; this is about *survival*. And in that case, you will have to be ready to do what is necessary to protect yourself. We have dealt with the morals of self-defense and the imperative of self-control at the beginning of the book. Pen techniques are gruesome and dangerous and should be used only in last resort. The reason is simple: *they only target the eyes, the throat and the carotid!*

IMPROVISED WEAPONS

The pen can be held normally to strike, but the preferable handle for stronger strikes is the 'Icepick' grip.

Strike, <u>preferably repeatedly</u>, the throat (on the side of the trachea), the side of the neck downward, the side of the neck horizontally, and the eyes. These must be crippling strikes for extreme situations. Think of the pen as a mini-knife and make *penetrating strikes*. Get psychologically ready for such a violent and unusual behavior, in case you get into a dire situation requiring it. It is not as easy as it may seem; most people recoil at the thought of such tactics.

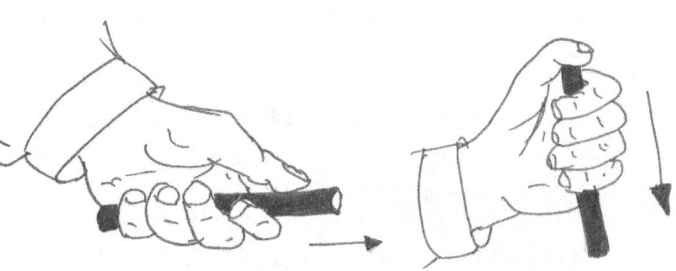

The regular and Icepick grip for pen strikes

Attack the Adam's apple by coming sideways below it

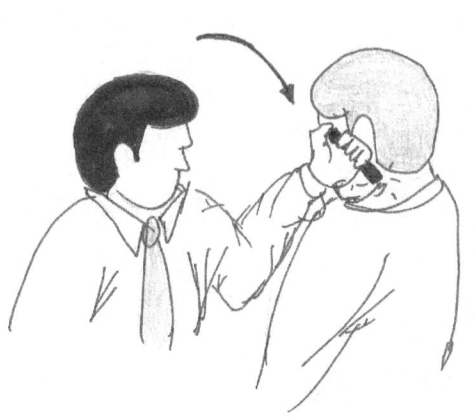

Strike the side of the neck diagonally downwards to hurt the carotid and nerve endings

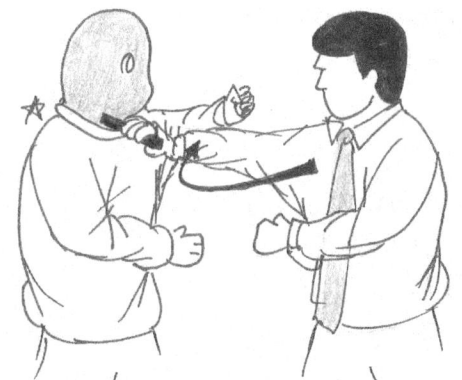

Strike the carotid directly in a horizontal strike; aim for the side of the neck

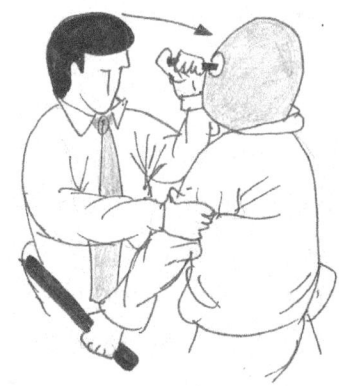

But the eye should always be target number one in life or death situations

And we shall **conclude with an example** that embodies the principles presented. See Illustrations at the top of next page. The Drawings show how you hold your pen in an *Icepick Grip* when confronted by a knife-wielding assailant. After downward-blocking a stab, you get control of the armed arm with the other hand and go for a Downward Strike to the assailant's *eye*. Totally justified.

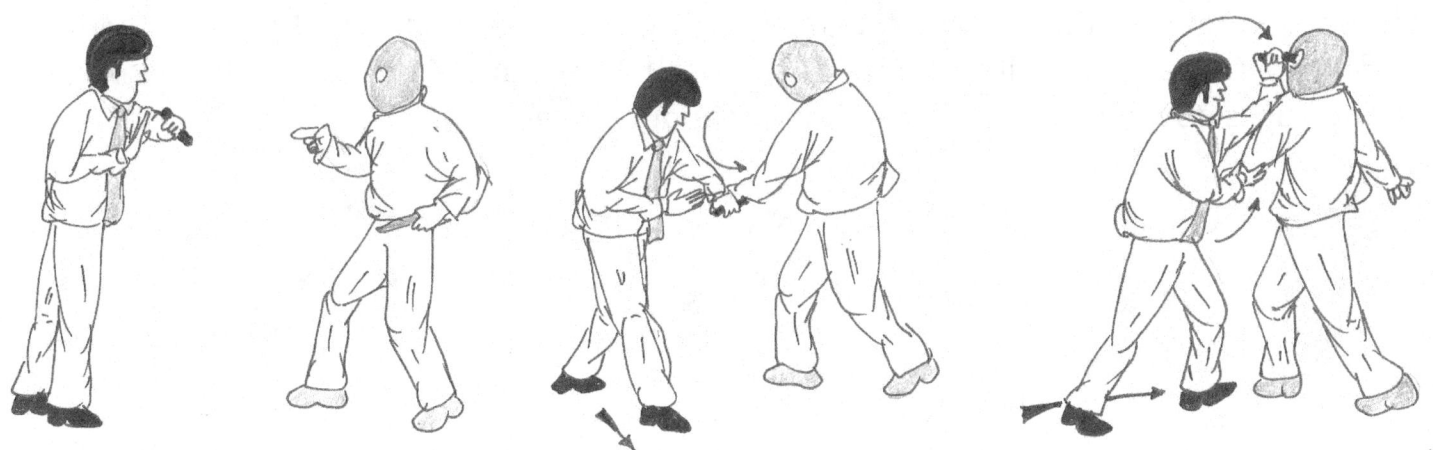

Icepick pen grip, block a knife stab and go for the eyes

Another useful everyday item is your bag. Whether a sport bag, a backpack, an attaché-case or a bag of groceries, you can use it as a shield or as a diversion. You could use it to strike the opponent, but unless it is weighted, it will probably not do much more harm than regular strikes that you can deliver. Although it must be said that the centrifugal force of wide moves can make it fearsome (*at the cost of the predictability of wide strikes*).
The author advises to restrict the use of such items for <u>shielding and diversion</u>, which simple principles will be illustrated below.

The first set of drawings shows how to **suddenly throw your back towards the opponent's eyes**. Start unexpectedly from a non-threatening and cowed stance to surprise him; explode into an energetic throw. As soon as you have thrown the bag, *get out of the center-line* by stepping diagonally forward. This is to evade a possible reaction. Immediately kick his groin as he is still unsettled by the high strike, as he still has his hands reflexively up or as he has your bag hindering his feet movements. From there, start a regular *Retzev*.

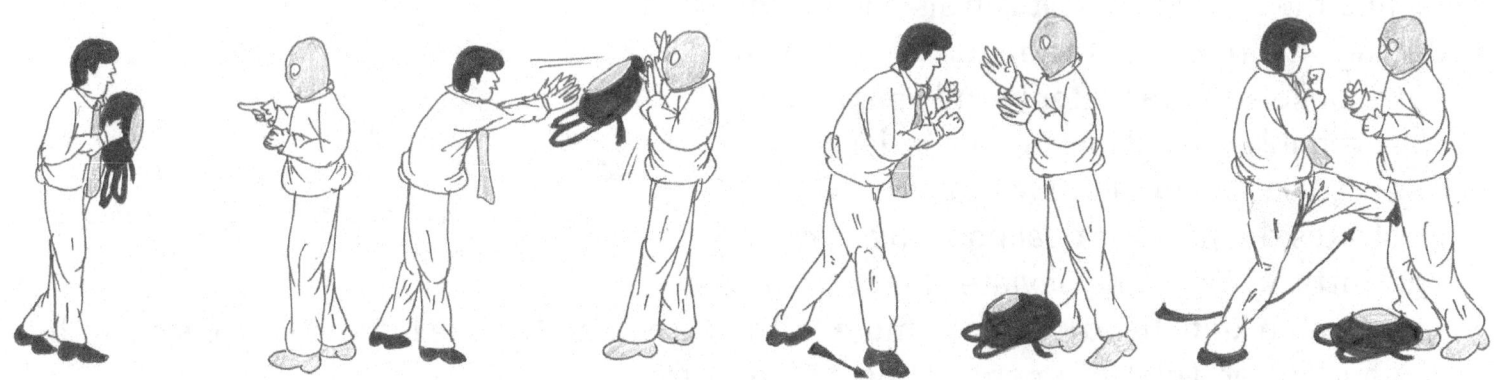

Throw your bag towards the assailant's eyes in order to allow for a groin kick

IMPROVISED WEAPONS

The second set of Drawings illustrates how to use a backpack **as a shield** to smother a knife stab. Deviate the knife and use its cover to kick the attacker's groin. The shield use of any bag is obvious but should be thought about for familiarization.

Use a bag as a smothering and deviating shield against a knife attack

Another excellent improvised weapon in case of need: the umbrella. We mean here the **long umbrella with a pointed tip**, not the short 'pocket-type'. The umbrella should not be used as a stick, but, again, as a *poking weapon* and hold with *one hand at the end and one hand in the middle* (as it is rather flimsy). *Krav Maga* is about maximum efficiency for your own safety, and hitting someone on the head with a flimsy umbrella will not do much damage. Even if you have a sturdier walking stick, wielding it around will only be efficient if you are an experimented fighter of cane fighting (*Arnis*, *Jo jitsu* or French '*canne*'). So concentrate on simple moves and maximum damage by *poking at sensitive points*. In life-threatening situations, you should preferably aim for the eyes or the throat. Again. But the pointed tip and the way you hold it can also do lots of damage if directed to the abdomen or the groin. Poke, poke away repeatedly and your assailant will probably go and look for an easier prey. The next set of Figures *at the top of next page* illustrates the possible dealing with a surprise knife attack. Block and deviate energetically the threatening knife hand with the umbrella and immediately poke his uncovered side with all your power. Think of a penetrating bayonet strike.

Poke the assailant's throat with the pointed tip of the umbrella held with both hands

242   **ADVANCED KRAV MAGA**

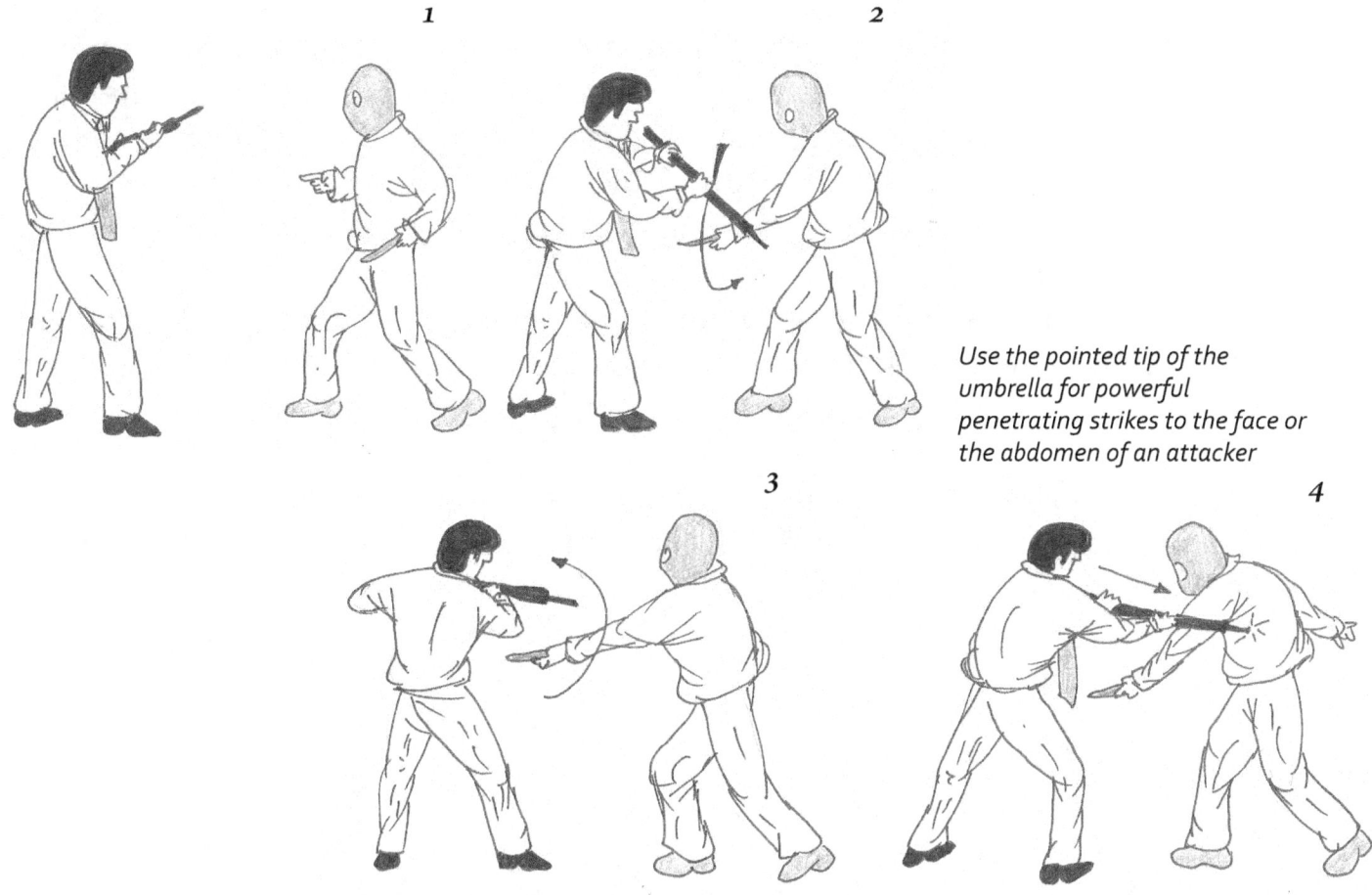

Use the pointed tip of the umbrella for powerful penetrating strikes to the face or the abdomen of an attacker

A sturdy walking stick can be used in the same way as the umbrella; the lack of pointedness is balanced by the stronger stick. As mentioned, use it also as a *poking weapon held by two hands* as described (unless you are a proficient stick fighter). Always prefer the eyes and throat as targets, if possible.

Use a walking stick just as an umbrella: go for the eyes and throat

<u>**The shorter umbrella is also an option, as is a rolled magazine or a plastic bottle**</u> which have all the same basic 'short stick' shape. Anything that looks like a short stick (*Tam bo*) can be used as a weapon: the short umbrella already mentioned, a plastic sports water bottle, a tightly rolled magazine, a small glass bottle,… ➡

IMPROVISED WEAPONS

The author does *not* recommend to use all those as you would a stick, as is sometimes touted. These items are not hard or strong enough to inflict serious pain to an adrenalin-filled opponent. Again, you should use those exclusively as *poking weapons to be directed at very sensitive targets*: eyes, throat and groin. Eventually, if you are strong and in control, the solar plexus and the nose could be targeted as well with strikes that would anyway need follow-up.

You should hold the makeshift weapon in such a way that you can use both extremities to strike according to the situation. So, do not hold the umbrella or the rolled magazine at one end, but better somewhere at a third of its length.

The Illustrations below show how you could strike the groin of an attacker launching a Haywire punch that you evade down. Follow up with another 'short stick' strike to the eye before starting your *Retzev*.

Use a short umbrella or a rolled magazine to strike the groin and face of an attacker

A surprising improvised weapon would be the jacket that is on your back. Of course, you would need to be holding it. If you have something of some weight in your pocket, it could eventually be used as a whip to strike the opponent's head. But it is best used *as a diversion or/and as a blinding tool*. Throw it over the attacker's head as he gets close and immediately attack as he is both encumbered and blinded; go for the head or the groin and start a *Retzev*. Even if the assailant can get rid of your jacket or avoid his head being covered, his dealing with it will divert his attention from your incoming strikes and kicks.

Cover the opponent's head with your jacket to blind him and distract him from your counter

The Figures below illustrate how you cover your attacker's head with a garment and tighten it enough to keep him blinded while you hammer-fist repeatedly the area where his nose should be. You can then attack his groin as he deals with both your jacket and his busted face.

Cover the attacker's face and try to tighten the cover for enough time to strike his nose area a few times

But remember that many other everyday objects can be used as improvised weapons according to the general principles covered in the previous examples. Look around you and your specific settings; think about it and imagine what could be grabbed in a time of need.

We will conclude with two more random examples.

If you are holding a ceramic mug, a glass, a glass bottle, a coffee pot or a decanter, what simpler than to break it on the assailant's head? Of course, keep striking after that until the threat is over ➤

IMPROVISED WEAPONS

Use anything of glass or ceramic and crash it on the opponent's head as the start of a Retzev

Our last example will be anathema to many readers, in this day and age of constant connection, selfies and social media. But striking the opponent's eye, head or face with the **hard edge of your smartphone** could help you win the fight. Think about it; it could be worth it…

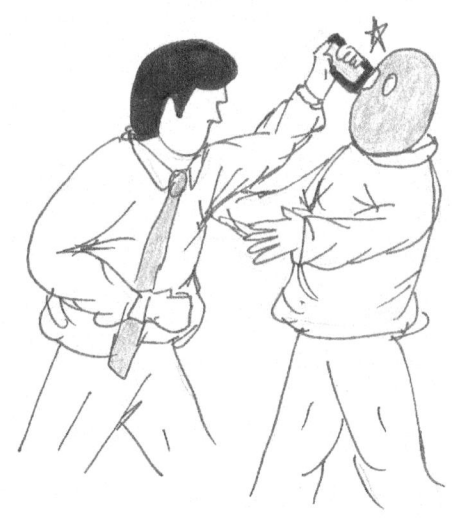

**We are what we repeatedly do.
Excellence, therefore is not an action but a habit.
~Aristotle**

246   ADVANCED KRAV MAGA

Afterword

We have now covered *Krav Maga* advanced techniques. But the work starts only now. "Knowing" the techniques and having practiced them a few times does not mean you have acquired them. In the real-life situation in which you could need them, it is only your muscle memory and instinctive reactions that will save you.

You will need to drill intensively all the techniques presented. Then, by practicing them in a 'free fighting' setting, you will be able to 'feel' the versions the most adapted to your temperament and physiology. It will then be time to focus on those techniques in order to make them quasi-automatic. Drill, drill and drill. Drill with a less-and-less cooperative partner, drill under stress and against several partners. Slowly and gradually, these reactions will become truly acquired and available for stress situations without having to think about them. But it will not be over yet! You now will have to keep drilling them from time to time, in order to keep them fresh in your mind and body.

Krav Maga and the will to survive 'just in case' are in fact, a life commitment requiring work and more work. A lot of intensive training *now* will not be an insurance policy for the next 20 years. Consistent and regular training is much more effective than intensive training. Keep training and the fruits will be yours to pick.

Good Luck and remember the words of a few masters, philosophers and champions before us:

- *I fear not the man who has practiced 10,000 kicks once, but I fear the man who has practiced one kick 10,000 times.* ~Bruce Lee
- *Success isn't always about greatness. It's about consistency. Consistent hard work leads to success. Greatness will come.* ~Dwayne Johnson
- *Success is no accident. It is hard work, perseverance, learning, studying, sacrifice and most of all, love of what you are doing or learning to do.* ~Pele
- *It does not matter how slowly you go as long as you do not stop.* ~Confucius
- *Pain is the best Instructor, but no one wants to go to his class.* ~Choi Hong Hi (founder of TaeKwonDo)

Complementary Reading: 'Krav Maga Kicks'

Our first book about Krav Maga did present the basic techniques, the kicks and self defense against unarmed attackers. Together with this work (Advanced Krav Maga), it covers all the essential techniques and principles of Krav Maga that you will ever need to know.

Krav Maga is recognized as one of the most efficient fighting systems around today. Based on common sense, it has evolved by necessity in a region ravaged by fighting for over a century. The first part of this book details and illustrates the preferred Kicks used in Krav Maga, and the second part presents the vital points to be targeted when kicking or striking. The Last part of this work is basically a full Krav Maga Self-defense course that also includes offensive techniques. The defenses against strikes, kicks, grabs, holds and chokes do often include kicking, but only when it is the most adequate reaction.

This book is the first to underline in print the important principle of **Retzev**, with dozens of examples of continuous motion until the opponent is fully vanquished. Suitable for beginners and trained Martial artists from other Schools. **Over 1500 Photos and Illustrations!**

If you have enjoyed the book and appreciate the effort behind this series, you are invited to write a short and honest review on Amazon.com… It has become extremely difficult to promote one's work in this day and age, and your support would be much appreciated. Thanks!

All questions, comments, additional techniques, special or vintage Photos about Kicks and Krav Maga are welcomed by the author and would be introduced with credit in future editions. Just email: **martialartkicks@gmail.com**

Books by the same author are presented in the coming pages.

Published by TUTTLE.

This illustrated guide to martial arts kicks provides the reader with a wealth of information on 89 different types of kicks from various styles. This martial arts book features kicks from Karate, Muay Thai, Taekwondo, Kung Fu, Kempo, Capoeira, Jeet Kune Do, and more. In a self defense situation there is no room for defeat. Readers will learn how to unleash a devastating barrage of kicks to throw their opponents off guard and leave every match in victory.

The Essential Book of Martial Arts Kicks has one purpose: to help readers hone their kicking proficiency so that they can readily deploy the most powerful tool in the fighter's repertoire. It contains contains thousands of photos and diagrams to show readers exactly how to perform all of the 89 kicks inside this book.

This encyclopedic reference is the first of its kind to present the entire range of basic martial arts kicks. Packed with full color photos, detailed diagrams and a companion DVD featuring 50 of the most powerful kicks, this book is required reading for every martial artist who wants to sharpen and expand their kicking skills.

Published by Fons Sapientiae:

Low Kicks are powerful, fast, and effective exactly what you need to defend yourself in a real life confrontation. And because they are seldom used in sport fighting, they can be a surprising and valuable addition to your free fighting arsenal. While they may seem easy to execute, not all low kicks are simply low versions of the basic kicks. There are specific attributes and principles that make low kicks work. Marc de Bremaeker has collected the most effective low kicking techniques from Martial Arts like *Krav Maga, Karatedo, Capoeira, Wing-Chun Kung-Fu, MMA,* and *Muay Thai*. In this book, he analyzes each kick in depth, explaining the proper execution and outlining applications and variations from self-defense, sport fighting and traditional practice: Hundreds of examples in over one thousand photographs and drawings.

Plyometrics and Flexibility Training for Explosive Martial Arts Kicks and Performance Sports Plyo-Flex is a system of plyometric exercises and intensive flexibility training designed to increase your kicking power, speed, flexibility and skill level. Based on scientific principles, Plyo-Flex exercises will boost your muscles, joints and nervous system interfaces to the next performance level. After only a few weeks of training, you should see a marked improvement in the speed of your kicks and footwork, the power of your kicks, the height of your jumps, your stamina and your overall flexibility. Hundreds of illustrations and photographs will guide you through the basic plyometric and stretching exercises. Once you've mastered the basics, add the kicking-oriented variations to your workout for an extra challenge.

Stop Kicks are among the most effective, sophisticated kicks a fighter can use. And because they hit your opponent at his most vulnerable, they are also the safest way to pre-empt or counter an attack. Stop Kicks are delivered just as your opponent is fully committed to an attack, physically or mentally, meaning it is too late for him to change his mind. Hitting an opponent in mid-attack gives you the added advantage of using his attacking momentum against him. Stop Kicks: Jamming, Obstructing, Stopping, Impaling, Cutting and Preemptive Kicks presents a well organized array of stop-kicking techniques from a wide range of martial arts. Learn Pushing Kicks, Timing Kicks, Cutting Kicks, Obstruction Kicks, and Block Kicks from the hard-hitting styles of Muay Thai, Karatedo, Krav Maga, Tae Kwon Do, MMA and more.

Whether you are on the ground by choice or you have been taken down, whether your opponent is standing or is on the ground with you, whether you are a good grappler or you are trying to keep a good grappler at bay, whether you were caught unawares sitting on the floor or you have evaded down on purpose, whether you are a beginner or an experienced martial artist...this book has the right kick for the situation. In **Ground Kicks**: Advanced Martial Arts Kicks for Ground-fighting from Karate, Krav Maga, MMA, Capoeira, Kung Fu and more, Marc De Bremaeker has created a comprehensive collection of Ground Kicks, with hundreds of applications for sport fighting and self-defense situation. Packed with over 1200 photographs and illustrations, Ground Kicks also includes specific training tips for practicing each kick effectively.

Stealth Kicks will introduce you to the Art of executing Kicks that your opponent will not see coming. This subject has never been treated comprehensively before. Whether you are a beginner or an experienced Artist, you will find suitable Kicks or tips to modify your current techniques to give them stealth. It will help you to score in Sport confrontations or make sure to come on top in real life Self-Defense situations. The *Feint Kicks* presented are based on misdirection: they will aim at provoking a misguided reaction that will open your adversary to the real kick intended. The *Ghost Kicks* presented are based on dissimulation and will travel out of your opponent's range of vision to catch him unawares. Together with general feinting techniques and specific training tips, hundreds of applications will introduce you to the sneaky Art of stealth kicking and will make you a better and unpredictable fighter. Crammed with over 2300 photos and drawings for an easy understanding of the concept of Stealth.

'Sacrifice Kicks' will comprehensively present the most important Martial Arts Airborne Kicks: Flying Kicks, Hopping Kicks, Jumping Kicks and Suicide Kicks. They have been dubbed 'Sacrifice' in the spirit of Judo's redoubtable Sutemi Takedowns in which one sacrifices his balance in order to throw his opponent down. *Flying Kicks* are not about showmanship, they are very effective techniques when used judiciously. They need not be necessarily high and spectacular; they can be surprising *Jumping Kicks* and *Hopping Kicks* executed long and low. And *Suicide Kicks* take the Sacrifice principles a little further: they are extremely unexpected techniques delivered airborne, but with little hope of landing on one's feet, unlike classic Flying Kicks. All these realistic maneuvers, coming from Karate, Krav Maga, Kung Fu, TaeKwonDo, MMA, Capoeira, Muay Thai and more, are described with applications and training tips. Over 1000 Photos and Illustrations.

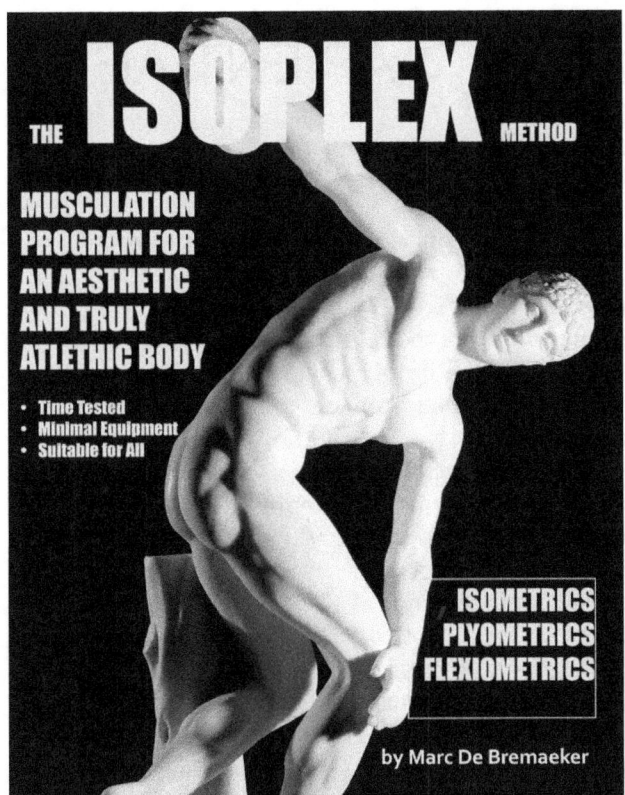

Isoplex stands for Isometrics, Plyometrics and Flexiometrics. The well-organized combination of these three training methods will give the serious trainee the most effective path possible to powerful and aesthetic muscles, in a minimum of time. The method is simply the optimal combination of those three basic tenets of fitness training. It is suitable for men and women. It is suitable for beginners, for athletes of all types, and even for bodybuilders. It is designed to build an aesthetic physique which is also conducive to sport performance and to personal health. ISOPLEX is in fact the modern and more scientific version of the training ideals of Greco-Roman Antiquity. As illustrated by many well-known antique sculptures, the athletes of old had aesthetic bodies based on core musculature and long, well-defined and necessarily efficient muscles. These synergistic training principles are and were universal. They were to be found in ancient Asian Martial Arts and in Body Cultures like Yoga, Chi Kung and many others. A truly athletic and functional body needed for realistic fighting was achieved by a mixture of Isometric exercises, intensive flexibility training and dynamic (Plyometric) drills. Martial Artists and Yogis will immediately grasp the connection. This is the way to train the body for effective and natural aesthetics, and that is what Isoplex concentrates on through an optimal and synergistic time-saving program.

With hundreds of Photos and Drawings and detailing Five complete weekly Programs for all levels.

Joint Kicks are probably the most effective way to neutralize an assailant in real-life situations. By attacking the opponent's articulations you ensure that they will not be able to keep on the fight; they will not be able to punch you with a damaged arm and they will not be able to run after you with a busted leg. Joint Kicks are basically regular kicks to be delivered towards specific targets and with the focused intention to cause damage. This is Martial arts in their purest sense and not sport techniques. In real life, you could easily encounter an assailant with a high resistance to pain. It could the high adrenalin levels, alcohol intoxication or drugs. But it will be very different from free-fighting in the dojo. If he is impervious to the pain of your blows, only by destroying the attacker's infrastructure will you be able to overcome him. The book reflects on the mindset behind Joint Kicks and presents numerous examples of their use. With over 800 Photos and Drawings.

AFTERWORD

OTHER GENRES FROM FONS SAPIENTIAE

AVAILABLE IN PAPERBACK AND KINDLE FORMATS ON AMAZON

The Manual is the definitive guide to Enhanced Concentration, Super Memory, Speed Reading, Note-Taking, Rapid Mental Arithmetic, and the *Ultimate Study Method* (USM).

The techniques presented are the culmination of decades of practical experience combined with the latest scientific research and time-tested practices. The system described herewith will allow the practitioner to:
- Read faster with higher comprehension.
- Remember any type of information instantly.
- Store information in long-term memory.
- Enhance concentration and focus.
- Access deeper levels of the mind.
- Induce relaxation.
- Rapidly perform complex mental arithmetic.
- Master the Ultimate Study Method (USM).

USM is a synergistic combination of established techniques for Concentration, Long-Term Memory, Speed Reading, and Note-Taking. It involves a systematic procedure that allows the practitioner to study any topic fast, efficiently and effectively. USM can be applied to all areas of educational study, academic research, business endeavours, as well as professional life in general.

Rain Fund: A riveting thriller

"...For the safety of the readers, this book ought to come with the disclaimer: leave this book read half-way at your own risk. Unless you are Superman, you won't be able to concentrate on much else until you have read the last page of "Rain Fund". The time has come for Patterson, Ludlum, Dan Brown et al to slide over and make space at the top for Marc Brem." - Shweta Shankar for Readers' Favorite

"...In the good tradition of Ludlum and Grisham. Five Stars" Aldo Levy

"Autistic geniuses charting financial markets; Mobster-fuelled Ponzi schemes; sophisticated hardware viruses; spies; and a rising superpower that strives for dominance – so realistic it is frightening."

www.ingramcontent.com/pod-product-compliance
Lightning Source LLC
Chambersburg PA
CBHW082315230426
43666CB00036B/2724